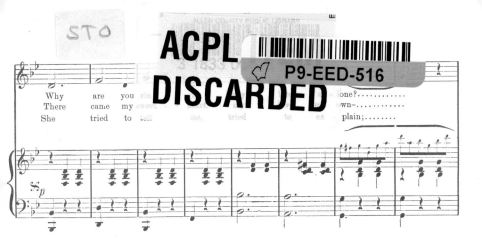

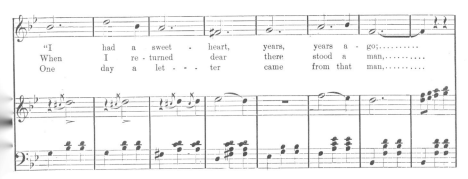

After the Ball. 4-2

After the Ball is a witty and personal but thoroughly researched history of modern popular music from "After the Ball" to "You Turn Me On," the 1965 hit song by the author himself that turned him (briefly) into a pop star.

It all began in 1882 when Charles Harris wrote "After the Ball," and about that time, Tin Pan Alley was founded. Soon songwriters and publishers were turning jazz, ragtime and blues into hit songs for an insatiable public.

Whitcomb carries the story into the twenties and thirties when radio and the talkies revolutionized the music business, and on through the birth of the record business and America's musical relationship with Britain— one of invasion, occupation and naturalization. Then came British rock and a musical invasion of the States.

This is pop as social history, art, fun, business, and even propaganda. Ian Whitcomb spent three years collecting material for this book, tracking down aged ragtime composers, Hollywood music men, song-pluggers, DJs and rock stars. What has emerged is an exhilarating, nostalgic and marvelously readable account of an art form which has both reflected and shaped the popular fancies, dreams and life styles of twentieth-century Americans.

Ian Whitcomb, who realized the universal fantasy by notching up two hit records of his own, is a history graduate of Trinity College, Dublin. Recently he has been involved with making three records: "Under the Ragtime Moon" (performer), "A History of Pop" (which illustrates Whitcomb's *After the Ball*) and Mae West's "Great Balls of Fire" (which he produced).

Ian Whitcomb

After the Ball

POP MUSIC FROM
RAG TO ROCK

SIMON AND SCHUSTER · New York

First U.S. printing
SBN 671-21468-3
Library of Congress Catalog Card Number: 72-93485
Manufactured in the United States of America

Thanks are due the following publishers for permission to quote from songs:

'Adam and Eve Had a Wonderful Time' (Seymour Brown, Albert Gumble). Copyright 1913 Jerome H. Remick & Co.

'Blue Room' (Richard Rodgers, Lorenz Hart). Copyright 1926 T. B. Harms, Inc.

'Children of the New Regime' (Ralph Reader). Copyright 1938 Cinephonic Music Co., Ltd.

'Dance Little Lady' (Noel Coward). Copyright 1928 Chappell & Co., Ltd.

'The Dixie Volunteers' (Edgar Leslie, Harry Ruby). Copyright 1917 Waterson, Berlin & Snyder Co.

'Hide & Seek' (Paul Winley, Ethel Byrd). Copyright © 1955 Progressive Music Publishing Co., Inc.

'How Ya Gonna Keep 'Em Down on the Farm?' (Sam M. Lewis, Joe Young, Walter Donaldson). Copyright 1919 Waterson, Berlin & Snyder Co.

'I Didn't Raise My Boy to Be a Soldier' (Alfred Bryan, Al Piantadosi). Copyright 1915 Leo Feist, Inc.

'I'm an Old Cowhand' (Johnny Mercer). Copyright 1936 Leo Feist, Inc.

Continued on page 299

Contents

1736956

Scene: a Greyhound bus, passing Garden City, Kansas on 10th July 1965

Full of hot flushes and a buzzing head, the writer was bouncing on this bus. Just one of the many acts in a rock 'n' roll caravan of stars being carried from state to state. Scattered around him were history text books, because he was preparing to take the finals for his degree in modern history and political thought to be held at Trinity College, Dublin that very autumn.

Tired of reading a book about *The Use of the Barricade in 19th Century Street Fighting* he picked up a Karl Marx paperback. Inside this he found the bourgeois being eliminated and the state withering away.

He was riding high on all hit charts with his record 'You Turn Me On', an orgasmic panting sung in falsetto. 'You can count on two years of gravy and bread off one stone hit,' a rock veteran had told him.

The writer was young, but he felt old and what's more his hair had been coming out in the Holiday Inn showers. Perhaps the pressure of the water?

During the classless-society passages in Marx his mind began to wander over the events of the recent past, arranging them in apple-pie order. The sights and sounds inside the bus – the poker players, the soul singers, the comics readers – darkened . . .

This teenie Margarita had knocked on his motel door a few nights ago, asking could she come in because a top-tenner had tried to rape her and the writer wasn't like the rest. He gave her shelter but he asked himself whether it was possible to be a fly-on-the-wall observer as he helped unzip her jeans. In Jacksonville, Florida, after taking two Contacs and a glass of sherry to fight flu he had found himself inviting the vast audience to knock down the police, mount the stage and have a good time. For this he was jailed. In Hollywood, stepping out of his car in order to take part as a featured guest in a Pop Awards show, he was ground into the sidewalk by police officers. They had mistaken him for a member of the public. In San Francisco he had held a sobbing girl in his arms after a Beatles concert. She knew that he knew the manager of the group. He was moved by this, but couldn't think why. Nor could he think why he kept punching people: he'd slugged the policeman who'd called him a 'punk' and the one-legged man who'd called him a 'Lady'. He'd tweaked the beard of the disc-jockey who'd called him 'Ian baby' . . .

Back to Marx: 'When classes disappear and the dictatorship of the proletariat dies out, the party of the first part will also die out and the Golden Age will take over . . .'

Suddenly, with a dull *thoppp!!*, a human book marker hid the print. One of the rock stars had placed his dong, his tool, his *wedding tackle*, right on the Marx.

The hot flushes became flashes. The writer felt these questions zoom into his head like a Warner Bros Looney Tunes trade mark: 'Who am I? What am I? Where am I? What is this business in which I am involved? Is there a story and am I part of it?'

'You Turn Me On', his hit, lasted him out two years – as predicted. During this time the above questions continued to haunt him. He frequented libraries, he looked up old-time songwriters, he pursued ragtimers. He remembered that once the college postman had asked him: 'What d'ye want to study history for? It's all happened and there's nothing ye can do about it.' He had puzzled over this for years, but now he realized that there *was* something he could do about it: *he could write it himself and in so doing he could find his place in the scheme!*

Part One
Happy
Alley Days

How Pop
Music Began

At the dawn of the century Chas K. Harris published a little red book of rules and secrets called *How to Write a Popular Song*. Just inside there was a picture of him – a dignified figure with his wax moustache, wing collar and frozen tweed suit. Not unlike a trading Kaiser Wilhelm. He was very proud of the business to which he belonged: song manufacturing.

So well had he studied his craft that he knew in advance how many sheet music copies his songs would sell. To his readers he advised:

> Look at newspapers for your story-line.
> Acquaint yourself with the style in vogue.
> Avoid slang.
> Know the copyright laws.

If the reader did all this he (or she) might become rich and famous in the world of popular music. It was a trade both respectable, profitable and artistic. Had not Mme Adelina Patti, the noted high-class singer, ended a recent concert with 'The Last Farewell'? And who wrote it? Chas K. Harris!

Rich and famous and working in New York, nerve-centre of world show business, he was a pillar of the *pop* music establishment. Pop – short for 'popular' and a trade term not for public use. Other pillars included the publishers Isadore Witmark, Jos. Stern & Ed Marks, Jerome Remick, Shapiro–Bernstein, Leo Feist. All were red-blooded Americans, hustling and bustling and jostling together in a couple of blocks they called 'Tin Pan Alley', feeding the near-by vaudeville theatres with all kinds of songs, flooding the western world with their wares: a million-dollar business. We shall examine the workings of Tin Pan Alley in a later chapter. Meanwhile we must delve around in nineteenth-century America in order to find out how pop music originated. First there was a wide-open country, then there was the city, the mass, the hunger for leisure-pleasure, the bold men who supplied its music, and finally ragtime!

Chas K. had been one of the first pop publishers to move from the hinterland into New York. In the early 1880s, in Milwaukee, Wisconsin, he had had a little shop with a sign advertising 'SONGS WRITTEN TO ORDER'. His work tool was a banjo and on it he carpentered songs for births, deaths, marriages, junkets – anything. Maximum price: 20 dollars. He worked hard, like a real Horatio Alger hero, and one day he arranged for his three-verse story ballad 'After the Ball' to be inserted into the variety show 'A Trip to Chinatown'. *Inserted.* The song had nothing to do with Chinatown, but insertion was getting to be standard practice. Good 'exposure' for your song, and if it 'clicked' then everyone was happy. Some shows were 'sure-fire' for years on the strength of one 'hit'.

'After the Ball' was an instant hit from the very first night. Harris, of course, was publisher as well as author/composer. He wasn't singer though. That was the job of actor J. Aldrich Libbey and he got a 'cut' of the 'royalties'. Within a year 'Ball' was bringing in 25,000 dollars a week; within twenty years sheet sales topped 10 million. It was translated into every known language. Harris had hardly another such hit – but he could live nicely off this single work. In 1929, at the end of his life and still in his wing collar, he sang the old song in an early sound film (helped out by a cartoon cat who called him 'Charlie').*

'After the Ball', written and published by Harris in 1892 was the first million seller to be conceived as a million seller, and marketed as a million seller. Harris's head was in the twentieth century, but his heart was in the nineteenth. The story and melody of 'After the Ball' were thoroughly Victorian: a little maiden

---

*By the way, like many notable pop writers Harris never learnt to read or write music.

4

climbs an old man's knee and asks him why he has no babies and no home. He replies that he had a sweetheart once but he caught her kissing another at a ball. He couldn't forgive her, wouldn't listen to her explanation. Years later, after her death, the man he caught her kissing tells him that he was her *brother*. That's why the old man is lonely, no home at all, because he broke her heart after the ball.

The chorus, in waltz time, went:

> After the ball is over,
> After the break of morn,
> After the dancers' leaving,
> After the stars are gone.
> Many a heart is aching,
> If you could read them all;
> Many the hopes that have vanished,
> After the ball.

Story ballads like 'After the Ball' were Harris's speciality. They were written for middle-class ladies to perform at home on the piano, only 'Ball' strayed much farther. Genteel parlour music had its origins in Europe but by the early years of the nineteenth century had found its glory in America. The piano, a triumph of engineering and a solid piece of furniture, was a sure sign that an American was doing well and going up. But *he* didn't play it. American musical men were considered effeminate. The playing of ballads was left to ladies, mostly young spinsters, or to touring performers from Europe.

There were more pianos in America than anywhere else in the world and there seemed to be more lady pianists. Novelist Anthony Trollope, jotting down his North American experiences, remarked that hotel drawing rooms invariably contained a piano played by a 'forlorn lady'. The instrument seemed louder, harsher and more violent than the European kind. Female voices 'rang and echoed through the lofty corners and round the empty walls'.

Performance was an accomplishment, not to be flaunted and never to be offensive. An 1851 issue of *Harper's* gave some 'Mems For Musical Misses': they must sit in a simple, graceful manner, never swinging the arms or turning up the eyes; they must aim more at pleasing than astonishing.

This genteel music market continued into Tin Pan Alley time. For example, 'A Day in Venice', published in the late nineties, combined business gimmickry with gentility: the purchaser opened the album to find a spread of free doilies.

The man who dreamed up the doily idea was a Harrisian. For this was the go-ahead progressive side of Chas K., inspired partly by the carnival tactics of P. T. Barnum but more by the extraordinary business fervour which filled America at the end of the nineteenth century. Business became 'life's greatest adventure'. 'Furnaces are glowing, spindles are singing their song', opined a Senator. 'Books are becoming wiser and music sweeter,' added a clergyman. All this optimism was made possible by the American Industrial Revolution. That great sweating engine, clanking away since the end of the Civil War, gobbling up the Virgin America so fast that by 1900 the USA had become Number One Industrial Power of the world! Pop music was a branch of that revolution.

The pop branch had worked hard. It had stripped-down catalogues, and complex sales methods. It was geared to scoring a hit. All this was a far cry from the sleepy days of genteel publishers such as Firth, Pond & Co. They had hits true enough – but they didn't cash in on them. They didn't plug. They had them almost in a fit of absence of mind. Lowell Mason's hymn collection did a half million over the years and Stephen Foster's 'Old Folks at Home' did a very slow million. There was no trumpeting and no award-giving.

The old firms had dignity and much too much music (one of them had over 30,000 different pieces). Like an old country store they kept everything somewhere, only they weren't sure exactly where. They had imported 'motto' songs, Swiss yodel songs, overtures, mazurkas, quadrilles, polkas, 'The Pope He Leads a Happy Life', funeral tunes, stacks of marches – including 'The Ocean Telegraph March of 1871', with a cover depicting the 'side view of the Atlantic Cable laid bare, showing protection of 18 iron wires, each 7 strands'.

Hymns were extremely popular. America was a collection of small towns with space in between and, until show-business got organized, the church was chief impresario and she liked hymns for her suppers, meetings and get-togethers. As long as the words were uplifting it didn't matter that the tunes were voluptuous. People sang 'What a Friend We Have in Jesus' even at work.

But in 1892 a strange thing happened. Not only was this the year of the first self-conscious million seller ('After The Ball'), but it was also the year in which Coca-Cola ceased being advertised as a patent medicine. It was no longer *improving*. It was now proclaimed a pleasurable soft drink. Fun is taking the place of moral uplift!

Tearful songs were next in popularity to hymns in those days. Tears were considered good and right and natural. And trembling, weeping, swooning were common occurrences. This was not just confined to America: Chancellor Bismarck of Germany wept often with Wilhelm I. Prime Minister Gladstone of England broke down in private and public.

Harris, American but a true Victorian, cried whenever he sang 'After the Ball'. Fellow songwriter Paul Dresser, a big man, played through his new effort 'On the Banks of the Wabash' to his novelist brother Theodore Dreiser and soon both had tears streaming down their cheeks. The nineties were to be called 'gay' but they were full of tears . . .

The pardon came too late, the letter was edged in black, the widower sat on his wife's grave with blinding tears falling as he sang of his lost pearl, the child asked the switchboard girl for heaven because her mother was there and the wires seemed to moan; the soldier's last words were 'Just break the news to mother', and the boy's last words were 'Don't send me to bed and I'll be good.'

Spreading a soft glow of feeling all over the body, these songs mirrored a cruel world governed by Fate. The listeners had a good cry and then, sensibly, got on with the job. Right into the early pop music years these heart-felt songs flowed, but their days were numbered. Pretty soon they were relieved by the tear-jerker. And the parody: 'Don't Go in the Lion's Cage Tonight', written in the

7

early 1900s, told of a circus mother who didn't heed her daughter's warning and conseqently had her head bitten off during show-time.

'Lucky Jim' (1896) is a curious piece – a transitional tear ballad, half jokey and half serious. In it, two pals are rivals but one of them, Jim, is always lucky. He marries the girl but dies and the narrator marries the widow. At last he's lucky too. But: 'Now we're married oft I think of Jim, boys – sleeping in the graveyard by the sea. Oh Lucky Jim! How I envy him!' Here we are with parody or tear-jerking or both. Anyway, we're on the brink of *decadence*.

Hymns and tear songs were only a small part of the huge and scattered American popular music scene before Tin Pan Alley. We shall look into the orifices where ragtime and beat developed in the next chapter. Meanwhile we continue to delve about in gentility. It was a gentility that didn't care too much for art. French chateaux were shipped in brick by brick, it's true, but they sat lonely in the desert. As for art-music, it had to be spectacular or uplifting. Nevertheless, there was an appetite for certain kinds of refined entertainment, and nineteenth-century America was crisscrossed by European performers satisfying big-hearted audiences. Oscar Wilde, on a lecture tour, was impressed with the hearty miners, but Booth Slezengar-Davies, the Welsh harpist, found the natives ' supremely vulgar' (stranded in Montana without a booking and with two arrows in his instrument). Charles Dickens, never without bookings, noted with disgust several gentlemen of Washington 'who in the course of conversation, frequently missed the spittoon at five paces'.

America was a plum. Audiences laid bare their hearts waiting to be massaged. One of the most popular roving entertainers was Englishman Henry Russell. Between 1833 and 1841 he roamed around the genteel circuit with his songs from the piano; self-penned melodramas including 'Life on the Ocean Wave' and many yearnings for the old village pump, the old family clock, the old spinning wheel, the old sexton. *Old* – essential ingredient of conservative popular song. Russell knew how to work an audience into high tension: he had a song about the axing of an old tree, with a chorus line which went 'Woodman, woodman, spare that tree!' This is the kind of thing that happened at concerts after he'd crashed out the final chord: old gentleman cries out, 'And was the tree spared?' 'Yes it was, actually,' admits Russell with an internal wink. 'Thank God!' sobs the aged party, 'I can breathe again!!'

On his travels round America, entertainer Russell often bumped into other European acts – Swiss yodelling families, German trombonists, trick pianists. He had an interesting chat with Norwegian violinist Ole Bull, who complained that he'd lost a good deal of his audience in New Orleans to a 'nigger fiddler'. This fiddler reportedly played a strange, awry music from the Bush. Could it have been early blues? Or ragtime? America was virgin, full of strange noises (later to be captured and tamed by Tin Pan Alley).

Meanwhile, the problem-task of bringing good music to Americans was vexing music reformers all through the nineteenth century. The idea was to stop Americans becoming American. They must be made to hear European classical music till they liked it. They must be taught how to play it correctly, that is, from the book. Yankee music teachers – coat-tails a-flying, mounted on wild horses – were dispatched to deepest Bush America to battle aberrations such as hillbilly mountain airs and fiendish jigs. This music may have come from Europe, but it was the wrong Europe, the uncivilized Celtic regions.

The blues writer W. C. Handy, musical director at an Alabama school in 1900, commented in his autobiography, '. . . there seemed to be an unwritten law against American music and any inferior song of foreign origin was considered "classical".'

When it came to classical music the most popular item in America was concert variations on 'Yankee Doodle'. But when it came to entertainment the Nigger Minstrels were tops. From 1840 to 1900 their 'chaste, unique and instructive music' dominated the European acts and even spread to the Old World – to the Adelphi Theatre in London in 1842, then to Queen Victoria herself, and eventually to Delhi via a band called 'The Hindu Ethiopian Serenaders'.

In the minstrel shows, their songs, dances and their presentation

9

of the Negro, we have pop music in the making. The main character, the Invisible Man, had been discovered in late eighteenth-century England when the Age of Reason was giving way to the Age of Romance. Captain Cook revealed that there were noble savages in the South Seas living naturally, uncontaminated by civilization. This golden age soon had its own music. In London, white Charles Dibdin immortalized the blackamoor as both sufferer and comedian in polite songs which he performed at salon recitals. In America, land of the new golden age where there were plenty of real blackamoors, Gottlieb Graupner appeared as the 'Gay Negro Boy' in 1799. He was a rave and many white 'black' performers followed. The impersonation became more authentic in the 1830s with the success of actor Thomas Rice and his Negro dialect song and dance, 'Jump Jim Crow':

> Wheel about an' turn about an' do jis so
> An' ebery time ah wheel about ah jump Jim Crow.

Yes, said Rice, this is what the darkies do. Even if it *was*, 'Jump Jim Crow' was uncannily like an old British folk song and an equally old British clog dance. The London *Times* reviewer even detected the 'Scotch snivel, the Hibernian whoop and the English guffaw'.

Rice inspired a number of rambling Jim Crows. They were all 'singles' until, in 1842, a depression drove many of them to merge into troupes, the most successful being the Virginia Minstrels. They seem to have been a noisy but cheerful quintet, making music from the banjo (of African origin) and the bones (of unknown origin), singing their own plantation songs and performing their version of a Negro dance later to be dubbed the 'Cakewalk' (see the next chapter for details on this dance). A little later Ed Christy and his Christy Minstrels established the traditional minstrel show form: the semi-circle of darkies with, in the middle, their jolly boss Mr Interlocutor. He served as a 'feed' or 'stooge' for the jokes (mostly puns) of tambourine-man Mr Tambo and bone-man Mr Bones. Between the jokes were songs and dances. Halfway through the show came the 'olio' in which individuals (sometimes in white-face) were allowed to shine. The finale consisted of some

10

gentle satire on topical events. These minstrel shows were originally a Northern phenomenon. In the 1850s the movement for the abolition of slavery was rapidly expanding. Jim Crow and his darky friends were often presented as pathetic and oppressed beings. Reason enough to get rid of the snoring South – so economically backward, too.

But there were other Negro characters popular in minstrel songs who weren't at all pathetic. Old Dan Tucker, Zip Coon and Jimmy-crack-corn-but-I-don't-care – they were sturdy frontiersmen, coloured Daniel Boones. Later there was Jim Dandy, another minstrel invention, and he foreshadowed the cocksure, city-bred Yankee Doodle Dandy, Mr Twentieth Century America himself, strutting to a Sousa march or a ragtime beat, out to astound the Old World. From black face into white face.

In the early minstrel songs both poor slave and rip-roaring coon lived in a pastoral idyll called the Deep South where life was one continuous story, where lily-fingered, pink-faced girls with teeth like pearls laughed, where the air was filled with the scent of magnolias. But by the start of the new century this gentle evocation of plantation life was vanishing and the minstrel show featured ragtime and vicious coon songs. As a form it was decaying: white-faced comedians abounded, sometimes there were performing snakes, and the olio (the middle bit) was taking over. In the olio the hits of the day were sung and new songs were plugged. Stars began to emerge from the communal ranks: George Primrose, Al Jolson, Eddie Cantor. The wandering minstrel show was soon eclipsed by fast, brash, citified vaudeville. But the colourful darky and the sweet southern never-never land became staples of pop music, as we shall see . . .

Ironically, the minstrel show lingered on in the South as an entertainment featuring real Negroes, right into the thirties. These shows had little to do with the original minstrel idea and were dismal affairs, managed by white men, often merely an excuse to sell quack medicines. W. C. Handy has described well the sordidness and violence of these decadent minstrel shows in the land of Jim Crow.

'Orange was the Texas town we dreaded most.' (Handy was

touring with the Georgia Minstrels.) 'Whenever it became known to the home-town mob that our show was routed their way, they would sit up all night waiting for the train to pass. Their conception of wild, he-man fun was to riddle our car with bullets as it sped through their town.' Handy's friend, the boy trombonist Louis Wright, was snowballed in a Missouri town by some white rough-necks. 'He retaliated swiftly, laying down a blast of curses.' Cornered later by a lynch mob he fired his gun into them. The sheriff arrested the entire minstrel troupe and gave Wright to the mob. 'He was lynched, his tongue cut out and his body shipped to his mother in Chicago in a pine box.' Jimmy Crack-Corn had come a long way.

It was a strange romance, this white obsession with the black. Nothing was to be done in halves. Today, even, the romantic blackman haunts pop. 'If the Negro were not there we might have to invent him,' wrote James Baldwin in our time. He is a figure either 'saint or danger'. He is 'the guilty imagination of the white people who invest him with their hates and longings'.

We jump back to early minstrel days. The success of Ed Christy's minstrel show encouraged Stephen Foster to write his songs – 'The Old Folks at Home', 'Camptown Races', 'Beautiful Dreamer', 'Jeannie with the Light Brown Hair', 'Oh Susannah!' Could anyone have actually sat down and put together 'Oh Susannah!'? That tune hummed in nurseries, dinned through Westerns! More likely it was entombed in rock and Foster dug it out. Actually he sweated hard to produce the *vaguely familiar*. Many of his songs failed. Then, as now, the successful popular song is the result of a marriage between pop man and public.

Foster is the first pop composer but he lived in prehistoric times, pre-Chas K. Harris, pre-Alley, pre-pleasure. He was from Pennsylvania, the son of a colonel. He dropped out of music school quite early and went and peeked shyly into the knockabout world of riverboats, blacks, roughnecks. He wrote about America (which was rare then) and his songs were spread by Christy's Minstrels. Some of them sold in hundreds of thousands.

But his publishers were sleepy and pop was unorganized. And

Foster was at first terribly ashamed of his vulgar songs; possibly he was affected by an attack in *Dwight's Journal of Music* which, in 1852, condemned his tunes as 'only skin deep . . . hummed and whistled without musical emotion'. Worse than that – 'They persecute and hunt the morbidly sensitive nerves of musical persons so that they too hum and whistle them involuntarily – hating them even while they hum them.'

This was the noxious weed which was the pop song, insinuating itself into the brain of even good music lovers, and sticking there like sellotape.

Foster eventually plucked up enough courage to cut himself off from the genteel world and become a complete songwriter. He married and started pot-boiling, turning out stuff that didn't sell. He tried writing straight lugubrious ballads instead of happy darky songs. He wrote a lot of songs about Willie, a dying boy. His marriage went on the rocks as the money ran out. He was drinking heavily. Broke and alone, he moved into a room in New York's Bowery, a rough neighbourhood. One day he fell over a washbasin. Somebody took him to Bellevue Hospital where he died on 13 January 1864.

A fatal calling was songwriting! In the 'Bohemian years' (before organization) many were the writers who ended tragically. James Thornton (also a singing waiter and monologist) often fell off the stage, once saw men with crab's legs, and went on to write the lovely lilting 'My Sweetheart's the Man in the Moon' and that close-harmony favourite 'When You were Sweet Sixteen'. He died broke in the thirties. Charles Graham ('Two Little Girls in Blue') died in 1899 in the Bellevue Alcoholics Section. Hart Danks ('Silver Threads among the Gold') died in a New York rooming house, leaving a note which read 'It's hard to die alone.' Paul Dresser ('My Gal Sal', 'Banks of the Wabash'), a really nice person, tried song publishing but his firm collapsed. He died broke and broken-hearted.

All these men, true romantics and good company, warned of the perils of the BIG CITY. Of the girl who had left her sea-side homestead for the *city and its strife* and now her picture was *turned towards the wall*. Later, she was found in the city, in the gutter. But somewhere a mother was waiting for her who had *seen better days* and she would be buried in the *old-fashioned country church*.

Afterwards, the writers met at the 'Grip' or the 'Black Rabbit', or other such saloons and dives in order to get down to some heavy mixtures: brandy mash, sherry cobblers, rum and gum. The big city, with all its pressures, created a killing schizophrenia – had they but known about schizophrenia. Hard to live the eternal truths here amongst the canyons of soaring skyscrapers and creeks of festering slums! In the latter lived the one-time plough-boy and the one-time Russian (fresh off the boat from Europe), feeding the machines by day, and by night needing refreshment that had a bit of spice. Left behind were the home-town serenading, the simple pleasures of candy-pulling and progressive tiddlywinks. Left behind, too, was the dim age of folk music when the song was part of the work – bringing on the rain, helping the crops, blessing the marriage. The new city folk needed instant entertainment. Ready-made. Off-the-peg. A tune for every mood, washing the gritty bits of hard life away.

Between 1880 and 1900 the urban population more than doubled. America was still a rural country, mark you, but the city was the future and New York the Santa Claus factory where the fun was to come from. Did the city folk need the city? *The city needed them!*

Vaudeville, begun in New York, influenced by England, was America's favourite entertainment by 1900. The olio of the minstrel show became the whole of vaudeville. Gradually the truly pastoral was eased out and the city slicker arrived, jeering at the rubes. '45 Minutes from Broadway' – went George M. Cohan's song – was hicksville and hopeless.

Tony Pastor was the first to use the dainty French word 'vaudeville', to describe the variety show he presented in 1881 in New York. It was aspiring middle class – what every American moved towards after he had been melted or absorbed. Pastor set the scene by having a prayer-room in his theatre and spruce ushers with undulating walks and high-pitched voices. His clientele, he claimed, were from the best families in the metropolis. Others followed the Pastor vaudeville. Keith & Proctor's started non-stop vaudeville and established the 'chain'. By 1900 they had 400 vaudeville theatres.

Vaudeville was an Irish stew of acts that included anything which might attract the public, from one-legged acrobats to John L. Sullivan (the fighter), William Jennings Bryan (the politician) and President McKinley's niece on crutches. What the acts needed desperately was cheap music and this was where the new pop publishers came in: vaudeville became the chief vehicle for pop song, with the genteel lady trade a poor second.

And Chas K. Harris stood between the two. At last we are back with Chas K.! And the dawn of the century! The dark nineteenth will recede but may keep bobbing back.

Harris looked to a bright future. He was optimistic. There was a cockiness in the air. You could touch it with your fingers. You could hear it in the roistering Irish vaudeville songs like 'Throw Him Down McCloskey'. You could hear it and *feel* it in the brisk, razzy All-American marches of John Philip Sousa. They said he was a foreigner but he wasn't. Maybe he was the son of an immigrant but he was born and raised and inspired by America. At 26 he was appointed conductor of the US Marine Band. He wrote marches for this band, including 'Stars and Stripes Forever', a neatly assembled flame of controlled fire, guaranteed to make the lame walk.

At his concerts Sousa had many requests for Harris's 'After the Ball'. But he had many more for the new 'Cakewalk' sensations. Especially syncopation numbers like 'Creole Belles' and 'At a Georgia Camp Meeting'. These appealed more to the body than to the heart, but Chas K. wasn't worried. Such things would soon pass.

In his little red book he wrote: 'The day of the rough coon song is over. Styles in songs change as quickly as ladies' millinery.'

Ragtime

Got more troubles than I can stand
Ever since ragtime has struck the land,
Never saw the like in all of my days
Everybody's got the ragtime craze . . .

Cakewalk music, it fills the air.
It can't be dodged because it's everywhere.
Once I didn't belong you see
But now you can't lose me!

I got a ragtime dog and a ragtime cat
A ragtime piano in my ragtime flat.
I'm wearing ragtime clothes from hat to shoes
I read a paper called 'The Ragtime News'.
I got ragtime habits and I talk that way
I sleep in ragtime and rag all day.
Got ragtime troubles with my ragtime wife.
I'm certainly leading a ragtime life!

(written in 1899 by Jefferson and Roberts)

A wave of vulgar, filthy and suggestive music has inundated the land. The pabulum of theatre and summer hotel orchestras is coon music. Nothing but ragtime prevails and the cakewalk with its obscene posturings, its lewd gestures. It is artistically and morally depressing and should be suppressed by press and pulpit.

(from the *Musical Courier*, 1899)

What is scurrilously called ragtime is an invention that is here to stay . . . Syncopations are no indication of light or trashy music, and to shy bricks at 'hateful ragtime' no longer passes for musical culture.

(ragtime composer Scott Joplin, in his 1908 instruction book, *The School of Ragtime*)

16

Ragtime

Ragtime is the American Creation and the Marvel of Musicians in all Civilized Countries.

(his publisher, John Stark)

Syncopation is in the soul of every true American. Ragtime is the best heart-raiser and worry banisher that I know . . . Someday I'm going to write a syncopated grand opera.

(Irving Berlin)

Ragtime, like ladies millinery, was Queen for its day – reigning hard until it died, succeeded by parvenu 'jazz'. THE QUEEN IS DEAD – LONG LIVE THE QUEEN! because this ragtime (a street word meaning constant, non-stop, marathon *syncopation*) once injected into the comfy body of nineteenth-century pop, set the heart-beat pumping, pulsing out a rhythm which, in 1900, was but a stately clatter, by 1917 a krazy zoo of jazz, by 1936 a streamline of sleek swing, and NOW is swollen into a thunder cloud of electronics pumped out of a smart city of amplifiers.

Poor ragtime! *Real, classic, timeless* ragtime – fine art form – has been much misunderstood, like Mae West. When I played a rag recently to a friendly rock record producer he knocked his knees, kicked his heels, crying 'A scooby-doo, a razzamatazz – you're just like Julie Andrews, man!' *Jesus wept!*

Ragtime reigned from 1897 till 1917,* the year that America went into the Great War, marching to ragtime. After this last stand the music seemed archaic: upright stuff for the upright piano, or player piano jangle (for in 1919 these automatic pianos outnumbered the human variety) or just comic accompaniment for Keystone Cop movies.

Mortally wounded by jazz age taste, pioneer ragtime publisher John Stark refused to attend a jazz concert by Paul Whiteman, King of Jazz, and broadsided by titling a 1921 rag publication 'Don't Jazz Me – I'm Music.' About the same time Joseph Lamb, reclusive writer of baroquey rags, submitted some of his latest gem-works to Alleyman publisher Irving Mills. 'Yes,' asked Mills,

*But the ballad *ruled*, as we shall see in the next chapter.

17

'but can't you write me some novelettes like "Nola"? That's what they want.' At the end of the twenties Bennie Moten, swing band pioneer, began a record with some two-fisted ragtime piano. Suddenly one of his side-men complained: 'Hey, Benny! Stop playing that *ragtime*! Let's get real low down!' ... They did and played the 'Get Low Down Blues'.

Classy old ragtime put down by the guttersnipes of jazz and blues!! Yet their time, too, would be over some day, just as soon as the city people, the mass middle class, decided they didn't need such music any more.

Ragtime had been torn from the Bush, ragtime was thrown away on to the pop rubbish heap. Ragtime was rescued years later by a few music lovers.

But now – ragtime in its historical context, a close look at the syncopated locomotion which caused such a commotion ...

In the ragtime era most people just danced, hummed, ejaculated 'It's a bear!' to the new music. Not thinking twice they taxied to ragtime balls where they balled the jack, walked the dog, won the prize. Others, whose livings were in jeopardy, howled 'It's a disgrace!' A select, precious few – those who wrote about serious music in journals and quarterlies, knew a B flat from an A sharp – argued whether ragtime was the real American Music or not.

Maybe Antonín Dvořák, classical composer, started the row during his American visit (1892–5) when he commented that 'In the Negro melodies of America I discover all that is needed for a great and noble school of music.' By the time ragtime had surfaced, a few years later, native academic Rupert Hughes wrote that 'Ragtime has come to stay' and soon 'would be handled with respect by the scholarly musicians of the whole world'.

This was fighting talk in the ivory studies! Into the fray rushed Daniel Gregory Mason, a New Englander and music writer, stating that ragtime was a mere 'comic strip', representing America's 'vices' and 'not a new flavour but a kind of curry'. His friend Dr Karl Muck wrote to him (in 1915, just before being expelled as an enemy alien), 'I think what you call here your rag-

18

time is *poison*. It poisons the source of your musical growth, for it poisons the taste of the young.'

Argument was fierce because the awful truth was that young America had produced no such thing as a truly American music until this ragtime poison. Here was a rude noise which had emerged steaming from the hinterland bush of brothels and dives, presented on stage, record and cabaret in a negroid manner by Jews very often, and so popular that even high society gentlemen such as Vanderbilt danced to it. Crude majority taste had fostered this syncopation, not the approved hot-house of the musical conservatory – and where crude majority taste dominated, *art languished and died*.

Anyway, wrote Mason, all this syncopated music wasn't even American; it was un-American. 'The Jew and the Yankee stand in human temperament at polar points ... Jewish taste has oriental extravagance and sensuous brilliancy.' Even so, he admitted, ragtime may well be a reflection of these raucous times, because it was without 'soul', without those noble and uplifting thoughts of progress towards a better world and regrets for a mis-spent past, without, in fact, all the *good* which 'good' music could spread. This new music was full of 'bangs and explosions, like a criminal novel'.

'Exactly,' joined Hiram K. Motherwell, as he entered the academic fight. 'Bangs and explosions' were important because this was the sound of the city, expressing its 'jerk and rattle, its restless bustle and motion, its multitude of unrelated details and its underlying progress towards a vague somewhere.'

Ragtime was more than a music. It was Our Time – the ragtime life with patent-leather shoes in many colours plus pearl buttons, a soft shirt of loud silk; female secretaries grabbing the snatched lunch, gobbling an evening meal made by just adding heat; all living on hot asphalt surrounded by autos, phonographs, movies and all part of a wider world which exploded daily in banner headlines –

ATLANTIC TIDAL WAVE CLAIMS 275 VICTIMS
IN GALVESTON!

19

HEIR TO AUSTRO–HUNGARIAN THRONE ASSASSINATED!

HARRY K. THAW SLAYS NOTED ARCHITECT IN LOVE TRIANGLE!

Society balls, even, were filled by circles 'of brilliant debutantes and impatient youths waiting for the first bars of some wonderful imminent dance music' (Henry James). That music was to come, as we shall see, and pretty soon the whole ragtime life burst out of America and into the Old World. In France imaginations worked full-time to describe rag as 'le temps du chiffon', music hall singers excitedly sang:

> Un deux trois!
> On lance le ventre en avant
> En t'nant les bras ballants
> Comme un orang-outang.

Avant-garde artists saw this 'chiffon' music as just the stuff to go well with fauve painting, because of all those gobs and smears of notes. Stravinsky rushed into manuscript with something he called 'Ragtime'. In Bradford, Yorkshire, England, J. B. Priestley, novel-ist in embryo, watched American ragtime acts at his local music hall and realized in later years that popular music could be prophetic:

Out of this ragtime came fragmentary outlines of the menace to old Europe, the domination of America, the emergence of Africa, the end of confidence and any feeling of security, the nervous excitement, the frenzy of modern times.

Herald of the Third World, Fauve Music, Sound of The City, America's Music, Poisonous Curry, Julie Andrews Razzamatazz, Pure Filth – this is ragtime. Who invented it? Where did it come from? In the first chapter we examined a rather genteel nineteenth-century America full of tears, yet with an edge of wildness. We now journey into another nineteenth-century world – out in the stamping beaty bush – ready to join regular America. We journey to find the inventors of ragtime ...

Many claim to have invented ragtime, just as many claim jazz and blues. But the inventor individuals have been lost in the folk fog of pre-history. You may figure that ragtime was African, an extension of the voodoo thump of the tom-tom, you may claim that it was nothing more than bar-room pianists getting fed-up with churning out the same old pop tunes and jiggling the melodies. You may say anything.

Most everything which makes us what we are today came out of that nineteenth century. Right now all I'm going to do is jab down a few comments and facts and then clear out of this territory, which I'll leave to experts with all the paraphernalia and patience. I may well upset them in the following, and will be cut in campus coffee bars.

Nineteenth-century America was full of musics sold and taught: march music, minstrel songs, parlour pieces, hymn tunes. Musics which came from *above*. At the same time, and much mistier in origin, was music from *below*; untaught, unsold; story ballads, jig and clog dances from the British Isles. Performance was all wrong, all unorthodox because it was self-taught. Mixed up in this great stew was the ex-African, and exactly what he brought over from Africa is not at all clear.

A whole rustic band of musical folk grew up who sang wrong, played the fiddle cack-handedly, ill-fingered the piano, and messed with unorthodox instruments such as the stove-pipe and the jew's harp. Wrong academically, right emotionally. All over the great sprawling virgin America, and especially in the South, were crevices and orifices unexplored by either teachers or salesmen.

For all we know, in this bushland there may have been folk dancing to 'Rock around the Clock'. But even if rock existed in some hidden valley there would have been no great demand at this point in time, and so this music would have had to lie quiet, charming but irrelevant.

Until they reached for the restraints of middle-classness, these bush people, black or white and poor, were not rhythm-resistant. At white revivalist camp meetings of the 1840s, preachers excited crowds of up to ten thousand with rocking 'call and response' services. Three-line hymns, half sung/half spoken, framed a sort of blue-eyed blues. The congregation shook, whirled, hopped, jumped for joy. Some cut loose to 'stamp out sin' with their own religious dance, or suddenly broke into eery tunes snatched from the sky.

In the black churches rave-ups were in rhythm. In 1823 a genteel observer ventured into this Third World, into a black Brimstone Church to witness a black Methodist preacher chanting a musical Hamlet: 'To be or not to be – dat is him question. Whether him nobler in de mind to suffer or lift up him arms against one sea of hubble-bubble and by oppossum endem.' Upon the word 'oppossum' the congregation cried out for 'Possum up a Gum Tree', a current slave hit.

Was this an African tune? To the genteel observer it sounded British. But the hymns with their bell-clear righteous chords were twisted and broken by the voices of these people, black and white, so that they re-emerged as brand new numbers. Sturdy old British ballads suffered the same fate; in 1830 Fanny Kemble, an actress, was boat-rowed by slaves who sang a wailing air, 'wild and unaccountable', which she later identified as 'Comin' thru the Rye'. More important, she noticed that this British folk song was accompanied by a rhythm section of rocking rollocks.

There were other isolated black performers who dazzled audiences with their weird playing. Ole Bull, the straight Norwegian violinist, complained to concert balladeer Henry Russell about the popularity of a Negro fiddler in New Orleans. Juba, a black dancer, got as far as Vauxhall Gardens, London, where he gave dancing displays with his hands in his pockets. Picayne Butler, also black, picked waltzes and polkas on his banjo to a New York audience in 1857 – picked them so hard he bust two strings.

All this is interesting and colourful. But out of this underworld of stamping, raving, wild hymn-singing, banjo-picking, jigging and 'Comin' thru the Rye' surfaced ragtime around 1890 – a music riddled with a rhythm called syncopation, but which also owed much to the harmonies of the gentler European world, the world bowed to by Chas K. Harris, and to the pattern of the march as developed by John Philip Sousa. Ragtime rumbled from out of the bush – but was to be written not for the banjo or stove pipe or guitar but for that dignified Victorian machine, the piano.

Wandering pianists were making a decent living playing for customers and dancers in what were called 'tenderloin' or 'red light' districts in the expanding cities. These districts housed saloons, brothels, clip joints, gambling hells, honky tonks, and jook joints. The popular piano style was termed variously 'barrel-house', 'boogie', 'honky tonk', 'jag-time', 'jig-time' and the pianists were 'professors' or 'fakers'. They could play anything. Stories are told by aged ragmen of legendary syncopated pianists who could rag the Messiah at 100 miles an hour, who could hold a pint of rye and still rag well, who were playing 13ths before they were invented, who had names like One-leg this or No-hands that. Most of the best tenderloin piano was to be heard in southern cities such as Memphis, Nashville, New Orleans and St Louis rather than the western San Francisco, the northern Chicago or the eastern New York.

One of these wandering honky tonk pianists, not content to celebrate just the passing moment, not wishing to kill himself with booze and the sporting life by playing mere dance music, fashioned this rough jagged/ragged time into a delicate form leaning to the concert hall rather than the hot crib. He was black Scott Joplin (1868–1917). His Joplin ragtime established the pop-to-art pattern that was later followed by both jazz and rock 'n' roll.

Before we look at ragtime as song and dance I want briefly to tell the story of Scott Joplin and his art-form, classic ragtime.

He came from Texarkana, Texas. A German teacher gave him some piano lessons; later he studied advanced harmony at college. He wandered around southwestern cities playing the tenderloin circuit and then in Sedalia, Missouri he wrote 'The Maple Leaf Rag' (named after the Maple Leaf Club, a local honky tonk). Before this he'd put together some standard pop – sentimental waltz songs and a 'Great Crush Collision March' – but 'Maple Leaf', published by local white John Stark, became a best-seller (1899). From now onwards Joplin concentrated on his ragtime, polishing and honing it into a set form. He played a little vaudeville, but avoided the sporting belt, made some money giving piano lessons – and wrote and wrote: thirty-three rags by himself (more

23

keep turning up), seven rags with others and a brace of ragtime operas.

In 1915 he tried out one of these operas, *Treemonisha* (a plantation story showing how the old voodoo superstitions must be discarded if the Negro was to get enlightened and modern). The Harlem audience was embarrassed by this seeming throwback to slavery days. And that was that. Next year he moved to a Manhattan hospital, his mind wandering. On April Fool's Day 1917 he died* – the year that vaudeville ragtime marched American soldiers into the First World War.

Joplin gathered other rag classicists around him like Arthur Marshall and Scott Hayden, who produced gorgeous lyrical rags. Also attracted to Joplin rag was the unlikely Joseph Lamb, a white Catholic who had never played in a brothel but wrote at home in a frame house in Brooklyn – after work, for he was in the fabric trade. Lamb produced his baroque beauties right into the Elvis Presley age, unperturbed. All these classicists were published and championed by ragtime knight errant John Stark. Mostly the rags were sent in untitled so that Stark could express the artistic pretensions of ragtime by calling them 'Grace And Beauty', 'Elite Syncopations', 'Euphonic Sounds'. He described 'Cole Smoak' as rendering up 'the interior thoughts of the soul'.

Joplin seems to have been, like Stark, a rather serious, dignified man, aware of his own worth. He opined that 'Maple Leaf Rag' would make him 'King of the Ragtime Composers' but he also knew that he would not be a pop hero in his own lifetime. 'When I'm dead twenty-five years people are going to recognize me,' he told a friend. Just over thirty years later he *was* recognized: Rudi Blesh wrote a fat and rich book about ragtime ('the true story of an American music') – dedicated to the memory of Scott Joplin. Another writer spent several pages analysing Joplin's rag 'Euphonic Sounds'.

Classic ragtime, then, was a self-conscious art form. Each rag was stamped with its composer's music marks; each rag was built to last. The finest demanded a delicate, unrushed performance by classically trained pianists. Joplin had published an instruction

*Not actually of a broken heart, but of an advanced form of syphilis.

24

book laying down precise rules: 'Exercise 5: the first ragtime effect here is the second note, right hand, but instead of a tie, it is an eighth note rather than two sixteenths with tie'.

Performed in the proper place – a quiet room on a well-tuned piano during a peaceful afternoon – classic ragtime is therapeutic. The fingers limber up as they dance over the keys. Diminisheds shake, sixteenths wobble, as you struggle through the luscious slices of the set form: first a fanfare flourish, then three or four strains with key changes announced by more fanfare flourishes. The brain swims in ecstasy, the feet tap. In 1900 a pianist trying out a rag could see before his very eyes the collision between old and new, the old oak replaced by the swaying skyscraper. As left hand marched steadily along with the safe old 'oompah-oompah', right hand syncopated, trying to trip up the traditional with cascades of battered notes. But thick German harmonies kept the whole exercise well-housed.

> Och Himmel the carpets wave up und wave down
> Und der light she go round mit a schwing
> Dot hot razzle dazzle – I can't find der notes
> Und der time he gone crazy by Jing!

Average pianists just couldn't manage real ragtime. Hands got tangled up, and besides, you hadn't any words and you hadn't any dancing. Really a very selfish exercise! In the 1890s most people preferred to enjoy 'coon songs' and to attempt a 'cake-walk' dance.

Today coonery seems at best quaint and at worst disgusting racism, so I shall just mention some statistics in an attempt to show the tie-up between this obsession for the black and the historical setting. From 1865 (the end of the Civil War), the ex-slaves had steadily emigrated from the countryside into the cities. The first dramatic increase in urban blacks was between 1890 and 1900 – and that was the decade of the coon vogue, when over 600 coon songs were published. By 1910 the urban black was becoming a fixture rather than a phenomenon: twelve cities with over 40,000 – and New York had had a 50 per cent increase. After 1910 the coon vogue vanished and ragtime became white-faced in both song and dance.

Happy Alley Days

In song the pastoral plantation darky of Stephen Foster days was replaced by the coon, ludicrous and threatening. Who wrote the stuff? – white or black? Both because this was the 'Age of Accommodation' for the Negro, a time for attempting to join the white world. Like the East European Jews, they were so low on the social scale they just *had* to make it, or sink out of sight. There was no question of rebellion; those with spunk were determined to 'move on up in the world'. Black society had its Elks and its clubs, such as 'Sons and Daughters of "I WILL ARISE"'.

The coon-song was of folk origin, but the vogue was commercially started by vaudeville pianist/entertainer Ben Harney, a black who passed for white. He claimed to be the inventor of ragtime, but a very different kind to the retiring Joplin's. The latter wrote a piece called 'Chrysanthemum – an Afro-American Intermezzo'; Harney wrote 'This Sportin' Life is Certainly Killin' Me'. That was a big difference, and in the ragtime era black performers like Ernest Hogan ('All Coons Look Alike to Me') and Irving Jones ('I'm livin' easy eatin' pork chops greasy') presented the happy zippy coon, whilst Joplin, serious and studious, presented the New Negro.

Harney was noisy and boisterous, tapping his feet as he delivered his rag songs to New York vaudeville audiences in 1896. His songs told of 'hot stuff' crap games raided by the police ('Mr Johnson Turn Me Loose') and worn-out floozies ('You've Been a Good Ole Wagon but You've Done Broke Down'). They were all his own work, he said, but who knows? Possibly they were his versions of bawdy honky tonk songs – things like 'Baby Let Your Drawers Hang Down', performed at Babe Connors St Louis club where the girls danced the 'Ta-Ra-Ra-Boom-Deray' – full of bumps and grinds – on a mirror floor.

Harney broke up syllables: 'Put a smile on each face' became 'Pugut agey smugile ogon egeach fagace', a private patter in ragtime. His racy terms and bashed-up English countered the stilted 'thee and thou' of the sentimental Harrisian ballad and brought slangy speech into pop. Published by the house of Witmark, Harney's songs became big hits and the coon vogue spread. Plump matronly May Irwin, white, was queen of the coon-shouters, reaching right to the very back of theatres with her stentorian (slightly off-pitch) voice in 'If You Ain't Got No Money Well You Needn't Come Aroun' (by A. Baldwin Sloane, composer of *The Wizard of Oz* and other extravaganzas).*

Coon-shouters were popular almost into the twenties, but real blacks were much enjoyed, too. Norah Bayes and Sophie Tucker liked to surround themselves with dancing coloured kids called 'picks' by the trade. They could make the difference between a socko show and a flop. A vaudeville promoter advised 'If the bill is weak add a dark act, and if that don't do hire some picks.'

What of the songs themselves? They ranged from the vicious through the enlightened to the eupeptic. They pictured coloured city balls as colourful and dangerous. Reed and Ward's chorus ran 'Leave your razors at the door, don't yer start no ragtime war'. But – 'If you want some black man's gore, don't carve him to the core but take a good size brick and do the job up quick.' Dockstader's Minstrels had a hit with their warning 'There's a Dark Man Coming with a Bundle'. Andrew Sterling told the grim song-tale of a poor white man hired by a 'kinky woolly head' to dig a hole in the road. A crowd of fellow 'kinkies' surround the digging white as the black employer proclaims 'I've got a white man working for me'. Furious, the digger grabs his employer and shoves him down the hole:

He grabbed another, sent him down to smother in the dusky gloom below.
They started scrapping, but he wasn't napping as he cried 'You all must go.'
When he got through he covered up the hole – they couldn't see the light of day.
'Remember, coons,' he said, 'I'm far above you don't let me hear you say –
"*I've got a white man working for me.*"'

*She utilized the media without fear, performing the first screen kiss with J. C. Rice in the peep show film *Widow Jones*, and making some cylinder and circular records of coon songs (her voice and the style suited the early recording apparatus well).

Happy Alley Days

On the other hand the coon was very down-to-earth in a nice cosy way, like a Hobbit. He loved food, was always hymning hambones, lamb, watermelon, bacon, possum meat. Life held no greater joy than 'the sound of chicken fryin' in the pan – dat's good enough fer me'. The country might be on the verge of war but the burning issue for coon-song hero Abraham Jefferson Washington Lee was 'for de lawdy's sake feed mah dog!!' These charming children! Carefree, with no nation! In the 1900s New York was full of Germans, Italians, Irish, with their separate cultures and 'Every Race Has a Flag but the Coon' (as J. Fred Helf and Will Heelan put it). So the Blackville Club devised their own flag made of red flannel shirt, with a chicken sketched on it, poker dice for eyes, wavin' razors round the head, a possum with a pork chop in its teeth, a big hambone with a banjo underneath.

On stage and in song, the new coon was a hit. In real life he was a threat and by 1900 there were fourteen states with segregation laws. Booklets warned of the 'beast' Negro, 'a menace to civilization', and anthropologists considered him cousin to the ape.

To be fair, not all the coon songs were nasty. In fact Witmark's, the publishers, asked customers to 'look over the Genteel Coon Deviation "Melinda's Wedding Day",' and sold thousands of copies of their plantation slumber song, 'Mammy's Little Pumpkin-Colored Coons'. Carrie Jacobs-Bond actually wrote an anti-segregation piece in 1903 which did quite well:

> Give de chillun equal chance to start out side by side
> An as dey grows up big an' strong along der paf dat's wide
> Dey'll come to know each udder an dat 'color-line' will fade
> An de Lord'll surely bless us fer de peace dat we has made'.*

But the most potent figure of all in the coon vogue was the sexy strutter, best-beast in city clothes – a hot lover boy, whose girl begged 'Pump away Joseph' on your 'Red Hot Member – with a Sting Like a Bumble Bee'. A liberated lover, able to chuck out his babe with the words, 'Take Up Your Clothes and Go'. She too could be tough and put her easy rider out in the rain, later pleading 'Bill Bailey Won't You Please Come Home?' Marriage wasn't mentioned.

*'Movin' in de Bes' Society'

28

So though the new coon was a far cry from the gentle puns of the minstrel show, he was close to the new vaudeville audiences who, in 1910, were enjoying white-face songs like 'Somebody Will If You Don't'. 'New' was everywhere – in Tin Pan Alley a new breed of writers mixed coon song and syncopation with slick street wit ('When Ragtime Rosie Ragged the Rosary', 'I Love My Wife but Oh You Kid'), and applied the coloured lingo-jive to all city types so that their songs were filled with 'dolls', 'babes', 'A OKs', as well as 'wisenheimers'.

Irving Berlin (born Israel Baline in Russia) assimilated the ragtime style well and served up white-face ragtime in his clever 'Alexander's Ragtime Band' (1911) which had but one tiny dash of syncopation. No matter – for now ragtime was almost anything that was up-to-date and peppy. No longer were there only hot coons. The hot coon was joined by Ragtime Cowboy Joe, the Ragtime Soldier Man, the Ragtime Goblin Man, the Ragtime Suffragette, the Ragtime Violin, the Ragtime Temple Bell, the Ragtime Wedding Bell, the Ragtime Bungalow, not forgetting Ragtime Shakespeare.

So ragtime wasn't simply coloured time in 1910 but also modern times. The witty and slangy vaudeville songs suited the ragtime age of sudden strikes, deep depressions, assassination. *Variety*, the show business trade paper, noted an increase in hissing, cat-calls and Bronx cheers and editorialized 'Rowdyism must stop'. Musically, band ragtime fitted ill-rehearsed pit groups who could cut loose with laughing trombone, whinnying cornet, skidding violin and percussion barnyard effects – the very opposite of Joplin's disciplined opuses. Nevertheless, ragtime.

Even better suited to the vaudeville pit band was a curious style distinguished by crushed notes packed in an unorthodox twelve bars called the *Blues*, which first appeared in 1912, became a dance and vaudeville fad in 1914, merged into jazz in 1919, but was of mysterious black bush origin (as usual). Nobody could discover the folkman who invented the blues, a music magnet pulling the singer's voice towards a blurred squashy raspberry note, apparently just below the correct one. The effect was of a sob, a wail, most undignified; but it sent good girls crazy crying 'Smear it! Smear it!' Three blues numbers were rushed into print in 1912: 'Baby Seals Blues', 'Dallas Blues' and 'Memphis Blues'. The 1912 blues wasn't such a regular 12-bar form as the blues of the 1920s – many of them were sub-titled 'ragtime novelty' – but the smear-note style was there, best performed on horn or voice. Stenographer of the Blues (later to be called 'Father') was W. C. Handy, educated black dance-band leader from Memphis, who wrote street moans down on paper. His bandsmen complained, 'You're always hanging about on street corners listening to beggars.'

Handy listened on a railroad station as a ragged Negro, the 'sadness of ages' on his face, plunked a guitar (pressing a knife on the strings) and sang, making 'the weirdest music I ever heard'. Handy listened at a ball whilst his band rested and a coloured group consisting of guitar, mandolin and banjo 'struck up one of those over and over strains that seem to have no very clear beginning and certainly no end . . . the strumming attained a disturbing monotony, a kind of stuff that has long been associated with cane rows and levee camps'. Maybe it was swamp blues or cajun blues or geechee blues, or embryonic rock? Handy listened hard, notated the sounds from beggars, cigar-box guitars, iron-pipe basses, Lard Can Charlie on his hot can – and decided that this was the stuff that people wanted. He got it published.

Soon Tin Pan Alley was producing as many blues songs as rag songs, Hawaiian songs and Dixie Songs. And many were tunes which could do service as blues, rags, marches, ballads, novelties – at one and the same time!

Handy wrote a colossal hit in 1914 in 'The St Louis Blues' (later an Abyssinian battle hymn, part of the repertoire of the Balmoral Royal Pipers and the favourite tune of George VI's Queen). The tune (and early blues had roller-coaster tunes) began with a *tango* and then fell into a *fox-trot*. These were the two most popular dances of 1914, the climax year of an orgy of social dancing which had begun in 1911 with the turkey trot.

Here we are at the final and most important aspect of ragtime. Not everybody could sing, less and less played instruments (except the phonograph), but everybody could dance these ultra-simple new steps. Shuffling, bouncing, hugging, neck-holding, the rapidly expanding ranks of the new middle class danced into marriage or fleeting alliance in the anonymity of dance halls, dimly lit restaurant dance floors, taxi-girl joints, all to the accompaniment of ragtime played by a novel organization soon to crystallize into the Dance Band.

A little back-pedalling is necessary here in order to explain the great change wrought by Dance Mania (1911–17).

The Dancing Professors of America formed a society in 1879 in order to regulate and teach correct dancing. At that time all accepted dances were imported from European society and were tricky to do, requiring the services of the professors and stiffly correct string orchestras. At one end of the social scale were the society balls where everything was work to rule whilst at the other end were unregulated dance halls – many integrated – where couples ground together all night, where Negroes evolved such dances as the funky butt and the buzzard lope.

San Francisco's infamous Barbary Coast consisted of just three blocks of dance halls. Reformers ventured in and noted that: (1) men danced with their hands in their pockets, often smoking pipes as well; (2) women hoochie-coochied with their buttocks; (3) monkeys hopped about and chickens clucked. Even the waltz and the quadrille had become lecherous affairs – which was full circle because they'd originated in Europe as lecherous affairs and only later been cleaned-up by polite society!

The dance professors pretended that such dance halls didn't exist. But gradually untamed Afro-American folk dances started creeping into polite society balls. The first to creep in soon swept out and all over the Western World. This was the cakewalk, a stiff-backed high-stepped prance – said to have originated on the old plantation (black servants parodying the high-faluting ball steps of their masters). Like the European ballroom dances the cakewalk required skill and great energy. Its accompanying beat was the same as that required for march, two-step or polka. Thus the slave-step fitted in with older, vigorous dances.

Even so, the *Musical Courier* attacked the cakewalk's 'lewd

Happy Alley Days

gestures', the American Federation of Musicians passed a resolution condemning the playing of ragtime dance music, and the Dancing Teachers Association of America blacked syncopated dancing. George Hall put his finger on the culprit when he wrote in his 1901 book *Pitfalls of the Ballroom*: 'Behold, the Night must light the Day! Africa must teach America!'

The cakewalk was a team effort done in lines, almost a light fantastic tripping compared with what was to come in 1911. Within the original black cakewalk there was room for individuals to fashion their own steps and it was from these inventions, these impressions of animals that the animal dances came. The dragging and shuffling of feet – the very opposite of ball ethereal tripping – the crouched body, all movement driven from the pelvic region – these were characteristics of African dance. George Hall had been prophetic!

Out of this communal Negro cakewalk came individual dance steps done by boy and girl, and it was these which appealed to 1911 Americans: bunny hug, turkey trot, grizzly bear, monkey glide, kangaroo dip, all these animal dances became the rage between 1911 and 1915. If such Afro-American dances hadn't been shot through with sensuousness they probably would have remained as delightful folk dances. After all, Eastern American cities were crammed with ghetto folk dances from the Ukraine, from Serbia, from Hungary. Men in skirts struck tambourines on the beat cleanly. A ghetto sensation was the all-male Georgian dance (from Russia) which showed a military patrol reconnoitring enemy territory.

But Afro-American bunny-hugging had the advantage of neck-holding. Girls could make lovey-dovey as equal partners with boys in the black folk dances. So the animal dances won popularity over the Georgian military patrol. They were easy to do – in fact many animal dancers simply invented their own steps right then and there on the floor. A New Jersey girl was jailed for putting a leg split into her turkey trot. Visiting Colonel A. Weston-Jarvis surprised his wife doing the sheep dip with a shoe salesman in their hotel bedroom. He shot both. At the trial he justified himself by claiming 'I put paid to suffragetting.'

Despite this opposition woman gradually took over the sexier steps until, in the Jazz Age she shook, shimmied and charlestoned whilst men just ogled.

Equal rights in dancing were, of course, a part of the suffragette movement. Only a minority were overtly political – the silent majority went about revolution in subtler ways. They wore hobble skirts and bloomers, they smoked, swam, drove cars, and ran away from home to become dance-hall hostesses.

Their men, husbands as well as lovers, were dragged along with them as they taxied to dance spots. In 1913, as the song said, 'My Wife is Dancing Mad!' and no restaurant could hope to survive without a dance floor* and a dance band. People danced at strange times of the day – lunch dances and tea dances – and in all kinds of places – even in Central Park.

Dancing was bang up-to-date. You didn't change into evening dress as in olden days. You could dance in street clothes, past plashy indoor fountains, and shiny cocktail counters. Indirect lighting added a touch of romance, aided by a slower, dreamier kind of waltz introduced into America by the hit operetta of 1907, *The Merry Widow*. Rough barnyard dances were fine for eupeptic love but waltzing could clinch it!

Dancing became an alternative world to that of the cosy hearth of home. A cosmopolitan cast of people habituated the new dance spots, freed from the corset of Victorian rules. Travelling salesmen tangoed like latin lovers, young girls left home to hire themselves out as taxi-dancers, gigolos sucking either canes or their thumbs – seal faces and patent leather hair – waited with lambent eyes for the tea dance to open. At the taxi-dance halls young girls from broken homes were hired by immigrants anxious to be Americanized, by cripples in search of love, by high society slummers. The attraction of the ragtime dance with the ragtime band in the ragtime dance hall was that immediate satisfaction, by instant contact, was promised. The circuit of dance halls covering all America constituted that urban hobo life of passing kicks so beloved of the city folk. The new rag girl saw men as 'easy dough', as 'saps' and 'suckers', as providers of fur coats and diamonds. The man took a back seat, and was to do so for the next decade.

*Reisenweber's boasted seven dance floors.

Happy Alley Days

Curiously, and superimportant, at the very same time as this dance-mania and emergence of superdoll, a social reform campaign, bent on crushing variegated America into middle-class respectability, reached its climax. For example the anti-saloon movement whipped up much support, eventually winning temporary prohibition in the First World War and permanent prohibition in 1920. Red-light districts were first segregated and then closed down – the Barbary Coast in 1913 and New Orleans's Storyville in 1916. Public dance halls had been under close scrutiny since 1910 when Mrs Israels and her New York Commission on Amusements and Vacation Resources for Working Girls (phew!) had investigated sample Cleveland halls and had found that a third of the dancers were inebriated, morale was lowered after midnight and that generally 'reckless and uncontrolled dances' were performed, thus turning an otherwise 'proper and helpful form of recreation into an opportunity for license and debauch'. Ordinances were passed forbidding hat-wearing, smoking and turkey trotting. Finally in 1919 the Walker Bill was passed, requiring halls to have a licence and one of three gradings.

Most Americans supported this moral drive, whilst quite determined to keep their fun providing that presentation was tasteful. Thus: the 'Roseland' ballroom, with roped-off 'hostesses', movies at the 'Bijou', and ragtime re-titled as 'novelette'.

But the dance hall reformers need not have worried unduly for millions of Americans chose to follow the graceful living style set by Irene and Vernon Castle. 'They were easily the most potent factor in the development of ballroom dancing as a public pastime,' wrote Fred Astaire in his autobiography. There were other society ballroom dancers and instructors but the Castles in 1914 were number one ideal married couple – that they danced too, was perhaps incidental. She was a willowy New Rochelle, N.Y., beauty; he was a well-mannered English gentleman. Both were decorative and decorous, up-to-date in the latest steps and fashions, but also well-versed in old world manners. High society, and the rest, adored and followed these entertainers, early members of that cafe society which was soon to usurp the trend-setting older 'high society'.

34

The Castles established a dance empire which included ball-rooms, Castles-In-The Air (on a New York roof-top) and Castles-By-The Sea (on Long Island) and Castle House where elegant dancing was taught. 'Do not wriggle the shoulders. Do not shake the hips', were amongst the orders. From out of the anarchic mess of social dancing came a style acceptably American.

For instance, everybody had been trying to dance the tango. Bones were broken, a youth died of it in a trolley car, the Pope denounced it. The dance had arrived from Paris by way of Buenos Aires, Cuba and Africa (where tangoing was a solo religious exercise). In its rougher form the girl was bent almost double by her pressing partner who sometimes planted a full frontal kiss. Plying for hire as demonstrators of the tango were corsetted dago types, causing much resentment from burly Americans. Vernon and Irene danced a much nicer version on the Broadway stage, re-moulding this bit of 'love-making set to music' into a rhythmic display of married good manners. Tango was snatched from gigolos such as Rudolpho Guglielmi (later to be the famous 'sheik' film star Rudolph Valentino) and given a French grace at tango teas. The band played 'Très Moutarde':

> Tango is the dance for me,
> I trip it merrily,
> Then have a cup of tea
> And dance some more. WHEE!

1736956

Similarly, the negroid animal dances were banished by the Castles as 'ugly, ungraceful' and, much worse, 'out of fashion'. A brisk walk done in four-four time was introduced: the 'fox-trot', the elegant animal who consumed the more riotous beasts, settled down to become a standard dance step.

Irene and Vernon were not only setting styles but also supplying a need. Exoticism, dago or Negro, was exciting to watch but hard to identify with. But the Castles' tripping seemed an extension of the ideal life. Every woman was determined to dance like Irene, and, also to move like her and to dress like her. So they bought Castle Hats and Castle Shoes. They bobbed their hair as Irene had. Every woman's companion was determined to be as unobtrusively elegant as Vernon, who supported Irene as she flew around the dance floor. In life, too, the companion would support her as she flew around her world.

General America was able to examine the couple in action because they toured vaudeville theatres with an act consisting of those very steps which only recently they'd demonstrated privately to New York's high society. The Castles became the highest paid act in vaudeville. Can you imagine? People paying hard cash to watch a man dance with his wife!

Back at home the audience could try out the Castle steps to the music of their record player. 1914 was a bumper year for dance records but the accompaniment, played by fifteen piece quasi-military bands, was correct but stiff. Nobody got very excited about Charles A. Prince and his Recording Orchestra, or the Victor Military Band. The regular ball orchestras were few and far between. They played only at the best houses. Most orchestras were hastily patched-together affairs consisting of concert musicians making a few dollars extra, or spirited amateurs. Anyway syncopation was tough to perform. Trained musicians of the old school couldn't or *wouldn't* master it.

The dance revolution called for a special accompaniment – a smallish unit of syncopation specialists playing night after night together and able to play suitable music for eating, talking and dancing. A style that embraced not only dippy foxtrot but also tango, maxixe and a clinging love song or two. Snappy. Stuffed with flutes, piccolos, harps, and so forth, erect in training and minus 'feel', the old fat string orchestras were no use. At their tea dances the Castles had been employing a specially shrivelled organization directed by the coloured band-leader, James Reese Europe: cornet, trombone, clarinet, two violins, some banjos, a piano and a battery of percussion instruments (called 'traps')* presided over by Buddy Gilmore.

*Drumming was a major attraction between 1914 and 1915. *Variety* reported a drummers' contest at the Strand Roof, New York, in 1915, in which Buddy Gilmore, of the Europe band, tied for first place with 'Battle Axe'. 'Bill Bailey' Jones of Reisenweber's cabaret came in second. All the contestants were coloured and the judges included show-tune composer Jerome Kern.

The Europe band played in unison as if they were alight. But Jim Europe was happier with a fifty-piece outfit playing rollicking marches and 'The Memphis Blues' with his Hell Fighters Band. They were a sensation when they played for the Allies in France in 1917.

Over on the West Coast, at the St Francis Hotel in San Francisco, a fellow called Art Hickman was experimenting with a regular dance band. By 1916 it had settled comfortably into trombone, trumpet, violin, piano, string bass; two banjos echoed plantation ragtime, a trap man provided a fire for the feet, and two saxophones harmonized soothingly bringing a refined sensuousness, and making more volume than fiddles.

The saxophone! During the roaring twenties the curvy saxophone played with a lot of wobble and a cute popping was to become the symbol of the Jazz Age. Then, in the thirties, whole sections of gangster-suited saxophonists swinging and swaying in high-precision Big Bands, spreading romance in waves of warm syrup or sending the fans with sheets of killer-diller riffs, epitomized chromium-plated all-America. And finally rock 'n' roll wasn't rock 'n' roll without a saxist in sun glasses honking and squeaking.

But here, way back in 1916, was this Art Hickman pioneering a modern-type dance band with a saxophone section even before the appearance of jazz bands! Actually the saxophone wasn't really so much of a novelty. It had become a standard military band instrument as long ago as the 1870s. Patrick Gilmore, the bandmaster whose concert band became very famous at that time, featured a whole quartet of saxophones. The minstrel shows and circus bands used them for extra blare, and around 1914 saxophone groups were a popular novelty act in vaudeville.

Quite often military and concert bands were called in to provide the music at large balls and dances where the usual string orchestra would have been too soft to be heard. So there were saxophones at pre-ragtime dances. But by 1914, with dance mania raging and cabarets, cafes and night clubs doing fast business, smaller cabaret bands were forming in the cities and a new trade was born.

Happy Alley Days

Hickman's stripped-down hotel band with its natty arrangements and heavy, almost soupy, saxophone sound was one of the
most distinctive and by 1917 it had gained a considerable reputa-
tion on the West Coast. Struggling dance bandsmen, servants of
the people – neither serious musicians nor ragtimers – were impressed by the snap and dash of Hickman's banjos, the yearning
harmony of his saxophones and the tap, patter and brush of his
traps. Impressive too was the hotel setting and the evening dress.
Art Hickman's orchestra was 'supreme in this new line'.

Florenz Ziegfeld, the great showman always on the look-out for
sensations, heard the St Francis Hotel band and invited them to
play in New York. In 1919 the band was at the Biltmore Hotel and
next year it was a feature of the Ziegfeld Follies show. But by that
time there were hundreds of other dance bands – some refined,
some jazzy, some symphonic. Fred Waring, Ben Bernie, Vincent
Lopez, George Olsen, Ted Lewis – veterans of the business by the
thirties – all had dance bands. Many were becoming personalities
in their own right. Some had organizations farming out bands for
every occasion.

The most celebrated of the dance band leaders was Paul
Whiteman (at one time first viola in the Denver Symphony
Orchestra). He had been sacked from his first dance band job after
one night because he couldn't get the beat, but he soon found his
calling was as an organizer of bands. He supplied them for hotels
in San Francisco, Santa Barbara and Los Angeles before he was
called to the East to play at the swank Ambassador Hotel in
Atlantic City. He brought with him his 'hot' cornet player, Henry
Busse (a German scarcely able to communicate in English), and
his ace arranger Ferde Grofé, keen to employ the devices of
classical music in dance music. All three men were conservatory-
trained, but this new business looked promising and they genuinely
wanted to tidy up rhythms and set the music on an even keel.

In 1919, while Whiteman was still in California, a dance band
under the direction of Ben Selvin had a million-selling record with
an instrumental called 'Dardanella'. The number, a ragtime
novelty by pianist Johnny Black with a little help from Alleyman
Fred Fisher, was invigorating not only because it was a good dance

record but also because Selvin had arranged it. A phrase here, a little bit of colour there. Dance bands scrambled to get recording contracts, and the record companies welcomed them. Paul Whiteman's Ambassador Band suddenly became an internationally known name with the success of their first record, 'Whispering' backed by 'Japanese Sandman' (issued in November 1920). And no singing on either side. Millions of copies were sold and pretty soon Paul Whiteman's face was appearing on the cover of sheet music. The Alley stuck photos of whole bands on music covers – dapper types dressed like yachtsmen, in blazers with brass buttons, creamy pants and matching shoes.

By 1922 Paul Whiteman had a press agent and a corporation worth a million dollars. Several Paul Whiteman orchestras were for hire. Tin Pan Alley had two rivals: records and dance bands. But both needed songs.

Alleymen didn't understand half the words of the dance steps – do the dog over there, hands behind back, forehead on knees, that's balling the jack – but nevertheless they went to work. From 1911 most songs had to be danceable and recordable so long story ballads with many verses were out. They drew on their imaginations for trips to 'The Motion Picture Ball', 'The Devil's Ball', 'The Old Maid's Ball', 'The Ragtime Ball', 'The Yiddishe Society Ball', etc.

Seymour Brown and Albert Gumble went back to the 'dark and pre-historic age' to describe ragtime dancing by Adam and Eve and Pinchme:

Adam and Eve had a wonderful time! Oh, a wonderful time back there.

The old turkey gobbler, he taught them to 'Trot'
And the other professor, the 'Grizzly Bear'.
All the birds and the bees used to sing in the trees,
Why, old Adam and Eve used to dance as they please
(I betcha!)
Adam and Eve had a wonderful time. Yes, a wonderful wonderful time!

39

Happy Alley Days

Ragtime and dancetime took their toll of the veteran writers. Edward Marks, the publisher, noted that none of his 1894 hit writers were producing winners in 1914. But a sharp new breed had appeared, ready to tackle anything. Typical was Fred Fischer,* late of the Imperial German Navy and French Foreign Legion. He'd mastered English rapidly and was into the age early with 'If the Man in the Moon were a Coon'. In 1919 he was still there 'and how!' with 'Dardanella'.

Fischer advised Alleymen of the ragtime era: 'Zong writing iss a question of zounds, not zense. If you create new zounds you make money. If you can't get new zounds den you must write mit der passion!'

*He dropped the 'c' at the time of America's entry into the First World War.

Inside
Tin Pan
Alley

A few months ago, ragtime expert Max Morath was on the phone talking to Irving Berlin. They were discussing ragtime and Berlin confessed: 'You know, I never did find out what ragtime was.' Nevertheless, he wrote it.

Yesterday the demand was for coon songs, today ragtime, tomorrow jazz – the business was there to service the public, their stock-holders – and Berlin was quick to point out that 'It isn't music that makes people, it's people that make music.' In the 1880s Remick's publishing company was asked by the Butcher's and Drover's Ball Committee for a suitable song. In a trice out came 'Only a Butcher', a tune that winged like a flight of wild geese. Chas K. Harris, conservative gentleman of our first chapter, published ragtime as well as class ballads and gave advice on how to write a 'coon song' ('the introduction or prelude should comprise four, eight or sixteen measures finishing on the dominant seventh chord'). There you are! You might also need your instruction booklet about playing the stuff. Quite easy – take your pick from the different left-hand parts available. You've your 'slow drag', 'cabaret', 'hatfield', 'double see-saw', 'thumb' and a selection of 'space-fillers' and 'trick endings'.

The popular music trade could take on all comers – all the mad men raging from the bush, screaming the blues, rocking to rag – and castrate them. The taming process had been successfully applied to 'Ta-Ra-Ra-Boom-Deray', which began as a brothel song danced with lewd gestures in Babe Connor's St Louis brothel and ended as a nonsense song on the lines of 'Hands, Knees and Boomps a Daisy'. A tricky bit of sexual athleticism – 'Ballin' the

Jack' became the novelty dance sensation of 1914. 'I ain't Gonna
Give Nobody None of My Jelly Roll' (or 'Keep your Hands off
of My Peter') became a song about a fat boy and his sweets.

'When I see we're shy on sentimental ballads, I sit down and
write one,' said Berlin in an interview. Although ragtime and the
dance caught the headlines, the real sellers from 1900 to 1914 were
the *big ballads*. It was a comfortable period during which Tin Pan
Alley reigned supreme in the entertainment world, pushing its
tall, dazzlingly coloured sheets with their art-work as captivating
as a comic and with rich Christmas cake advertising copy on the
back:

Publisher Will Rossiter introduces his clients to lyricist/poetess Miss
Beth Slater Whitson, who wrote 'Meet Me Tonight In Dreamland' *and*
'When I Met You Last Night In Dreamland':* . . . This little lady is
just like a beautiful flower filled with goodness and it seems to be her
mission on earth to give out good thoughts to others . . . She lives in a
pretty little farm-house down among the purple shadowed hills of
Goodrich, Tennessee. You will be interested to know that Beth, hardly
out of her teens, is the main support of her parents and brothers and
sisters, and her earnings are from these beautiful song poems.

In this lush sheet music era a medium-sized hit was a song
selling around 600,000 copies, whilst a smash hit started at a
million and might sail as high as 5 or 6 million. David Ewen, a Tin
Pan Alley expert, has calculated that between 1900 and 1910 there
were over 100 songs which did the million. Gradually the publishers, in cut-throat rivalry, managed to cut the price of each
sheet from 40 cents in the nineties, to 25 cents by the turn of the
century. By 1910 the price was as low as 10 cents a slash. Now not
only ladies had pianos but also working men.

*Dream songs became so popular and so numerous that warehouse men
were forced to number them as 'Dream Song 1' or 2 or 3 to avoid confusion.
The cycle songs and 'follow-up' or 'answer songs' have a long history, trace-
able back at least to Stephen Foster days when 'Old Folks at Home' was
pursued by Professor Sigsbaum's 'The Old Folks are Still at Home'. During
the coon song era the plea of Bill Bailey's lady-lover of 'Bill Bailey Won't
You Please Come Home' was answered by 'Since Bill Bailey Came Home'.
Like most of the old Tin Pan Alley regalia this practice is now only preserved
by the Country Music field.

And the staple survival food was the ballad, not ragtime. Most of the songs today associated with the 'gaslight' or 'gay nineties' period and still sung in pubs, pizza parlors, Lawrence Welk Shows, around pianos, at clubs when the electricity fails, on sinking ships, and possibly in moon rockets, were written during the first twenty years of this century, the heyday of the Alley.* Here are a few of these veterans:

1900: 'A Bird in a Gilded Cage'
1902: 'In the Good Old Summertime'
1903: 'Ida! Sweet As Apple Cider!'
      'Sweet Adeline'
1905: 'In the Shade of the Old Apple Tree'
1909: 'I Wonder Who's Kissing Her Now'
1910: 'Let Me Call You Sweetheart'
      'Down by the Old Mill Stream'

These last two sold at least three million copies each when they were first published and have gone on to edition after edition. They're both ideal for 'barbershop' close harmony, full of olde-worlde Walter Scott courting which, by 1910, was fast becoming a charming relic of the golden rustic past. Maidens were beginning to be referred to as 'chickens', and 'it' and 'doing it' is creeping in. So, even in 1910, nostalgia for the nineties, for the 'good old days', is here in pop. Nevertheless, woman is still hymned about by the man; she isn't yet cabaretting, taking over.

At the same time the sleeker, stream-lined ballad – unspecific and exportable – is starting to be popular. I'm thinking of 'You Made Me Love You' (1913) and 'Melancholy Baby' (1912) in which the verses tell no story at all, and are about as useful as a little toe.

The ballad, conservative backbone of the industry, never really

*The shivering, shimmering, goose-pimple-provoking harmonies of tunes like 'Meet Me Tonight in Dreamland' built like a sturdy brick house, are the perfection of the ballad years. Bigger men than me have loved these tunes, defending them fiercely with the tear in the eye. Louis B. Mayer was always asking 'Where are the old tunes?' (one wit looked under the desk). Jerry Lee Lewis and blues veteran Furry Lewis both play 'Let Me Call You Sweetheart' whenever they can.

changed and spans the whole of pop history. I'll just make two calls along the years: 1931 and 'Tears' (revived in the 60s by Ken Dodd), 1965 and 'Yesterday' by Paul McCartney.

Having made this rather long introduction, I now want to take you inside the institution called Tin Pan Alley, during its brief golden period, before inspecting its finest hour, which was the First World War. After this the pop story gets shriller, as ragtime reaps the whirlwind . . .

Why were the railroad flats around 28th and Broadway called 'Tin Pan Alley'?* Many and conflicting stories – a British folk-song researcher told me that the phrase was coined in Georgian times to describe the flourishing London 'broadside ballad' trade. But if I start getting too scholarly we'll end up in the Middle Ages, and maybe skid back even from there!! (and I'm really getting a terrible attack of twentieth-century 'progressive itch'. I do want to clear out of the nineteenth.)

The most plausible (and most colourful) explanation of the origins of the phrase is this one: Monroe Rosenfeld, a tear-jerker specialist and journalist, wrote a series of comic articles about the new business for the *New York Herald*, and thought up the collective title 'Tin Pan Alley'. The publishing houses were clustered on top of each other. Every window was open. Almost every room had an upright piano, being played. The Babel of different embryonic tunes all playing at once in the song factory must have struck Rosenfeld as being reminiscent of tin pans being clashed. That's one story.

Many of the pioneer pop publishers started their business life as salesmen. Isadore Witmark had sold water filters, Leo Feist was in corsets, while Joe Stern and Ed Marks had peddled neck-ties and buttons respectively. Often, the publisher was also the songwriter; after a hard day's work in the Alley he had to trudge around the Gotham night spots lugging a briefcase-full of sheets. Ed Marks ('Mother was a Lady', 'Little Lost Child') tells of these rounds in his autobiography. The Alhambra Music Hall was expensive be-

*By the 1920s the Alley had shifted uptown as far as 42nd and Broadway, following (as always) theatreland.

cause you had to buy drinks for the boys in the band and there were twenty-six of them. At the Haymarket, where bullets often flew, you could only get in by joining a club called the 'Welsh Rabbits', and then there was another round of drinks for the boys. A chorus of 'Mother was a Lady' was the reward.

All this leg-work and heavy drinking got to be too much for the pioneers. Besides, by the turn of the century business was booming. The publishing chiefs now sat at desks and delegated work to underlings, in a trade that was becoming increasingly more complicated. A good Alley firm had a honeycomb of tiny cubicles, each with a piano and a staff writer (probably wearing a visor). Word-men would be hovering about, shifting from cubicle to cubicle throwing in a line here and a word there, all under the eagle eye of the professional manager. Few hits came to the publishers through the post. Outsiders filled the mail boxes with manuscripts (encouraged by Harris's book) but these were generally hopeless efforts. (Max Winkler of the Carl Fischer company remembers getting a thing called the 'Subway Waltz'.)

The staff writers used more 'perspiration than inspiration', turning from theme to theme. Some had once been newspaper columnists, all read the daily papers. They kept their ears close to the ground, listening for current catch-phrases. Ragtime composer Eubie Blake remembers Irving Berlin watch him play piano at a restaurant. The latter wore a melancholy but intense expression. At other times he could be found sitting alone in a cafe, within ear-shot of a talkative bunch. Suddenly he'd jot down some lines.

Versatility was very important. No time to waste being moved by your song. Al Piantadosi, of the new breed, was a good chameleon – now writing the tear-jerking 'Curse of an Aching Heart', now the mother's plea against war which cried 'I Didn't Raise My Boy to be a Soldier', now the stirring march song 'Send Me Away with a Smile'. Harry Von Tilzer wrote over 3,000 songs; Berlin wrote so many hits that for years the fiction went round that actually they were written by a coloured boy, kept prisoner in his office.

Tunes, like jokes, are limited. A kind of folk fund existed, writers dipping in every so often and coming up with something already copyrighted. That was the big difference between the old folk music and this modern industrial folk music: the Alleymen knew all about copyright, the folk didn't. 'Do you like my latest tune, Benny,' asked the songwriter. 'I've liked that tune for years,' said the publisher. It was a wise song that knew its own author. Monroe Rosenfeld recognized the folk nature of the Alley very early and sub-contracted his ideas to other writers. Others went through costly law suits and rarely won. Most hit songs were (and are) faintly reminiscent, but with some new twists. The best example of the communally-made hit song full of folk memories – but heavily copyrighted as an original effort – is 'Yes! We Have No Bananas'.

(Strictly speaking, this is a jazz age novelty – outside of the period discussed in this chapter. But Tin Pan Alley throve on for three more decades, repeating the practices begun in our period.)

'Bananas', a world-wide smash hit written in 1923, is rather seminal to our story because it is the archetypal patchwork industrial folk song, entirely without feeling. So crazy was 'Bananas' that songwriter James Thornton had his heart broken, and ace music hall comic T. E. Dunville drowned himself in the Thames. But more about that later on.

Here's the story: Frank Silver and Irving Cohn saw the phrase 'Yes! We Have No Bananas' in a cartoon strip by Tad Dorgan, and thought 'that's a good title for a song'. The cartoonist claimed copyright ownership on the phrase, but it was later discovered that 'Bananas' was a saying picked up by US troops in the Philippines from a Greek pedlar.

A story was put together by the writers Cohn and Silver about a Greek fruit-store owner who always answered 'yes'. A tune was added, but before publication most of the staff at Shapiro-Bernstein contributed little bits . . . a word here, a note or two there. Amongst the contributors were Hanley and MacDonald ('Indiana', 'Trail of the Lonesome Pine'), Lew Brown ('Best Things in Life are Free', etc.), and Shapiro and Bernstein themselves. Amongst the phrases that went to make up the patchwork tune were selections from 'The Hallelujah Chorus', 'My Bonnie', 'The Bohemian Girl', 'Aunt Dinah's Quilting Party' and 'An Old-Fashioned Garden'.

This, then, was how the folk fund worked.

Some Alleymen, like George Gershwin, could write out rhapsodies. Others, like Irving Berlin, couldn't read music and played in one key. It didn't matter. Berlin's key was F sharp and he had a special piano that could play in any key at the flick of a switch. Lewis Muir's key was C, and when demonstrating 'Waitin' for the Robert E. Lee' on a transposing piano, had to have an assistant waiting for his shout of 'Now!' as he rolled from the C verse into the F chorus. Geo. Meyer always had trouble with his vamping left hand, and mostly played his tunes in the treble. Joe Young just snapped his fingers.

This was a bad time for the less flexible older writers, the specialists in story ballads. Monroe Rosenfeld threw himself out of a window (but recovered and limped ever after). Arthur Lamb, writer of 'A Bird in a Gilded Cage', was reduced to hawking his water colours to sympathetic publishers. Richard Gerard became a New York Post Office clerk and, in 1927, was still carrying a card stating that he was author of the 'World famous song "Sweet Adeline"'.

But there was a bold and brave woman who worked outside of the Alley and managed to succeed. Carrie Jacobs Bond, a widow, kept getting her songs returned by the publishers so she started her own firm, the Bond Shop, in her bedroom, in the Chicago boarding house which she ran. 'Just A-Wearyin' for You' was a national success. 'I Love You Truly' became a regular at wedding receptions. One day in 1910 she was visiting friends in California and they decided to go for a day's motoring. It was a lovely, peaceful, happy day. Whilst she was dressing for dinner she wrote down some verses for her friends' amusement. Later they were set to music as 'A Perfect Day'. The song became a standard and was the favourite of President Harding's wife. Carrie Jacobs Bond became a national figure, singing for Teddy Roosevelt and in 1941 was selected by the General Federation of Women's Clubs as 'one of two composers, representing progress of women during the first half of this century'. She died in Hollywood in 1946, the envy of many an Alleyman.*

Inside the Alley there was little time for awards and prestige as yet. Selling was being developed into an art form. Now, instead of the publishers legging it round the dives and halls, the vaudeville headliners were driven in limousines to the 'professional parlor' where one of fifteen demonstrators would sing them all the latest songs. Song copies were now given away free to the artists. Stars were given co-authorship of songs they promoted, and heaps of presents (Al Jolson once got a race horse). Many singers were on the payroll of publishers. On top of all this the industry waged a cut-price war: in 1907 one New York department store sold 20,000 sheets in two hours at one cent a piece.

This rampant free enterprise was costing the industry over a million dollars a year and in 1916 the buccaneers got together and decided to police themselves, and codify behaviour. The Music Publishers Protective Association was formed (later taking on the job of self-censorship).

With the growth of the industry came the science of plugging. It called for bright Yankee Doodle boys. They were racy types, who liked to gamble and were natty dressers. Mickey Addy, a plugger who started in 1914, and was still plugging in the days of rock 'n' roll, wore a fresh carnation every day and actually set dress trends, introducing the polo-neck sweater around 1914. (Later he introduced different coloured trouser legs, but this never really caught on.)

Pluggers were originally called 'boomers' because they had to be able to sing their wares. Lower East Side synagogues were searched for boys with large lungs and rabbinical voices who could be planted in vaudeville audiences, and trained to get up at a certain moment and sing a certain chorus.

The pluggers, armed with their sheets, swarmed out of the Alley houses, some taking to the streets in truckloads, singing in groups to the sidewalk crowds. Young Jack Robbins, aged sixteen, (later to form the powerful Robbins Music), won his spurs by com-

*L. Wolfe Gilbert tells us she spent most of her last years in a golden chair beside a white spinet piano in a room adorned with flowers.

mandeering a hay wagon, donning farmers' clothes and driving down a busy Chicago street advertising 'It's an Old Horse That Knows Its Way Home'. Mickey Addy used to campaign with a band consisting of three Hawaians and three Americans, all armed with megaphones. Their prime spot was Sunday night at Coney Island, a popular New York resort. There they queued up with other pluggers taking part in 'Publishers' Night'. The German manager welcomed them: 'Good evening, gentlemen! Now, you represent Leo Feist so you will follow Remick's at 9.30.'

They infested not only theatres and resorts but also political rallies, cycle races, billiard saloons and lavatories. This last venue proved to be unsuccessful. A plugger began to sing a few bars of 'Won't You Come and Flirt with Me?' and was promptly arrested for procuring.

They were never scared of new inventions. They loved them as a new vehicle for song exploitation. Ed Marks made up a series of photo slides telling the story of his song 'The Little Lost Child', and these were slipped into movie shows between reels. The plugger was there to conduct the audience. Many immigrants learned to read from these song slides, which also printed the words.

Like the men who founded the movie industry many of the early Alleymen were immigrants or the sons of immigrants from middle and central Europe. Irving Berlin, and L. Wolfe Gilbert were from Russia, amongst the many who'd fled the anti-Jewish pogroms of Tsar Alexander the III. Fred Fisher came from Germany; Jimmy Monaco from Italy; Jack Yellen from Poland; Jean Schwartz from Hungary. They came during the great immigration period between the years 1880 and 1910, when 20 million arrived. Two thirds of them stayed in the cities and this in a period when there was a growing xenophobia called All-Americanism, caused by depression, the closure of the frontier, the new imperialism, and the intense fear of the rural people for the big cities. Native-born Americans labelled the immigrants 'dangerous and corrupting hordes'. They were failures, beaten races, God's rejected.

Finding the established businesses such as banking, law and medicine closed to them, the immigrants opened up the rogue industries of mass entertainment. At this gutter level they could start from scratch, become their own bosses. And they had an advantage: they were not lumbered with an older culture. They left the Old World ways behind them. They were progressive. They liked new things. There was much coming and going in the early days in the sub-cultures of movies and pop. Marks nearly went into business with movie-man Marcus Loew. Carle Laemmle (founder of Universal) ran a music publishing house in his early days. Harry Cohn was once a song plugger.

1910 ragtime, shunting and progressive, was city music which they found easy to write. But they were also good at assimilating all the American myths, particularly about the South. L. Wolfe Gilbert, late of Odessa, Russia, didn't know that there weren't any levees in Alabammy, but he wrote about them in 'Waitin' for the Robert E. Lee'. Irving Berlin, having no home at first, made the world his home, writing songs about Spain, Italy, Cuba, and even Russia (in 'Russian Lullaby').

Pop songs were a part of the show-business family, many of whose stars were Jewish, soaked in the wailing Yiddish synagogue style – the massive heart, the cry in the voice. Al Jolson, Norah Bayes, Sophie Tucker – the vaudeville singing stars who made Alley songs into world hits – echoed that shaking cry, at the same time fusing it into an All-American pop style which contained ragtime, blues, ballads, jazz. 'My Mammy' was at once Momma, undisputed boss of the Jewish family *and also* Mom, all-American dispenser of pork chops and green apple pie.

Did the Jewish show people (most of whom were immigrants from Eastern Europe, considered lower than the lowest by the already-established German-Jews) share the blues with the Negroes? Were both the suffering peoples music rebels wailing against the wall of oppressive America? Certainly there were similarities in the music of synagogue and cotton field, but in the great outside, pop-city suffering music soon became merely an ingredient in the American pot-pourri. And rebels they certainly weren't in this land of promise.

Though the immigrants were at first excluded from Anglo-Saxon America, they had no intention of upsetting that society, no schemes for burning down the club. Rather, they wanted to join it. Many had fallen on their knees on first sighting the Statue of Liberty. They had carefully read the booklet *How to Become an American Citizen*. They anglicized their names so that Izzy Baline became Irving Berlin, Billy Rosenberg became Billy Rose. Harry Jolson, Al's brother, wrote: 'As Asa and Hirsh we were Jewish boys. As Al and Harry we were Americans.'

Good Americans too, anxious to adopt the folk-ways of American middle-class life, to become so very American that they were more American than the old Americans themselves. No Yiddish slang here. Patriotic: Irving Berlin wrote 'God Bless America', the second national anthem. Their conformity was to stamp the future history of the once-roguish, once-vulgar pop business. By the late fifties the pop pioneers, now settled family men, viewed rock 'n' roll as the obscene junk of the new barbarians – forgetting that once upon a time they had been cursed as sellers of cheap nonsense.

Much of early Alley pop was musical journalism. Issues of the day were made into songs and the hits were as true a reflection of what the ordinary man was thinking or feeling, as the popular newspapers of the day. But they became as quaint as yesterday's newspapers, too. Berlin was a bit more poetic about it, versing that 'popular song you will never be missed' – but Chopin and Liszt will live on. However, he added, the consolation was that a 'rose lives and dies in the very same way'. In 1925 he admitted that his 1911 hit 'Alexander's Ragtime Band' sounded like a funeral march.

I want now to look at the way these songs mirrored their times. For instance, immigration:

The first great wave of immigrants had been Irish, escaping from the Great Famine and the general beastliness of life in Ireland. These early Irish–American songs had pictured the immigrant as a working 'stiff', who loved a shenanigan. In James Thornton's 'Irish Jubilee', newly-elected Senator O'Rafferty throws a party in a bar-room with a thousand kegs of beer. His guests include men whose teeth are in pawn, who eat ice-cream and cold cream and dance to a band which plays horn-pipes and gas-pipes (a good example of vaudeville pun humour). Another song describes Mrs Murphy's party where Tim Nolan shouts out: 'I can lick the Mick that threw his overalls into Mrs Murphy's chowder.'

As the Raffertys and Nolans hoisted themselves up in the world so the stage mick, in red strap whiskers and guzzling beer from a can, was howled off by the Hibernian Societies. Ireland now became a celtic Dixie, the best songs being written by Ernest Ball, of Cleveland, Ohio. His 'Mother Machree' and 'When Irish Eyes are Smiling' can be heard even today in Dublin pubs.

The Germans, in songs, had bands and drank beer. The Italians were a happy, sunny lot. But the Jews were money-grubbing, hand-rubbing old men who wore crepe hair and ran pawnshops. Alley writers – all things to all men – reflected this stereotype. The 'Yiddishe Society Ball' has Abie Stein ordering wine when he was broke. When the waiter brings it Sam says 'Can't you take a joke'. Louie Fink, who thinks he's smart, says 'Bring me some more *à la carte*', and all the guests go around the hall 'trottin' for nothin''. This is a fearful song, which only lately I was allowed to sing – after the family skeleton was revealed to be a Jewish great-grandmother.

As the immigrants melted into Americans so the race songs vanished. When Fanny Brice sang 'Second Hand Rose' she used a Yiddish accent, but when Barbra Streisand recorded the same song the accent was gone and so were some of the more Jewish lines.

Moving from the race situation, flipping through the dog-eared sheets of these tune tabloids, we glance at the headlines – 'Just As The Ship Went Down', a song-poem of the Titanic sinking. Event songs lasted well into the twenties, celebrating Lindbergh's flight ('so take your hats off to plucky lucky Lindbergh, the Eagle of the USA'), discussing the Scopes Monkey trial, mourning Valentino's death ('There's a New Star in Heaven Tonight') and William Jennings Bryan's death ('Bryan Believed in Heaven That's why He's in Heaven Tonight'). In the thirties these event songs continued being produced, but fewer were hits – 'Brother, Can You Spare a Dime?' and 'My Forgotten Man' being the most notable amongst those few. The Second World War was largely missed, left to hillbilly writers. Women's Lib and moon landings remain tuneless.

Although the Alleymen pounced progressively on to new inventions they took a more old-fashioned attitude in the songs that they produced about these gadgets. They domesticated them, using them as new means of carrying on the old ways. For instance, 'Come Away with Me, Lucille – in My Merry Oldsmobile', 'Come, Josephine, in My Flying Machine', 'There's a Wireless Station down in My Heart', 'Take Your Girlie to the Movies If You Can't Make Love at Home'. And a pile of 'telephone songs', with lovers or babies calling up their loved ones at home or in heaven or in no-man's-land. Science was humanized.

The 1906 song 'College Life' gives a vivid picture, set to a stirring march, of that world where 'mother and father pay all the bills and we have all the fun'. Freshmen had things poured into their ears, or were made to gobble their gloves and shoes. On the football field 'we have the greatest fun of all – breaking their bones and biting them. We will find a fellow who is thin and tall and kick him in the shins.' Finally: 'If anyone is left alive the football team will do the rest!' 'College Life' was pretty accurate, for the year before it was written, nineteen school footballers had been killed during the season.

By 1914 heavy nostalgia had set in (and stays for the next thirty odd years). City folk enjoyed 'In the Town Where I was Born' which told of that one-horse village, where Dad told stories, Mother knitted, you pitched new-mown hay, there were no taxis or midnight cabarets and girls weren't called 'chickens'. Irving Berlin turned in a yearn for the return to nature and the commune with 'Gee! How I Wish Again That I was in Michigan down on the farm.'

However, that very same year he wrote 'This is the Life' in which Farmer Brown came to town, took in the sights and shouted 'I love the cows and chickens but this is the life!' Definitely: 'no more picking berries – me for cocktail cherries!'

1914, once described by Professor Gildenblatten as the 'zenith and nadir of civilization', was a pretty slick year for the pop business. Ragtime and the animal dance were elbowing away at the waltz ballad. The new woman appeared in the songs, smoking a cigarette on the cover, easy prey for fast-talking dapper types in soft shirts. One-liner gag songs were the rage: 'If I were the Ocean and You were the Shore I'd be Kissing You All the Day', and 'It's Going to be a Cold, Cold Winter but I'll Never Freeze When You're Around.' Tempting girlies were warned 'If I Don't Get You I'll Get Your Sister', or even ordered 'Do It Now!'

They were real stunners, quick-fired out of the side of the mouth, guaranteed to knock an audience dead. They were the musical fore-runners of *Rowan and Martin's Laugh-In*. But within the trade it was generally admitted that the British music hall songs were much better, far subtler. However.

Show-business thickened and quickened. Twenty-six vaudeville houses in New York. Dance halls springing up, packed. Tango teas at the Hotel Astor. Cabarets everywhere. Meals accompanied by music, to the annoyance of gourmets who complained of cold soup and lack of nuts – but Maxim's was making as much as 25,000 dollars a week off this food-and-music crowd.

The music attracted the people – but the owners and producers of this music made not a penny because, although the 1909 Copyright Act gave them the right to 'perform publicly for profit', it was impossible for individuals to run around from coast to coast checking all public places where their songs were played, demanding a few cents here and there.

But there was no doubt that pop music was the real attracter of the audiences. Then and now. Many shows were kept afloat by their songs. Silent films were never silent – they were accompanied by music, without which they were dreary affairs. Radio lived off pop. Talkies succeeded because of the hit songs in *The Jazz Singer*. *Easy Rider* was jammed with group songs. The most popular video cassettes will be those featuring singers, not old movie dramas. Why do people see *The Sound of Music* and *The Jolson Story* over and over again? It's the tunes, mostly.

But in 1914, although Europe had its performance rights societies, collecting money from restaurants, circuses, cafes, pubs, theatres, etc., American writers and publishers had no such societies. A copyright law protected them in theory, but in practice it lay silent. Encouraged by his friend Puccini, the theatre composer Victor Herbert, backed by Sousa, decided to form the 'American Society of Composers, Authors and Publishers'. (Rather high-flown, but then these weren't ordinary men of the Alley – plain wordsmiths and tunesmiths – but theatre people whose works were printed on better paper than the Alley pop.) They began with a test case. They sued Shanley's restaurant, an expensive New York place, for playing Victor Herbert scores without payment. Shanley's claimed that they didn't charge for the music, just the food. The case dragged on till 1917 when Supreme Court Judge Wendell Holmes ruled that this music was part of the atmosphere, as attractive as the food. Therefore they must pay up. The society (ASCAP for short), led by their lawyer Nathan Burkan, had many years of fierce battles ahead, fighting the other show business forces: at various times the Association of Motion Picture Exhibitors, the American Federation of Musicians, the Vaudeville Managers Protective Association, the radio networks and finally, in 1940, the biggest battle of all against the broadcasters.

The money involved ran into millions and millions of dollars. In 1921 the first sums were divided amongst the ASCAP members, and by that time most of the publishers had joined up. The men who made ASCAP were fighting for their livings. They were embattled in their medieval-like guild, keenly aware that the world at large didn't appreciate them. As they established themselves, as the money rolled in, so they dropped the purely survival approach and adopted a high cultural pose. Now they were more than craftsmen, they were artists, guardians of American musical culture.

But before ASCAP established itself, Tin Pan Alley became a responsible citizen by performing its first national duty. America entered the First World War. The Alley provided the music.

Alleymen versus the Allemands

Dixie, coons, ragtime lover boys, babes. Whatever caught the popular fancy could be melodied and dressed with words by the Alleymen. The butchers, even, had been rhapsodized in 'Only A Butcher'.

The shape of the song was firmly established. First a vamp ('till ready') then a verse, setting up the story, and finally the chorus with a punchy, catchy opening phrase, a few bars away from home in the middle, and then back again to that punchy catchy opening phrase. It was neat and tight!

The business of marketing these packages was firmly established, too, as we have seen in the previous chapter. By 1914 Tin Pan Alley, like show business as a whole, was far better organized to cope with the great masses than the Federal government. They had learned that the rugged individualist was fast becoming a myth and that there was growing a swirl of people, cursed as 'the horde' by Old Americans, classified later by sociologists as the urban mass, the lonely crowd. These were the people who went to make up the mob that moved in blocs, crab-ways or drifting like tumbleweed, or raging every which way like a mad dog. Sometimes, as 'suckers', you could catch them and make them sing like a mixed chorus of geese and crows. In 1914 they were turkey trotting, hugging like bunnies, lynching, striking, ceasing to learn how to play the piano. Growing shriller.

Here we had, then, a seething mass and a well-organized music business, capable of tackling any topic. Many of the Alleymen were anxious to prove themselves as good Americans, putting their mongrel backgrounds behind them. And many of the Alleymen looked, in those days of ideals, for some noble cause, something bigger than babies.

Tin Pan Alley, the song factory, had all the machinery for making a super piece of propaganda artillery! Woodrow Wilson, a reader of detective novels, a fan of vaudeville, and president of the USA in 1914 (elected two years before) was well aware of this show-business machine. But he had no intention of joining the World War, which had just begun in Europe.

Actually, there was a precept, the Monroe Doctrine, which advised the United States against interfering in the affairs of wicked old Europe. And war itself was an un-American activity, no part of the paper rules which had established the Republic. The Civil War was unfortunate, but dying proof that war was wrong. The Spanish–American War of 1898 had appeared as a sunny exercise, lived by Americans through newspaper reports. Largely a fun thing, with Teddy Roosevelt charging a hill far from home, yelling and without his glasses. (The writers of 'Goodbye Dolly Gray' just missed *that* war, but, quickly shipping copies to England, were in time to catch the Boer War.)

By 1914 the soldier was a rare sight in the United States. The war in Europe was distasteful, the kind of barbarity that the immigrants had escaped from, but news from the fronts was published in the papers, together with detailed maps. Progress was followed avidly by the millions of German-Americans. Songwriter Fred Fischer, late of the Imperial German Navy, saw an early victory for the Central Powers (Germany, Hungary and Austria). Americans, many only recently arrived from Europe, moved checker armies across maps of the war. If anything, Germany was favoured for much of American life was of German origin: the beer made by Anheuser Busch, by Budweiser; the wiener (middle of the ubiquitous hot dog); the hamburger. These Germans were comfy people who made the comforts of life, who were friendly, fat, comic and could even make love. (Irving Berlin recorded, in 1914, his 'Oh! How That German Could Love'.)

Ballard Macdonald pictured a World War of food in his song about Herr Gustav Snider, a local provider of groceries, who stuffs his brain with too much war news. Hearing a din in his store one night he rushes downstairs to find his provisions battling each other in the First Great Grocery War:

> There were egg shells bursting near and far
>   Above the Russian caviar,
> A Bismark herring by itself
>   Was pushing all the French peas off the shelf.
> Frankfurters fighting all over the floor
>   Howling and growling 'We're the dogs of war!'
> And a couple of tough Vienna rolls
>   Shot a poor Swiss cheese all full of holes,
> In the terrible war in Snider's grocery store.

For boys of mixed parentage this newspaper war could become a headache. The problem was posed in 'The Land of my Best Girl', in which the hero's father is German, his mother is French and his best girl is English. Which side should he support?

This was the mood of the country in 1914 when the war was distant and the nearest Germans were jolly. But the following year, as the war news increased, the general attitude became dovish. Bryan and Piantadosi reflected this in their very popular 'I Didn't Raise My Boy to be a Soldier' ('respectfully dedicated to every Mother, everywhere'). Sensibly, they reasoned that 'there'd be no war today if mothers all would say "I didn't raise my boy to be a soldier".' Ex-President Teddy Roosevelt, anxious for America to join the war, scoffed and said that the mother might just as well sing 'I Didn't Raise My Girl to be a Mother'.

But though he had a large following he was unable to defeat President Wilson in the 1916 election, with his campaign slogan 'He Kept Us out of the War'. Son of a church minister and one-time President of Princeton University, Wilson seemed an unlikely leader. His appearance – he looked a bit like a short-sighted stoat with a nasty smell under its nose – was not heroic. Yet he was hymned in ragtime ('We're going to celebrate the end of war in ragtime – be sure that Woodrow Wilson leads the band') and congratulated by vaudeville star Norah Bayes as the world's great mediator, proof that the pen was greater than the sword.

She sang all this in 'We Take Our Hats off to you Mr Wilson' and, on the record, she interjects a personal comment just before the last line: 'I was over there in Europe and I know how terrible everything is' – sung on one note, priestly, with the orchestra hanging on to the chord. As if the song form was constricting her and she had to bust out and speak her mind. Like many of the songs about the war, she seems to be very passionate, too. At last! A great issue!

1916, the year of Wilson's re-election and Bayes's stirring heart-felt song was also the year of the Battle of the Somme, in which hundreds of thousands were killed. But Wilson just advised 'Be Prepared,' and the Alleymen turned West, across the Pacific to the newly annexed state of Hawaii, far, far from Flanders. Soon Hawaii was to become useful as a re-fuelling station for the fleet but now a sudden craze for hula girls had sent the Alleymen scurrying imaginatively to this sun-drenched isle of paradise Crusoe-style, away from the clangour of rude modern life. This craze was fanned by the appearance in America of Hawaian bands who toured vaudeville halls, wooing audiences with the pleasing plunk of the ukelele (a sanforized guitar) and the gulp-provoking swoop slides of the steel guitar. Like the popular jug bands, this was a grand novelty which was soon to pass as a sensation only occasionally revived (except in the rural areas where this steel guitar settled down to become a traditional country music instrument).

During the Hawaiian craze Alleymen told of straight chaps who dropped out of business life, lured by the call of the swaying hula girls who were able to 'yacki, hacki, wicki, wacki, woo!'. In 'They're Wearing 'Em Higher in Hawaii' ladies-wear buyer Henry Meyer takes a 'flyer' to Hawai-er in order to study fashions. Turned on to the pleasure principle by the girls, he stays there as a weaver of grass skirts. Furious, his boss embarks for the islands but on arrival quickly freaks out and decides to move his entire business to this island paradise.

Then the Alleymen turned South to satisfy a yen for Dixie. They sang of Sunny Tennessee (this even reached the British lines in the

Happy Alley Days

Western Front) and of missing that 'Mississippi Miss that misses me'. The world might well change and decay in this twentieth-century rag, but 'In 1960 You'll Find Dixie Looking Just the Same'. Mammy would still be wielding that frying pan with skill, whilst old black Joe rocked you with a Dixie melody.*

In a manner of speaking, the Alleymen were caught on the beaches and amongst the magnolia, when Wilson declared war on the Central Powers in April 1917. Of course, he *had* instigated a 'Preparedness' campaign the year before, but, nevertheless, it was something of a shock to find this man of peace, the reformer who had determined to 'set America free' from the industrialist robber barons, joining the squabble of the Old World. His conscience had been wrestled with and *now he knew what was right*. It was America's duty, not just to set America free, but to SET THE WHOLE WORLD FREE – to 'make the world safe for democracy'. To go to war to end war. To kill to end killing.

Outside of his mind there were other, less lofty reasons for America joining the Allies. He loved English literature; American industry was supplying the Allies with munitions; unrestricted submarine warfare by the Germans was threatening the US economy. Also, British propaganda was skilful. British agents revealed a Mexican/German plot to invade the US. Viscount Bryce distributed pamphlets telling the lurid story of a corpse factory in Germany where dead allies were melted down to make soap tablets.

Wilson, committed to war, now irised in on the enemy without and within. The heady crusade for democracy became a witch-hunt for anything German. Thus, Wagner was banned, German measles became Liberty measles and poor sauerkraut became Liberty cabbage. The authorities swooped on anybody who opposed entering the war. Wilson himself spoke against those who wouldn't join his team. 'This intolerable Thing, which we now see

*Curiously, when I ask Alleymen who wrote during this period why Dixie and Hawaii should suddenly have become all the rage, they look at me bewildered and then, pressed for an explanation, mumble something about it being 'the thing' or 'what people wanted'. Generally they find it very hard to remember back that far. 'Aren't you more interested in today, kid? Look, I got a great new song here that you can really rock up.'

so clearly as the German power, must now be crushed. Woe to the man or group of men that seeks to stand in our way in this day of high resolution!'

Licence was given to those who wanted to settle old scores in this new name of Democracy. Socialist leader Eugene Debs was jailed, so was a man who giggled at recruits rehearsing clumsily with rifles. Clergyman Henry Van Dyke volunteered to hang any man who opposed America's entry into the war. The American Security League determined to hunt down those who criticized the YMCA. Puritanism was mixed with the drive to conformism when drink was outlawed in most states and a standard haircut – short back and sides, or 'crew-cut' – took the place of flowing hair and beards. Free speech was banned.

Privately the President realized that his war move would 'overthrow the world we had known' and the nation would 'forget that there was ever such a thing as tolerance and the spirit of ruthless brutality would enter into the very fibre of national life'.

Songwriters came quickly to the breach. George M. Cohan, more of a Broadwayman than an Alleyman, who had made the Stars and Stripes the heroine of his song 'You're a Grand Old Flag', wasn't lazing in Hawaii or Dixie. He was first off the mark, right after Wilson fired his war declaration, with 'Over There'. Once, dressed as his character Yankee Doodle Boy, he had strutted the stage wrapped in Old Glory herself, rattling melodically out of the side of his mouth. Now, as war became the backdrop, as fiction became documentary, Yankee Doodle Boy was transformed into All-American boy. Cohan knew only four chords – but they were very good chords – and he shuffled them and settled them beneath a marvellous bugle call of a tune. 'Over There', first hit of the war, called on Johnny to get his gun on the run, then warned not only the Germans but also the Allies that 'the Yanks are coming!' Leo Feist, the publisher, bought Cohan's battle cry for 25,000 dollars. Norah Bayes, finished with peace mongering, plugged the song strenuously, applying semaphore arm movements which she had hitherto kept for her coon shouts rags. 'Over There' became the accepted phrase to describe the Great War. It was recorded by the Great Caruso, and was described by Wilson as 'a genuine inspiration to all American manhood'. It was also a million seller.

America now experienced 'big government' for the first time, as agencies took over every aspect of life. Pop music, not commandeered, was overseered. By government order the use of the Flag on sheet music covers was prohibited. George Creel, a busy booster, took charge of war propaganda and his Committee on Public Information used film, book, lecture, and song to propagate the correct war spirit. A song book was issued and song leaders sent all over the country to conduct gatherings in community sing-outs. At the same time and in the same spirit Leo Feist Inc. (motto: 'You can't go wrong with any Feist song') issued their collection of copyright war songs. In vaudeville houses war song contests were held, the material being supplied by publishers and presented by pluggers, some with the advantage of being in uniform.

This was not a conspiracy between the Alley and the Government, but maybe it was a voluntary 'arrangement'. The War Industries Board, for instance, allowed supplies of paper to the publishers because music was 'essential to win the war'. In an economy drive the publishers shrank the tall sheets, and they stayed that way even after the Armistice, forever. Right alongside the music patriotic slogans were printed, such as: 'Eat more fish, eggs, cheese and poultry. Save beef, pork and mutton for our fighters.'

These, then, were good days for the Alleymen. They were at once doing their bit and doing nicely. They buckled down to it with vim, producing more songs between April 1917 and November 1918 than at any time before or since in this the most musicful of wars. They pulled with the crew – no battle-poopers here! – in their rollicking tank-ship, which contained all the pop styles and cartoon characters developed so far in our story: the babe waved her Johnnie goodbye off to war in march-time, twisted and bent by touches of ragtime (making its last stand) – but he dreamed of her and she dreamed of him in waltz-time. All of this was encased in the set form of the ballad.

Alleymen versus the Allemands

The sense of noble purpose, *this crusade*, inspired some Alleymen to ethereal splendour. As Wilfred Owen, the British poet, found his true subject at last in war, so did these writers. 'Somewhere in France is the Lily' bubbles the blood – I have seen it rock upright pianos. A march which knows where it's going. 'Belgian Rose', promising 'hands across the sea' rescue to a wronged little country, turns the barber-shop ballad into a hymn set in a church of chilling 7th chords. 'Hello Central Give Me No-Man's Land' has the telephone put to good use because the baby is calling up her daddy over there. The tune soars high and pummels the heart.*

Getting down more to brass tacks, songwriters urged melting-pot Americans to forget that foreign past. Just before the war grumblers had been told 'If You Don't Like Your Uncle Sammy Then Go Back to Your Home O'er the Sea!' Now Irving Berlin, putting away any remembrances of Russia, urged 'Let's All be Americans Now'.

War strategy and tactics were compressed into handy phrases, rather like the slogan buttons of today. The navy boys were going to 'knock the Heligo – into Heligo – out of Heligoland'. On land all was fairly simple, too: 'Just Like Washington Crossed the Delaware General Pershing Will Cross The Rhine'. Finally 'when we all go swimming in the Rhine, we'll hang our clothes on Hindenburg's old Line'.

But much more popular were the songs which saw the war not from the high vantage of a General, in grand sweeps, but from the worm's-eye view of the ordinary man. The writers ignored the tank which won the war, believing in people rather than machines. So it was 'Oh How I Hate to Get Up in the Morning!', the rookie soldier's lament. 'They were All out of Step but Jim', crowed Jim's mother proudly to her neighbours. A girl, seeing her boy off

*This is a song which has always given me goose-pimples. I sang it in clubs but never really dared let go. This seemed uncool at the time. So I camped by putting on a baby lisp. I was coy and was rewarded with laughter. Then one night I sang 'No-Man's Land' in this manner to songwriter Dick Sherman (who wrote the score of *Mary Poppins*, *Chitty Chitty Bang Bang* and more). He listened and commented 'Yes, you're talented – but why do you make fun of a song that can be very moving?' He was right, but the time is not quite right.

to war, quipped to her friends 'If He Can Fight Like He Can Love *Goodnight Germany!*' Who wanted to be a big shot anyway? 'Would You Rather be a Colonel with an Eagle on Your Shoulder, Or a Private with a Chicken on Your Knee?'

Sometimes, I feel, the writers were cerebrating too much, sitting in their tiny cubicles in the Alley, pencils poised, brains racked. Their war became one monster pun, with efforts like 'Your Lips Are No Man's Land But Mine'.

Sometimes, too, they got carried away by this war theme and upset the authorities. 'I Don't Want to Get Well – I'm in Love with a Beautiful Nurse' and 'There'll be a Hot Time for the Old Men When the Young Men go to War' were considered encouragements to dodge the draft or even desert. Both were banned and copies seized. The Alley was warned that peace songs were taboo.*

War aims clarified, the Alleymen sent the boys off to war with rousing raggy marches set to words that befitted their home. Thus, city slickers sailed to 'Goodbye Broadway, Hello France' and country boys to 'Goodbye Ma! Goodbye Pa! Goodbye Mule!' Figures from the Alley myths joined, hovering about like ghosts. There was old Alexander, from way back in 1911, taking his ragtime band to France. There were no Hawaiians, but the Dixie Volunteers appeared as 'peaceful sons' who'd 'shoulder guns' and marched all the way from the 'land of old black Joe'. However, the sheet music cover showed these sons to be blue-eyed Dixie boys, not red-hot raggedy coons.†

The US Army swelled to 4 million men, and included Alleymen like Irving Berlin. At Camp Upton he wrote and performed in an all-soldier revue called *Yip Yip Yaphank*. Major General J. Franklin was reluctant to attend, but afterwards declared 'Berlin

---

*However 'I Don't Want to Get Well' was a smash hit in England in the autumn of 1918.

†This reflected reality. W. C. Handy wrote in his autobiography that his black band was all ready to play for the war parade in Memphis but they were never invited to do so. Instead Old Black Joe was reduced to shuffling along at the side of the grand procession carrying buckets of water. Handy says Joe was there to 'assist some white gentleman should he fall from exhaustion along the line of march'.

is as good a soldier as he is songwriter.' The Army considered that a singing army was a good weapon and Army song leaders were appointed, amongst them Geoffrey O'Hara, who in 1914 had lived in the bush with the Navajo Indians researching and later recording their songs. As a song leader he led the men in choruses of his great stuttering song success 'K-K-Katy'. This was very quickly parodied into 'K-K-Kay Pee', a complaint about the drudgery of 'mopping up the k-k-k-kitchen floor' in the 'm-m-m-messhall'.

'If You Don't Like Your Uncle Sammy' became 'If You Don't Like Your Beans and Hard-tack'. Not as sardonic as the parodies of the British Tommies, with their 'If you were the only Boche in the trench and I had the only Bomb,' but then the doughboys had not yet experienced life on the Western Front.

One who *had* been 'over there' was Lieutenant Gitz-Rice of the First Canadian Contingent. He copyrighted the trench song 'Hinky Dinky Parlez Voo' and re-arranged the old music hall song 'Hold Your Hand Out, Naughty Boy' (chanted by the British Expeditionary Force in 1914) so that it came out sideways and the cry was now 'Keep Your Head Down Fritzie Boy – If You Want to See Your Father in the Fatherland'. This officer was a familiar figure around the trenches, where Tommies would often warn him 'Git yer own 'ead dahn, Gitzie-boy!' He brought the flavour of the war, as he savoured it, to the American public via his records 'Fun In Flanders' and 'Life in a Trench in Belgium'.

Furnished with songs, led by Army song leaders, off went the Singing Army to end the Great War . . .

Wilson had declared war in April, 1917. By June one million three hundred and ninety thousand doughboys arrived in France. Just in time, for Britain was a few weeks from starvation. Commander-in-Chief Haig had prayed for victory before the Americans arrived. The German generals hoped for the same thing.

As they swept into the battle ground, bands blazing, they astounded the war-weary Allies. A young subaltern, Guy Ffernshawe, described this in his diary:

Happy Alley Days

Impressive no end were these clean-limbed Yankee boys with their heads regularly shaped. Tall (not stunted by malnutrition or stooped by factory life like our Tommy Atkins), gangling idealistically over the torn French soil and swaggering – or was it *reeling*? – to a tipsy military band tooting a ragtime march. Brass bullied away with positive notions, euphonium broke wind in my face with a rigid bass, snare drum machine-gunned wildly. Who but the sallow intellectual still 'if'fing and 'but'ing could now doubt the rightness of the Allied Cause?

Tommy Atkins, the British soldier, liked to sing too and had been singing since the start of the war back in 1914. But not songs about the Allied Cause. Instead he tended towards those unrelated to the grand issues, marching to the front to 'Hello! Who's Your Lady Friend?' and especially 'It's a Long Way to Tipperary'. This last, probably the best-remembered song of the First World War, was actually published a few years before it began. Florrie Forde, the music-hall chorus singer, had tried it out in a Christmas panto-mime, but it had failed to click. By some mysterious folk process, the troops decided to adopt 'Tipperary' (no more than an average stage-Irish song) as their 1914 war anthem. Most war-aimed British songs (e.g. 'Belgium Put the Kibosh on the Kaiser', 'Your King and Country Need You') were never heard outside of a music hall theatre. Soldiers on leave despised these home-front entertainers. Officer Siegfried Sassoon longed for a tank to burst into a theatre, trundle down the centre aisle lurching to a ragtime tune and blast the whole sham to kingdom come. Yet it would be unfair to blame singers and songwriters, for they hadn't a chance to go to hell in France. Many were felt to be more useful at home writing 'buck-up' songs and were placed in the Royal Navy Air Service, which required their wearing a splendid uniform and serving aboard H M S *Crystal Palace* – permanently dry-docked in South-East London and known in the trade as 'the ship they couldn't sink'.

Out at the front the British soldiers kept their singing for when they came out of the line, striking up a cheerful refrain to accom-paniment of mouth organ, tin whistle, concertina. In the evening, off duty, they liked songs that reminded them of home ('There's a Long, Long Trail a-Winding', 'Take Me Back to Dear Old

66

Blighty', 'Keep the Home Fires Burning'), or which were simply damned good tunes and nothing to do with home or war ('If You Were the Only Girl in the World', 'Moon My Moon', 'For Me and My Girl'). Ironically, one of the most popular of these ballads – 'Roses Of Picardy' – which told of roses, poplars and a girl with sea-blue eyes, was set slap bang in the area where thousands were being killed and wounded daily, sometimes hourly.

By the time the Americans arrived songs at the front weren't war sirens but only songs. Some were downright unhealthy! Tommy Atkins had been mumbling a piece of nihilistic nonsense which ran 'We're 'ere becos we're' ere becos we're 'ere becos we're 'ere', ad nauseam! All at once the Americans with their ragtime offered 'go-getter' advice about finishing off this business. Alfred Bryan, Cliff Hess and Edgar Leslie had sent it all the way from Broadway in a package:

> When Alexander takes his ragtime band to France
> He'll capture every Hun, and take them one by one.
> Those ragtime tunes will put the Germans in a trance;
> They'll throw their guns away, Hip Hooray! And start
>   right in to dance.
> They'll get so excited they'll come over the top,
> Two-step back to Berlin with a skip and a hop.
> Old Hindenburg will know he has no chance,
>   ('I haff nein chaaance!')
> When Alexander takes his ragtime band to France.

Ragtime – no doubt about it – was the answer! But, in those days, the alternative culture wasn't strong enough. These suggestions were laughed at, enjoyed – and afterwards everybody *got back on the job.* Poor ragtime had hoped to put an end to war, and be chief music-provider at the Victory celebrations. As one rag had put it in 1915:

> Everybody soon will sing in rag-rhyme.
> England, France and Germany – even folks in Italy –
> The aristocrats and the diplomats marching hand in hand
> (See them tip their hats to those ragtime melodies).
> Everyone's in harmony.
> We're going to celebrate the end of war in ragtime
>   – Be sure that Woodrow Wilson leads the band!

67

Happy Alley Days

But this was not to be. Ragtime was tottering in 1918, a tired expression for a misunderstood music, root of all subsequent pop. Now jazz and blues, her poor relations, were creeping in – even here, in France. US military bands were amazing the Allies with displays of this jazz. The orchestra of the 158th Infantry Regiment under the direction of 2nd Lieutenant A. R. Etzweiler entertained open-mouthed troops with a version of Tiger Rag, now called 'Le Rugissement du tigre'. The new sound, crazy and sloppy but peppy and tingly, had started in the South, it was rumoured. Jim Europe, the coloured lieutenant conductor, led his band to the Tuileries where they took part in an Allied Military Concert. All the other bands played the classical music of their native land – but Europe couldn't compete with that so he conducted his soldiers in the 'St Louis Blues'. Allied bandsmen crowded round the bandstand agape. So this was the classical music of the USA!

Did the doughboys actually sing anything when they went into battle? One who'd fought at Belleau Wood told me he found himself humming 'That Tumbledown Shack in Athlone', which was odd because he came from Denver, Colorado. John J. Niles, in his book *Singing Soldiers*, says that the city white boys tended to sing the ready-made Broadway songs, whereas the coloured boys made up their own songs (but these may have been unpublished blues). I think most everyone sang or hummed something.

The American intervention tipped the balance in favour of the Allies. In November 1918 the Central Powers surrendered. So the doughboys returned home in wild boat-loads to beating of bells and the eager, patriotic lips of the Liberty Ladies who were rewarded with the 'french kiss', one of the many new ways of life picked up in France. The wise-weary look worn by returning soldiers was well expressed by Alleymen Abe Olman, Jack Yellen and Geo. Meyer:

> Every time he looks at me
> He makes me feel so unnecessary
> Oh! Just think of it Clarice,
> He spent two months in Paris, and
> Oh! Oh! Johnny's in town!!

Perhaps they had a heightened awareness of the possibilities of life. The farm seemed impossibly *drab*. 'They'll never want to see a rake or plough – and how the deuce d'you "parlez-voo" a cow', went Walter Donaldson's 1919 hit. One thing was quite clear and that was 'NO MORE MORAL ATTENTION SONGS'. Signs went up back-stage in vaudeville houses prohibiting war songs.

Peace brought Dixie whooshing back (although it had hovered in the background, shooting out a hit here and there, during the war period). Dreamy and lulling, singing that 'Dixie is Dixie Once More'. Even the Blues caressed – as in Roger Graham's 'Flower Garden Blues', which pictured a morning glory climbing up the garden wall to kiss a wild sunflower ten feet tall, watched by gossiping geraniums and hollyhocks.

But peace could not suddenly shut off the stream of righteous energy released by Wilson's war propaganda experts. A Red Scare swept the country, although it was estimated that there were no more than 60,000 communists in the USA. Justice was done summarily, by lynch mobs. In New York bands of soldiers and sailors roamed the streets looking for radicals, reds, socialists, or people they didn't like the look of. Leo Feist Inc., chief publisher of war songs, turned to the enemy within and encouraged citizens to follow the example of the soldiers and sailors: 'Let's Knock the Bull out of the Bolsheviki', written by Johnson, Schuster and Piotti, suggested:

> With anarchy and bloodshed, our freedom is at stake
> So let's wipe out each cause of it and trample on the snake.

But indignation quickly lapsed into celebration of back to 'normalcy', a word coined by Warren G. Harding who became President in 1921.

The war had flashed by and was now put away. The Alleymen had responded to the clarion call. In the days of twenties normalcy, this militancy was regretted. 'My Buddy' pined for the dead comrade; 'That Old Gang of Mine' noted that the old street corner gang had been decimated as they'd hit the von Hindenburg Line. And Billy Rose, who also wrote 'Barney Google' remembered the Unknown Soldier:

69

There's a grave near the White House
Where the Unknown Soldier lies,
And the flowers there are sprinkled
With the tears of mothers' eyes.

I stood there not so long ago
With roses for the grave
When suddenly I thought I heard
A voice speak from the grave.

'I am the Unknown Soldier'
The spirit voice began,
'And I think I've got a right
To ask some questions, man to man.

'Are my buddies taken care of?
Was their victory so sweet?
Is that big reward you promised
Selling pencils in the street?

'And that baby that sang
"Hello Central Give Me No-Man's Land",
Can they replace her daddy
With a military band?

'I wonder if the profiteers
Have satisfied their greed?
I wonder if the soldier's mother
Ever is in need?

'I wonder if the kings
Who planned it all are satisfied?
They played their game of checkers
And eleven million died!

'I am the Unknown Soldier
And maybe I died in vain
But if I were alive and my country called
I'D DO IT ALL OVER AGAIN!'

Books about the 'good old songs' always have acres of colourful
stories behind the songs, so I'm going to finish this section with
one. I always devour these stories because they help to put some
flesh and blood into songs which have become over-familiar, and

thus tired. My story is about 'Melancholy Baby', a favourite of drunks on bar-pianos. Ernie Burnett, who had studied music in Austria and then returned to become a vaudeville pianist, wrote the tune in 1911 and it became a big hit. Burnett went to war in France and fell amongst a heap of bodies. His name tag got swapped with a corpse's, so the stretcher-bearers thought he was somebody else. He wasn't able to identify himself because he'd lost his memory. After the war a band of entertainers visited the hospital and one of the girls sang 'Melancholy Baby'. Burnett (or Jones, or X) suddenly shot up in bed and claimed 'That's my tune!' The lead singer explained that Ernie Burnett, the composer, had been killed in the War. Working from the knowledge that he'd composed the tune, Burnett gradually found out about his past life, and was re-incarnated, as it were.

I tell this story because, as we plough into this pop business, figures and facts are going to crop up increasingly, together with the awful inventions of science such as radio and talkies and gramophones and electronics. Humans may get lost somewhere.

Part Two
Between the Wars

Introduction

And now, as we enter this lush choc-a-pop period – all-roaring in the twenties, all-purring in the thirties – as we leave rickety old ragtime behind and before we reach my modern times of rock, I can feel the hot anticipatory breath of a reader over my shoulder.

For this is the time when the older generation will instantly recall memories through the time machine of an old song. This is the time when, looking back from today, all those evergreen standards were written, when dance music was sweeter, when you could dance all night, and life was 'amusing' and 'civilized' and 'sophisticated'. A high plateau, or comfortable couch, of popular music. Tuneful songs like they don't write them anymore – in a world whose ideal was graceful living in the suggestive society. Songwriters might dig the side lovingly but never frontally assault.

So I can feel that older reader over my shoulder wondering 'What songs is he going to mention? Mustn't forget "Dancing with Tears in My Eyes" because that reminds me of that tooth I had removed. And "Red Sails in the Sunset"? You hummed that while Harold was born.' 'D'you remember when we had Bing on the gram. singing "I Surrender, Dear", out on the moors near the M.G. and you popped the question?'

Everybody is an expert on pop music.

What follows is my own time-trip then and you may dismiss it as the journey of a madman. I never lived through this era, but I can get awfully nostalgic over it . . .

Behind all the razzamatazz there seemed to be a reposeful ideal: to live happily and cosily in the little white house in Honeymoon Lane with your pal of a wife. Excitement was provided by the rapidly expanding entertainment empire, presented in newspaper, talkies, on record and radio. Gertrude Ederle swam the Channel; the serum was brought to Nome making a hero of the dog Balto; the stock market crashed; Violet Gibson shot Mussolini in the nose; the Prince of Wales drummed with Paul Whiteman's band; Britain declared war on Germany.

Tin Pan Alley grew up. A new breed of songwriters, writers of Broadway scores, set a high standard for the old piano-pumpers of the Alley. Song became more intricate, more literary, more musically complicated through the works of a select company of musical comedy composers and lyricists. The master jewellers of the profession who set the new standards were Jerome Kern, George Gershwin, Richard Rodgers and Lorenz Hart, and Cole Porter. They broke out of the 32 bar prison, and tooled popular song into a miniature art. The key word of the twenties was 'syncopation', but by the thirties this had given way to 'sophistication', which meant beating about the bush with a feather duster. In the industry these men were the tops at this sophisticated stuff. Tunes were bedded with restless modern harmonies, such as flattened fifths and thirteenths. Words were skilfully put together by men armed with thesauruses, who could joke in French, bring in references to the Mona Lisa, and speak of 'feminine rhymes' and 'sprung rhythms'. Vanishing, it seemed, were the good old days of Alley piano-pumping ear-men who played with one finger on pianos which changed key at the touch of a lever. Only Irving Berlin made the big change and held his own with the new lettered men. By the end of the thirties sophisticated songs, crooned tastefully, held Alleymen in thrall and even the general public cheerfully understood the phrase 'strictly "entre nous"' in the 1938 hit 'Thanks for the Memory'. Or did they?

But quite another kind of sophistication was high-rising at the same time, quite a different kind of 'growing up'. The pop industry was consolidating, empire-building, *power-structuring* – using the new devices of radio, electric recording, microphones, talking pictures and the old one of monopoly. Our little ragtimey dance band fattened until it became the many-tiered wedding cake orchestra of Paul Whiteman (up to 30 players, ranging from violinists to bicycle pump experts). By the time that swing appeared, dance bands had become stream-lined organizations manned by well-drilled executive players, guided by managers, booked by giant agencies such as MCA, fronted by canny businessmen musicians – like conservatively suited Tommy Dorsey or Benny Goodman.

Show business in general became the leisure arm of Big Business. Pop was promoted as a leisure activity with the same high seriousness which went into the promotion of Mah Jong, Contract Bridge and Crossword Puzzles. Was it accepted as seriously by its public? Yes, but as yet there wasn't enough free time around for people to take university degrees in it. At the end of the thirties over three quarters of the nation's hit songs were controlled by the movie business. Hollywood had bought up Tin Pan Alley. Radio made the hits by air-play. *Variety*, the old show-biz weekly, was a *Financial Times* vitally concerned with the stock market; in 1929 it had banner-headlined the Great Crash 'WALL STREET LAYS AN EGG'.

On the whole, though, the Depression was a good time for show business. By 1935 everything was very rosy: Americans were spending 4 billion dollars a year on amusement (almost 10 per cent of their annual income).

The business sophisticates were more futuristic than the song sophisticates, whose stunning wit and satire and careful piano craftsmanship was the jewelry of a vanished age – *moderne* rather than modern. For the average Alley cleffer times were getting more complex – you were less your own master, more at the mercy of mechanics and arrangers. But still the demand for material was there OK. In fact, more demand than ever before, since the electric machines gobbled them up so fast. The smiths quickly re-worked the old faithfuls (novelty, rhythmic and sentimental ballad) spreading sunshine over badtime. They now met in their special section at Lindy's (on the right as you went in) in New York. Their Hollywood fellows ate at the Brown Derby, but pined for Broadway.

American pop music spread over the globe via record and movie, pushing aside native product so that popular music became associated with America. Whilst visiting Brazil, songwriter Harry Warren, creator of 1930s movie song hits, was presented with a beautiful boat of hide, hand-made by an Indian in gratitude for writing 'The Shadow Waltz'. In Milan he heard a street merchant whistling 'September in the Rain'. Cole Porter, passing through Zanzibar in 1935, saw East African ivory dealers listening attentively to a record of his 'Night And Day'.

The golden age of American pop came to an end in 1939 – if we must date it. That year the mighty ASCAP, controller of songs, refused to let radio, controller of plugs, have any more vital song fuel unless she paid more money. Radio called in the Third Estate – hillbilly music, lower class 'nasal whining'. Rock 'n' roll was not far off! . . . the barbarians were at the gate! But that's another chapter and that's a gross simplification.

With ragtime behind us and rock before us, we now plunge into verdant detail of this high plateau of pop.

Jazz

'What is this *jazz*?' asked a judge during a 1917 white-slavery case – and didn't stay for an answer but recessed for lunch. Even today jazz is a slippery animal to trap and one jazzer's jazz is another jazzer's junk, so I'm blessed if I'm going to get involved in this dangerous subject!

But the boys of the Alley never stopped to analyse, they just ran along. In 1917 'jazz' was THE COMING WORD, taking over from tired 'ragtime'. Jazz was what you called your rag, now.

Although the Great War was raging the industry wasn't devoted solely to the production of war songs. Relaxation from moral attention was supplied by song trips to Ireland, to the silver sands of Hawaii and to the sunny lands of Dixie. Jazz had originated in Tennessee, then waited – *oh baby* – waited for her popularitee, so the song said. This jazz was part of the romance of Dixie, land of ragtime and minstrels. From New Orleans? Impossibly romantic!

The French tried to destroy this theory by stating that jazz was 'first made by ten thousand cats on Paris roofs during a fourteenth-century plague'.

Between 1917 and 1919 ragtime was quietly eased off the scene, as jazz – the southern sensation – entered. The distinction between the two was fuzzy. Shelton Brooks, the coloured composer/writer, had described Rufe Johnson's Harmony Band in the rag days of 1914 as including a 'trombone moaning'. Four years later he raved over 'That Dixie Jazz Band' with 'that trombone moaning'. Could it be that 1914 Rufe is leader of the 1918 Jazz

Band? A year later, when Scott Fitzgerald's 'Jazz Age' was launched, 'The Jazz Baby' revealed her family background as a rag-trombone-playing father and a rag-cabaret mother who'd met at a tango tea. A syncopated wedding was followed by a Jazz Baby. And now you has jazz!

More down to earth was song plugger Sol Truck who simply opined to me in 1970: 'Rag, jazz, swing, rock 'n' roll was just new handles we gave Joe Public for old sounds. Before rag we called that beat stuff "tipple". You know, home-made hollering by the coloured folk.' Another plugger, Mickey Addy, such a pace-setter with his dress habits, was premature with his jazz; he had organized the 'Three Leaf Jazz Band' in 1914 – just four years too early!

But the word 'jazz' had been floating around sub-culture for decades before that. Possibly it came from Africa, possibly France, possibly from legendary player Jassbo Brown. By the time of our century the word had two general meanings – 'Jazz it up!' meaning 'Will you please speed up that tune?' And 'I sure jazzed that gal!' meaning 'I certainly gave that girl a good bout of sexual intercourse!' Folk spoke and didn't write so the word was at first variously spelled by journalists as jass, jaz, jazz, jasz, jatz, jascz.

The latest intelligence I have is that the word is actually an abbreviation of a hotted-up version of the spiritual '*Jassed* a Closer Walk with Thee'. However, scholars are still working on exactly when, where and who.

However, 'Jazz' became a pop word in New York from late in 1916 onwards. So that's when it starts concerning us. 'Jazz' was the subject of tattle on the cafe scene. The unit that made the music was called the 'jazz band' and it was only one of the many 'novelty' sensations which were popular in cafe-cabaret at that time (jug, Hawaiian and Redskin bands were amongst the other sensations).

The most musical, the most successful, the canniest of these early jazz bands was a five-piecer from New Orleans calling itself the 'Dixieland Jazz Band' and later the '*Original* Dixieland Jazz Band' – to distinguish itself from the dozens of other noisy combos rapidly forming in northern cities and streaming up from the South.

Was the Original Dixieland Jazz Band (ODJB) the first jazz band? Who knows! – for who knows what jazz was? But they appear to have been the first band to use the word 'jazz' to describe a kind of music. And their front line (cornet, trombone, clarinet) was to become the classic set-up for future New Orleans jazz. They came to set the style.

Even in their home town before pop fame, they were celebrated and envied. New Orleans appears to have been packed with all-purpose bands, black, white and indifferent. Bandsmanship was as popular in Southern cities as it was in Britain's industrial North. Bands at parades, bands at marriages, bands at funerals, bands at births, bands in brothels, bands at political conventions, bands at picnics. Bands with all manner of instruments: sandpaper players, toilet pipe experts. Bands that were content to play for a bag of food and a keg of beer. Bands that tried to play ragtime and couldn't make it, so they faked it; that played wrong notes so often they became right notes. A rag-bag hotch-potch gumbo with a theft chest repertoire of tunes from many sources. For example, the ODJB's 'Tiger Rag' was supposedly patched together from 'London Bridge is Falling Down' plus a waltz bit, a quadrille wedge and a slice of the 'National Emblem March'. A ragtime composer (Joe Jordan) was pained to discover his 'Teasin' Rag' bagged and bowdlerized by the ODJB and slipped into their 'Original Dixieland One-Step'.

Out of this free-for-all folk jungle came the seemingly anarchic, but actually very controlled, music of the ODJB. In 1916 this country brass band played a date at a Chicago cafe. Other southern bands, playing in a roughly similar way, had played Chicago before the ODJB and failed. The ODJB caught on at once. A listen to their records will prove how exciting and extraordinary they are. In 1916 they were sensational.

Al Jolson, a very big star, saw their act. He was so moved that he burst into tears, and got them a peach of a date at Reisen-weber's restaurant, an important venue in New York. Pretty soon they were the latest craze, with folks standing in line for this *new music.* Actually, as we've seen, it had roots but that was of no concern to the fans of the band. Yes, their music was and is good – but the O D J B had a lot more than music going for them!

Nick La Rocca played the cornet left-handed and shimmied as he blew. He described their operation thus: 'You see I cut the material, Shields (the clarinettist) puts on the lace, and Edwards (the trombone player) sews it up.' Chordic backing was provided by vamping Henry Ragas. Tony Sbarbaro worked his vast set of traps (cow bells, temple blocks, and the largest kazoo in the world) setting the pulse.

They were much louder than any other novelty band (louder, in fact than the US Marine Band). They seemed like a street band playing indoors. ('You could almost smell the horses,' commented a witness.) They were much faster and more sloping than ragtime bands – somewhere mid-way between the upright two-two of ragtime and the steamy roll of four-four that was eventually associated with jazz. They seemed to be all playing a different tune, making it up as they went along, yet all finishing as one man. Critics linked this improvisation with the irresponsibility which loomed up in 1919.

In fact the O D J B were very canny country lads who had carefully rehearsed every number, and, guided by shrewd manager Max Hart, were very adept at supplying the news-hungry press with juicy quotes. 'None of us know music,' boasted Eddie Edwards, trombonist and note-reader who taught the boys the new show tunes. 'I am the assassinator of syncopation,' stated leader La Rocca, with glee.

The press added their own fantasies. A reporter described notes that 'blat and collide', excellently imagined 'violins snickering and shrieking', metaphored the drums into 'heavy artillery', the piano into 'a torpedo boat destroyer', the whole ensemble into a 'pack in full cry'. The band provided more headlines by appearing at a concert wedged in the bill between Caruso and evangelist Billy Sunday, by wailing the blues in court during a copyright case, by soothing the wild animals in Central Park Zoo for an experiment supervised by physiologists.

In visual appeal they followed in the razzamatazz tradition of

John Philip Sousa, but they had the benefit of a slicker, faster press and the new emerging art of press agentry. Also, the war spirit, which continued even after Armistice, was on their side. Anarchic music appealed to the new generation. Unfortunately, though they billed themselves as the 'Creators of Jazz' they couldn't copyright their 'invention'. Dance bandsmen and vaudevillians had rushed to Reisenweber's to absorb the tricks. Earl Fuller, king of traps, quickly cut his band down to five and started making barnyard sounds similar to the ODJB (but nothing like so musical). Jimmy Durante, at the Alamo Cafe, adored the new music and imported genuine New Orleans players to add to his ragtime piano. Soon record companies were cashing in on the phenomenal sales of the ODJB's records (they had the first million seller in 'Livery Stable Blues') by issuing products made by 'straight' house orchestras but with 'jazzy' names. Thus: The Plantation Jazz Orchestra (echoes of the minstrels), The Futurist Jazz Band (heralds of 'futurism' and 'modernism'); Harry Raderman's Jazz Orchestra squealed with 'Make That Trombone Laugh' backed by 'Slide, Kelly, Slide' and a hit of 1920 was 'The Yelping Hound Blues'. The emphasis was on noise and novelty and by the early twenties there were hundreds and hundreds of cacophonous jazz bands all over the country. What jazz was exactly nobody quite knew. But one thing was very clear: it was darned easy to play and if you played it you were *popular*.

Drums were still the main attraction. Well-equipped operators were able to boast not only mere drums but also baby-cry gadgets, coconuts, watchman's rattles and garden flyswatters (these latter later became drum brushes). Other instruments gave drums stiff competition though; girls liked boys who played saxophones best. Next in line were trumpeters, trombonists and clarinettists, in that order. Drummers were too fast and pianists came in last. But singing ukelele players – dark horses – were a cinch for getting her hot on the back porch, if the truth be known. Singers, always the singers, but jazz seemed to have little singing. Was there such a thing as jazz singing? Show business said that there *was* and vaudevillian George Jessel became 'The Jazz Singer' in the

Broadway play, whilst another vaudevillian, Al Jolson, became 'The Jazz Singer' in the 1927 movie.

For vaudeville jazz was a bonus – plenty of 'business' (bashing drums, playing a sax and smoking two cigarettes at the same time) but a wee bit dangerous because after 1919 most acts tried to go 'classy' (even acrobats wore evening dress). However, with a title a drop of class could be injected: Sophie Tucker, once the 'Mary Garden of Ragtime', surrounded herself with jazz bands black and white and became 'Queen of Jazz'. Ted Lewis, ex-clarinettist of the Earl Fuller Jazz Band, toured as the 'Top-Hatted Tragedian of Jazz', the Hamlet of the Halls, posing the eternal question 'Is everybody happy?'

The dance band business came to terms with jazz in its *watchman's rattle* and *hyena trumpet* form. Back in the second chapter, you may remember, we left Paul Whiteman with a million dollar corporation. His fellow musicians Henry Busse and Ross Gorman together with other society bandleaders like Vincent Lopez had witnessed and digested the music of the ODJB. Over in Chicago, members of the Isham Jones orchestra liked to study King Oliver's Jazz Band, one of the many black bands made of New Orleans jazzers. The collective playing, the driving beat, the almost human sounds coaxed from scientific instruments – all these qualities were genuinely admired by straighter musicians. But most dance musicians agreed that even the best jazzers lacked finish; they were frequently out of tune (especially the Negroes with their wretched second-hand horns and lack of decent music schooling), they were limited in style and rhythm. Few patrons of dance bands wanted to shimmy and shake *all* night long.

During the pop-jazz craze of the early twenties, the Paul Whiteman band had attempted to make music out of the air in the jazz manner. Unfortunately the notes came out all wrong, so in future they were written down. Skilled arrangers such as Don Redman of the Fletcher Henderson Band, and Bill Challis of the Paul Whiteman Orchestra, caught the hot burns and fade-aways, the flares and warm raspberries which blasted from the little jazz bands, and scored them. Carefully placed here and there in the

84

arrangement of a melody, the explosions of jazz added a dash of pepper to dance music. At the same time the dance bands were developing a musical style of their own. Died-in-the-wool jazzers came to love the sound that Freddy 'Mr Silvertone' Martin pressed out of his saxophone. Louis Armstrong said he was inspired by Guy Lombardo and his Royal Canadians, purveyors of 'the sweetest music this side of heaven'. Jazz licks and phrasing were only a part of modern dance music, which also included harmony choruses, key changes, nutty surprise endings with tiers of Chinesey chords. All that and a wide selection of music ranging from blues, through ballads to light opera!

If jazzers wanted to make it in the dance band business they'd have to learn to read and to play with accuracy. The ODJB added a saxophone, sounded like heaps of other mediocre dance bands, squabbled internally and disappeared. But other jazzers joined bands as house hot boys ready to break out with a solo at specially indicated times.

By 1930 bands had swollen considerably. Whiteman had thirty-four players. Red Nichols's once all-hot outfit of five was now fifteen. Bandsmen were expected to be at the date on time. They were employees in a growing business. Many grew little tooth-brush moustaches, adding a few useful years to their appearance. Leaders had to be disciplinarians. It was said that Isham Jones resembled a country attorney rather than a dance band leader. He ruled his band 'with an iron baton'. Too much jazzing and practical joking was not to be tolerated. Bands were serving the public not only music for dancing but also unobtrusive music for dreaming, reading a book, doing a crossword puzzle, falling asleep.

Bands were everywhere. George Olsen and his Music appeared in Broadway musicals; Paul Whiteman's orchestra played for the Prince of Wales (the Prince sat in on drums). Laurel and Hardy two-reel sound comedies were accompanied by continuous dance band music. Duke Ellington provided the music track for Ub Iwerk's 'Willie Whopper' cartoons. Vaudeville was said to be dead in 1930 but dance bands filled theatres during the next decade with shows that came to include singers, vocal groups, dancers, acrobats, and MCs. Old-time vaudevillians were dismayed because many bandsmen refused to wear make-up and insisted on appearing in casual clothes, e.g., sweaters and bags. Whiteman's orchestra made an impressive sight with its glittering array of instruments and rows of players – the genial headmaster with his school behind him. Henry Busse hit the highest note in the world, and one man played a bicycle pump. (On the other hand, together the band could play the '1812 Overture'.) Waring's Pennsylvanians had tambourines which glowed in the dark. Guy Lombardo's outfit set and kept the all-time high attendance record at the Savoy Ballroom, Harlem. All the world loved a good all-round dance band, it appeared.

The pop music industry, growing more complex and powerful all the while, dropped pure jazz once the novelty value had worn off. Tin Pan Alley was exasperated by jazz bands who played their own folk-library of tunes, unpublished and not written by Alleymen. (Samey-samey blues were hard to copyright.) When the jazzers did play standard Alley stuff they usually garbled the melody by tootling as the mood took them. Radio executives, attempting to cater for a family audience, had little time for jazz bands either. Electrical recording (introduced in the mid twenties) enabled sweeter orchestras to be recorded. Victor banned the word 'jazz' from its catalogues. The musicians' union had no love for jazz bands; regular dance bands had had to cut their numbers down to conform to the craze for little bands, whilst the market had been flooded with horrendous kid amateurs bashing drums and fooling with saxophones (the trouble was that the sax was easy to learn). Dance hall owners found that five-piece jazz bands were all very jazzy but in their vast (and growing vaster) halls they simply couldn't be heard by all the patrons. Anyway, in 1925 a more refined version of the dance hall became popular: the modern ballroom, catering for the whole family. A few years later housewives were turning up at these ballrooms in their thousands for 'tango teas', and housewives didn't want jazz. Quite enough noise in the home as it was, they felt.

Women contributed most to the decline of jazz music. Oh, in the beginning they embraced it as a fashion. A new hat, a new drink. Those tomboys, the flappers, leapt on it joyfully, shimmying and charlestoning. Observers reported that jazz made some women violent. Girls and matrons jumped on top of tables screaming and tearing their clothes off whenever cornettist Nick La Rocca of the ODJB let fly with some of his hot licks. The illegitimate birth-rate rose dramatically. Mrs B. Dorbandt was (rightly) fined for allowing her three-year-old daughter to shimmy publicly. These women were the most strenuous jazz lovers of all. You'd think they were really into a revolution with jazz as their Red Flag. But actually they were cunningly making use of the style. Solo charlestoning – self-expression – swiftly became smoochy duetting in their hands. They fox-trotted their chosen male to the tune of 'All Alone' down the garden path and into the rose-covered cottage. Thus were boys with a genuine interest in the technicalities of music betrayed by their girl partners. 'God! look at that bunch of corny old rackety jazz records' she exclaimed, as she turned out the basement in the late thirties. Scarcely an hour and the trash can was crammed with McKinney's Cotton Pickers, the City Blues Blowers ... Poor jazz hadn't got a chance!

But to get back to the early twenties. Jazz was only a part of the Jazz Age. The phrase was coined by writer and 'flaming youth' F. Scott Fitzgerald, to describe that rebellion of Youth versus Age, which found its first self-conscious expression between 1919 and 1927. Of course, those of you who remember the chapter on ragtime will shake your heads because you'll know all this revolution in manners and morals happened back in that ragtime era: the ladies smoking in public, dancing with abandon; the hints of sex, the growing restlessness. Even petting parties and casual drinking have been dated back to that extraordinary 1910–16 period. But from 1919 the word 'revolution' became trendy what with the Bolsheviks and the fear of anarchists in America. New young articulates sprang up to tie all these changes together into an outlook or philosophy. 'The shooting war was over but the rebellion was just getting started' wrote Hoagy Carmichael in his autobiography. In the *Atlantic Monthly*, 1920, a youth put the gripe squarely: 'The older generation had certainly pretty well ruined this world before passing it on to us.' Scott Fitzgerald felt the trouble was that they *hadn't* passed it on, but it was only a few years 'before the older people would step aside and let the world be run by those who *saw things as they were*'. That was the core of the new philosophy: to tell the truth, to be unhypocritical, to live life more fully – then anything was possible in the rosy jazz dawn! His book *This Side of Paradise*, with its revelations of petting and drinking among the young, shocked parents but thrilled kids. *Paradise* became the *Playpower* of its time. Other books told similar bald facts. *The Plastic Age*, a novel set in a college, had 'jazz' closely connected with 'sex'. Quickly the entertainment industry recognized the new liberated girl and boy. In the comics appeared Harold Teen, Flapper Fanny, and Syncopating Sue. In the serious papers the word 'teen-age' was coined, at least by 1924. Flaming Mamie, Betty Co-Ed and the rest were celebrated by press, motion picture and popular song.

The revolution, so dashingly expressed by Scott Fitzgerald, never touched on politics or world issues. It was about self and self's relation to 'good times'. He saw the 'fulfilled future' and 'wistful past' mingled in one 'glorious moment'. And that moment was to be enjoyed right now. So he and his wife Zelda set out to live that moment at a succession of parties and junkets. Her slogan was 'Let's DO something!', her ambition was 'to be very young always and very irresponsible'. *His* ambition, or at least his idea of heaven, was to throw a 'stupendous house party that went on for days and days with . . . a medical staff in attendance and the biggest jazz orchestras in the city'.* Like many other jazzing couples the Fitzgeralds were casual to the point of rudeness in their social manners. They arrived three hours late for dinner parties, sometimes crawling in on all fours, they tried to undress in the theatre, they jumped into public fountains. Thousands of others were being careless and casual and blasé, too.

To make for tension, the puritan crusade – noted in our ragtime chapter – was marching ahead. Dance halls were licensed, red light districts closed down and Prohibition became the law of the

*See note on Dance Marathons on p. 92.

88

land (actually by general consent) on 16 January 1920. Far from wanting stupendous house parties or irresponsibility, the majority ambition was business progress in a country of well-trimmed domesticity. President Harding announced America's need as 'not revolution but restoration, not surgery but serenity'. His successor President Coolidge bluntly stated that 'the business of America is business'. The advancement of businessmen as heroes had begun even in 1916 when the chief of Coca-Cola had been elected mayor of Atlanta. In 1925 ad-man Bruce Barton wrote a best-seller naming Jesus Christ as the founder of modern business.

Thus the jazz life clashed with the business life and its Calvinist morals. The *Ladies Home Journal* asked 'Does Jazz Put the Sin in Syncopation?' and demanded 'Unspeakable Jazz Must Go!' The fall of 1,000 girls in Chicago between the years of 1920 and 1922 was traced to jazz. The stories poured out of the presses – Mrs Fred Tracey was awakened from an eighty-day trance by a jazz record played near her bed; students learned to type to jazz by tapping out in time the pattern RXPG-STOP-RXPQ-STOP (this is rather hard to type to a beat but maybe I have the wrong record). These stories were on the side of jazz, but after a few years the novelty and the controversy palled. By 1930 most of the flaming youths had settled for wives and the quiet life, taking clubs instead of cars on to the golf course, eating rolls at dinner instead of hurling them about. The *New York Times* announced 'Jazz is Dead'. As early as 1930 Hollywood was looking back nostalgically on the antics of the roaring twenties as in *Reaching for the Moon* which had Bebe Daniels swaying her hips and rolling her eyes as she did her stuff with 'There's no low-down lower than that.' Aiding and abetting her was Bing Crosby, poised between his wild youth as Joe College and his placid crooner years as Joe Average.

When Don Alfonso Zelaya, son of the former president of Nicaragua, and student of 'musical vibrations' issued a statement on 1 April 1926 that if 'jazz was not curbed it would turn American children into a bunch of jumping jackals' he was referring to the Fitzgeralds, the Flaming Mamies and their friends. But another kind of jazz was holding forever the minds of young people for

89

deeper reasons. The Reverend Stelzle came fairly close to some of these reasons:

> Jazz is an attempt at individual expression, protest against machine methods, against the monotony of life. It is *their* dance and they find freedom, liberty and release in it. Each generation must settle its own problems. I will not accept the verdict of the past.

For *dance* read *music* and you are nearer. The trouble with most of the jazz attackers, according to this breed of jazz-boys, was that they simply hadn't heard *real* jazz. The real McCoy was mostly played by black bands, they said. Chicago was beginning to fill up with New Orleans black bands and looking for the real thing was an adventure because you had to sneak into coloured dives and cafes and dance halls. To be a true jazzer was something like being an early Christian, living in the catacombs. You were really outside society. It was on top, overhead, overground. White kids in short pants watched King Oliver and his band and shivered to the shouts from Louis Armstrong's trumpet. Many became hooked on this jazz – and they came from all classes. There was Bix Beiderbecke, middle class and Lake Forest Academy educated. He had followed Nick La Rocca around for ages, but he idolized him solely for his playing. There was Hoagy Carmichael from Indiana University who had fallen off his chair and under the table when he first heard Armstrong on record. There were Jewish slum kids like Mezz Mezzrow who longed to be black. And there were others like Benny Goodman, Glenn Miller, Jimmy Dorsey, and Tommy Dorsey, whose minds had been seared by the ODJB, King Oliver, all the hard jazz bands so that their musical language was based on sounds which to the older generation were mere noise. These jazz-based musicians entered the dance-band business but had to bide their time until after the Depression. Then a new generation were ready for their stream-lined chug-chug Dixieland which was to be known as 'swing'.

Armstrong himself saw his music as just an enjoyable way of making a living. He loved playing so long as he made the folks happy: '. . . doing my day's work, pleasing the public and enjoying my horn'. He was to become a show business star as accomplished as Al Jolson, whom he greatly admired. But to Beiderbecke and co. this real jazz was an end in itself, deadly deadly serious. The music was everything. Nothing else mattered: girls, food, politics, clothes. Beiderbecke slept in his clothes in a shabby room littered with baked bean and sardine tins. He and his close circle giggled in ecstasy at Armstrong's record of 'Heeby Jeebies', after a few puffs at some 'muggles' (pot). Another pleasure was watching ants crawl slowly over bed blankets. At the end of his short and tragic life Beiderbecke used to like visiting the city morgue, and watching flying movies like *Wings* and *Hell's Angels* over and over and over again. When he died they said jazz was dead.

The serious approach to jazz was taken by another group quite different to these hot jazz boys. This group approached jazz not as rebel, outlaw music but as a new art form which might become concert music, might even become what ragtime had failed to become – AMERICA'S MUSIC.

Experiments with this 'folk music of the machine age' had begun in 1919 when bandleader Vincent Lopez presented an 'evening of jazz music'. Several more experiments introducing 'gutter music' into the concert hall were attempted with varying degrees of success. Even Al Jolson gave a recital of mammy songs in white-face at Boston's Symphony Hall.

But it was bandleader Paul Whiteman (once viola player with the Minetti String Quartet) who threw the most lavish and successful of the jazz concerts. The hefty, avuncular Whiteman, known endearingly as the 'jazz jelly', was familiar with jazz licks and classical tricks. His 1925 Aeolian Hall, New York, concert of symphonic jazz marked the high point in this search for the true American Music. Here the slut jazz-woman was made into a lady. She was Eliza Doolittle and Whiteman was Professor Higgins.

The orchestra, currently appearing at the Palais Royal, played the 'Experiment in Modern Music' in the afternoon. 'Midnight music in mid-afternoon' was the thrilled murmur from the audience, who were made up from the 'soup to nuts high collar' trade, with a sprinkling of those intellectuals still hopeful that America could produce some art and wasn't all philistine 'boobs'. They

91

included Gilbert Seldes, discoverer of lively arts such as movies and jazz, and Carl Van Vechten, champion of Bessie Smith's blues.

Whiteman explained that his object was to show that 'tremendous strides have been made in popular music from the early discordant jazz to the melodious music of today'. He hoped that 'eventually our music will become a stepping stone which will be helpful in giving the coming generations a much deeper appreciation of better music'. The concert was, then, educational. Unfortunately the example of the 'discordant jazz', a version of the 'Livery Stable Blues', was hugely enjoyed by the audience. Very 'Rabelaisian'. The programme included some pieces by operetta composer Victor Herbert and ended with 'Pomp and Circumstance'. The flares, slides, sinuous harmonies and rattling drum beats made by the grey-spatted twenty-two-piece orchestra, made classicist Ernest Bloch beat his hands with delight, and Gilbert Seldes tap his briar pipe against the knee of his trousers.

The high spot, the 'pièce de résistance', was George Gershwin's 'Rhapsody In Blue', especially written for the occasion. The composer himself played the piano. It was thrilling, warm music. Some marvellous tunes linked by classical devices. But was it jazz, or modern music? Was it a rhapsody and was it blue? It *was* excellent pop and the sheet music sold a million copies.

And what happened to symphonic jazz? Later Whiteman tried more experiments. A piece called 'Monotony' conducted by a towering metronome. A Mr Delamaster wrote variations around the old favourite 'Honeysuckle and the Bee' and had the thing performed by the Chicago Symphony Orchestra. Touring around, too, was a strange dance/concert band going under the title of 'Yerke's Syncopated Symphonists'.

Well, concert jazz fizzled out long before the end of the twenties but the issue of American Music was to be raised and raised again.

Note on Marathons

Fitzgerald's idea of heaven was realized in the *dance marathon*, an extraordinary rogue sport/spectacle which, during its short history from 1923 to 1933 (when it was outlawed) became a profitable, but very low, branch of show business.

Here, briefly, is the story: in 1923 the first modern marathon was held at the Roseland Ballroom, New York (the ragtime era had had its marathons but they were puny beside this one). As the non-stop fox-trotting reached day three, disapproving church and mayor called for the police. But Mr Brecker, Roseland's boss, had been tipped off about an impending raid and quickly put an escape plan into operation. The eighteen remaining contestants were hustled into a removal-van and raced to the coast. There they were transferred to a 60 ft boat, which at once put out to sea. All through this operation the dancers had kept up their jiggling. Out on the Atlantic waves, aboard the floating dance hall, they jiggled on to the music of a portable phonograph. A winner might have been acclaimed had not the hall been boarded by the pursuing police who had commandeered a high-speed motor launch.

Dance marathons in the twenties were but a part of general endurance sports (e.g., flag-pole sitting, walkathons, hanga-thons, kissathons) but during the Depression they emerged as the most popular and most profitable. Indeed they rivalled even the mighty movies. Millions visited their local dance halls to partici-pate as artist or audience in this live and cheap form of entertain-ment, which promised thrills in colour to the sound of dance music. There were births, deaths and marriages at dance mara-thons. The contest could last days, weeks, even months. Heroes were born and stars appeared, but none made it into the over-ground world of entertainment. And most of the marathon pros had already failed in vaudeville or on Broadway. One girl had been, for a brief moment, a star of the Great White Way; another was Hoot Gibson's sister.

Radio stations relayed the action via hook-ups to the mike, wielded by a friendly M.C. 'Folks, who's the next to go? If you're in the market for laughs be here Friday when the kids are going to sleep before your eyes on the very floor!' Kids! – they always called them kids although many were minus top hair and/or waist. Contestants for the few hundred dollars prize money could win audience approval (and thus boost their morale) by a display of their talents: crooning out a tune, telling jokes, doing a dance routine. But the dancing itself provided the most human excitement – 'A more sorrowful sight you wouldn't want to see, folks! A more dramatic picture could not be unfolded in your local motion picture theatre!!' said the M.C. because right there on the floor Fay and Larry, who'd lasted fourteen days and fourteen nights, were doing what the fans called 'squirrelling'. *She* was clawing his T shirt and *he* was smiling at green fields and jabbering to himself. 'Wyeth's Surgical Powders – for Sore or Blistered Feet' was spelled out on their shirts. Wyeth's would not be pleased, would probably drop them.

This sort of drama was for the night-time. Mornings were slow, but business picked up in the afternoons when mothers (often with children) arrived, many armed with inflatable cushions and picnic spreads. Personable M.C.s attracted scores of female fans. In the New Jersey area M.C. Ted Brown, an elegant dresser with a honey voice, was known as the 'Marathon Fashion Plate'. He answered the question 'Why marathons?' this way: 'Because the little human things in life properly exaggerated lend comedy appeal to the nature of the harassed man and woman of average temperament.'

Though the M.C. enjoyed glamour he also had to watch the dancers carefully to make sure rules weren't broken. They were many and they were strict: no smoking, no spitting, no slacks, no shorts, no sleeping on the dance floor. But teeth extraction was performed during contests by trained medical men. Two minutes in every hour for hygiene calls. Ten minutes each hour for rest. Compulsory showers every twelve hours. Eight hot meals a day. The first 200 hours were the worst, said the veterans. After that you just hung on till the final 'grind'. That was pure hell. The band speeded up the music and you had to keep up too. Sometimes couples had their legs taped together for a 'Walkathon Grind'. But the worst was when they harnessed two couples together – one couple facing the other – and then, at the sound of music, made this bloc move in all directions.

The dance marathon business flourished. Hundreds of pros toured the country. Radio, dance musicians, merchants, public –

all liked marathons. A weekly, the *Marathon News*, was published; *Billboard*, the show-business paper, devoted a section to news from the endurance field.

A marathon held in Santa Monica turned out to be the most successful and spectacular because denizens of the near-by Hollywood film colony decided to patronize the show. During its seven-week run visits were made by such stars as Mary Pickford, Ramon Novarro, Ginger Rogers, Charlie Chaplin. A few, including Eddie Cantor and the Marx Brothers, performed short acts. 3,500 dollars was contributed by the stars to the prize money. Casting directors hovered about from time to time but no talent was discovered. One of the winners was an Illinois lad who'd pinned his hopes on discovery. Earlier he had made an ill-fated but imaginative attempt to crash into the movies by having himself mailed from Chicago in a wooden crate with a label addressed to a major Hollywood studio and the description 'Statue'. His plan was to leap out on arrival and demand a contract. Near San Francisco, however, his thirst was so great that he cried and banged his box until rescuers came and rescued him.

Although the stars enjoyed marathons their employers, studio bosses and distributors, disliked this business intensely. It was keeping people away from movie theatres. It was rivalling the 'real-life' depicted in the movies. Warner Brothers' sales manager stated that movies 'keep the world in love with love, even during periods of financial depression, when the stress and strain of life operates to deter men from marrying. *It is a fact that civilized man cannot live without motion pictures.*' The movie empire was the most powerful force in the entertainment world. Pressure was applied to the government to outlaw dance marathons. Reasons were not hard to find: crooked promoters had got the business a bad name; doctors warned that the 'toxic poisons of exhaustion will mount up and make them (the marathoners) old wrecks in a hurry'; in 1932 a twenty-six-year-old youth dropped dead in a New Jersey hall after 48 days and nights of dancing.

In 1933 a law made marathon dancing and endurance sports illegal.

Records

From jazz, the folk music of the machine age, we pass to the machine music of the urban folk age. Talking machines, talking pictures, records, radio sets, microphones, were all utterly dependent on pop music. Those deadly bits of tin and nuts and bolts and ohms and volts and slithers of invisible electricity, all of them owing their success to shaggy lumps of human kind like Fred ('Chicago') Fisher who threw his typewriter out of his skyscraper for a laugh. Or Joe ('They're Wearing 'Em Higher in Hawaii') Goodwin who had to be tight before he could write lyrics. Or Al Jolson who was so moved after recording 'Dirty Hands Dirty Face' that he broke down. Those boss machines couldn't operate without the fallible song people! But those machines slowly and surely destroyed vaudeville's flesh and blood shows.

The friendly Frankensteins soon sat, homely as a Toby Jug, in a parlour corner. A radio set made to look like a globe; a phonograph masquerading as an antique cabinet. It was easy to make them work, but how they worked was another question, mysterious wizardry. When I was very young I believed a band of dwarfs played the music behind the fabric of the gramophone speaker, and that radio air-waves darted between buses, hopped over houses to reach my set. Lenin, too, discovered the mystique of electrification when he got a shock whilst attempting to change a light bulb.

The magic-gadgets *moulded* pop music as well. They were both servant and master. Here are a few of the changes they brought about:

(1) Rise of the star, who was known by all the world but who knew precious few of the world.

(2) Therefore an increase in distance between performer and audience.

(3) And much more reliance on professionals.

(4) Resulting in a temporary banishment of home-made music.

(5) Rise of the bland universal well-made song.

(6) Fall of sheet music and piano empire.

The jazz craze of 1919–24 coincided with the fattest years of the record. 110 million records produced in 1922 and most of that jazz or dance or both. Any band worth a fig had to be under contract. Victor had Paul Whiteman; Columbia, Ted Lewis; Okeh, Vincent Lopez.

We've seen some of the reasons why jazz caught on. But another important one was that jazz bands – loud, brassy, blarey – recorded well. Without records jazz would have spread more slowly through dance hall, concert hall and catacomb. Tin Pan Alley transcribers found it impossible to write down on paper. How do you put down dee diddle de dee dee doh doh dah daaah dah dah performed on a triple-dented trumpet in syncopated 6/5 time with glissandi all over the place? I can't even write it.

Recording horns trapped some of the ODJB's glorious moments and turned millions on to jazz all over the world. Out of the 'Viccy' came that passing, glorious moment. You could listen to it in the secrecy of your room. You didn't have to venture down to coloured town, or gangster-ville. Nick La Rocca talked straight to Bix Beiderbecke. The scientific toy spouted the chatter of jazz with its farts, cries, and yah yah yahs.

Truly, these were the talking machine years! Proudly, the *Talking Machine News*, in 1922, wrote, 'in the last two years the vaudeville stage has lost much of its importance as a medium for song popularization'.

But the machinery of the *industry of human happiness* hadn't been intended by its inventors for amusement. When Edison and others* devised the phonograph, around 1877, they hoped it

*Edison's recordings were made on wax cylinders. It was Emile Berliner who invented the flat disc, in 1887.

97

might be of service as business tool, dictating machine or telephone aid, or maybe a toy. But in 1894 records were produced for the entertainment market, so the pleasure principle had won again, and the talking machine became magician rather than clerk. Still, the record companies, Columbia and Victor, who bossed the market from the early 1900s, half hoped that their classical records would take their place in cultured homes alongside the Shakespeare set. Edison himself, who built the first machine, quickly progressed from his very first recording of 'Hulloo!' to the heights of Beethoven and Haydn (cut on location at New York's Metropolitan Opera House). But that the real gold lay in pop songs was proved by the enormous sales of the works of ex-slave George Washington Johnson. He had but four songs – 'The Laughing Song', 'The Laughing Coon', 'The Whistling Coon' and the 'Whistling Girl'. This 'Original Haw Haw Man' sold all over the world, doing especially brisk business in China and Central Africa. A certain Major Cyril Fosset reported from a jungle outpost to his superiors in 1902: 'The new box of laugh records arrived today and performance eased what might have been a tricky situation with the natives. They seem to prefer these to the Reverend's piano recitals of Gilbert and Sullivan.' Hee-haw and chortles were universal, like jazz.

This type of music recorded excellently. The tin horn turned out to be rather butch, with a special fondness for xylophones, banjos, all brass instruments and shouters. Bull-voiced matrons May Irwin and Sophie Tucker, together with piercing-voiced males, Henry Burr and Billy Murray found lots of work with the record companies. Burr started doing hymns in 1904 and by 1927 had passed on to dance-band vocals; Murray, known both as the 'Denver Nightingale' and the 'Camden Budgerigar', began his recording career in 1903 and was still on the job in the 1940s.

By 1910 it was quite clear to the record companies that the classics only brought in prestige and that the steady income was to be made from sales to the 'Cracker-Barrel Trade',* to the 'Good Old Coon Song – Sousa – Monologue – Sentimental Ballad –

*Farmers.

98

Bunch'* and to the nickelodeon arcades.† Four years later, in 1914, BOOM! – dancemania in full madness. The regular old record buyers were joined by dance-crazy millions. Here were the biggest business boosters of all. Tangos, hesitation waltzes, two-steps, and animal dances moved across the sales counters swiftly. Demand exceeded supply after only a few months of 1914. St Louis cried out for more. Chicago too. New York would have to ship and right quick. Anything danceable – even Redskin tom-tom records were proving popular! 'Talker' men answered the call. *Spokane, Washington*: a Columbia talker talks a Methodist minister, well known blue-nose, into leaving his store with six tangos under his arm. *Chicago*: Victor salesmen circulate at dance demo asking viewers 'Are you a dancer? Have a Victrola? Have you dance records?' *Memphis, Tennessee* (blues and hillbilly centre): a couple do the two-step dressed in full evening dress, aided by wigs and masks, right in the store window.

Piano sales slumped. Vaudeville theatre managers posted signs backstage warning 'Recording harms your throat'. Live musicians felt threatened by the talker boys who were advertising that the 'Grafonola' or 'Victrola' takes the place of the orchestra. What a parlour party you could have with this ready-made home orchestra! A tantalizing suggestion was made: 'With a talking machine, a bunch of records and a select party of trusted dancers ALL THINGS ARE POSSIBLE'. At some of these 1914 tango parties guests were dressed only in *lingerie*.

Just twenty years old and this new industry had made the talking machine part of the furniture in nearly every home, and every class. 'They are the poor man's piano-player and the rich man's variation on the player-piano,' said the *Talking Machine News*. Conventions were held at Atlantic City where the talker boys raptured about peachy great roadside billboards advertising their machines, about the civilizing effect of their work in the Philippines, about world markets ('Ireland is a fertile field for sentimental and other reasons.'). The talkers and their wives ended the

*Tin Pan Alley pop customers.
†The nickelodeon was a fore-runner of the juke box.

celebrations with a vaudeville show, during which they sang some of their trade songs:

> Be a booster friend of mine
> – It cannot do you harm
> 'Twill give you prestige every time
> To tell where you are from.
> Don't be ashamed of what you do!
> Get in line! Speak out and show
> That you're a *talker* thru and thru
> Get pep! Get out! and GO!!

After the war martial discs were sold off as mementos of the 'dark days of history' and jazz continued the dance boom. Threatened pop people found that a partnership was possible: dance bands thrived on records, records thrived on dance bands; Alley publishers enjoyed a 2 per cent royalty off their recorded songs; even the Starr piano company got into the act with their 'Gennett Records'. Vaudeville theatres filled their houses by advertising record stars ('See Jack and Irving Kaufman, the phonograph stars you have so often heard and may now see.'). The singers made their entrance through giant prop. phonograph horns.

But the easy days were over for the record industry. Radio burst out as a new pop medium in the mid twenties, hitting record sales mightily because it was free and the sound was smooth not tinny. Quickly the principle of radio was applied to recording and in 1925 electrical recording became practical. Inner harmonies and bass could now be heard, stentorian-voiced singers weren't necessary any more, and now it was possible for friendly song delineators like Gene Austin and Whispering Jack Smith to be captured. However, radio ruled and made the hits. Radio even consumed records – the Victor company was taken over by the Radio Corporation of America in 1929. Then the Depression really ruined the market with record sales slipping to 600,000 in 1932 (compared with the 110 million of 1922). RCA considered the record business to be dead, but a couple of years later they issued an afterthought. This was a turntable which could be attached to your radio set (should you be bored by their programmes).

By 1939 things were much, much better. There were even million sellers again. 1939 is the end of our period in this chapter and I picked that year partly because of this record revival. We're trembling on the brink before diving into disc jockeys, and all that.

This record revival was due, first of all, to the Depression lifting and a new generation of jumping, forgetful kids. But the industry had helped too. A new company, Decca records, (set up with the help of British money) had introduced the thirty-five cent record (they used to cost seventy-five cents) and lured Bing Crosby, the Dorsey brothers, the Mills brothers, Guy Lombardo, Arthur Tracey and other hot artists onto their label.

Secondly the nickelodeon re-appeared as a streamlined super salesman and entertainer with a jivey name – 'Juke Box'. A tubby temple of chrome, the juke (taking its name from southern black joints) spread right after Prohibition ended in 1933, until by 1939 there were 225,000 of these buxom beauties. They were strategically placed around the country in bar, tavern, joint and honky tonk. Dry spots liked them, too. Jukes created a pleasant mood for spending money in drugstores, department stores, excursion boats. Railroad stations found they spread relaxation, gave waiting passengers something to do.

The juke consumption for 1939 was 13 million records. At the same time jukes acted as audition boxes and thus stimulated record sales. 'The Music Goes Round and Round', 'Three Little Fishes', 'Beer Barrel Polka', 'A Tisket A Tasket' and the double-meaning fish/sex song 'Hold Tight' were some of the hits created by the juke box and her feeders. Jaunty little pieces, with hum-along words not to be bothered about. They say the juke made stars of Orrin Tucker (his band and vocalist, wee Bonnie Baker) and Glenn Miller.

Who were the feeders? Most apparent and glamorous were the youths who loved to spend a juke-box Saturday night loafing in the corner drugstore, spending time with the chick, sipping at a soda, while the other guy fed the machine. Bass boomed out, boogie beat pumped the tune along remorselessly like a moving staircase. The average juke-box operator (a new pop character, ears and eyes close to the ground in best Alley tradition) ran fifty machines which he maintained and stocked himself. He made the chrome dazzle and saw to it that the real hits were inside, no dogs. An old-time (1939 vintage) coin operator told me this:

You'd foot it from joint to joint making your rounds. A whole sort of drinking village there was in these bars and taverns. You know what they did was they *used* their music – they didn't sit make and say 'How clever! How very artistic! What a rhyme and what a chord!' Know what I mean? Porter was something you found on Grand Central station. Rodgers and Hart could have been lawyers for all they knew. They liked to dance to the juke, talk to her, maybe they screwed under her influence later. They tell me that Crosby was responsible for a lotta back seat conceptions. Anyway, my customers took their tunes in lots a ways: some guys set up as tin-pot bandleaders, sittin' by that box all night long – tendin' and feedin' coins. Pickin' the music. I noticed there were certain what I like to call *loot tunes* – you know: *bread bringers*. I'll give you an example: the Poles dug polkas, Swedes they liked folk dances. They tell me that in Texas those one! hup! two! hup! German, you know, marches sold like hot pizza. But I was puzzled by the sock sales in my Chicago territory of this hillbilly nasal corn. Some of my platters were ground smooth as pebbles. That stuff about home, mother and God sure got 'em! That stuff about leaving home and bumming around in honky tonks or riding the freight train, hearing the lonesome railroad whistle. I'm a big band man myself. And – weird as hell – many of the people who liked this corn weren't even country hicks as far as I knew.

Since the Great War the rural folk had been gradually migrating to the big cities. The Depression increased this black and white migration. California, especially, was filling with Oklahomans fleeing dust storms and drought. These born losers brought few belongings, but they did bring a desire to hear the old songs, simple, gutsy, shit-kicking. And those in the cities who mucked in with the rurals rather enjoyed this new music.

Even so, 'hillbilly nasal corn' wasn't on the surface of regular pop in 1940. Historian Bill Malone writes that hillbilly music was still 'a distinctly regional phenomenon'. For instance Jimmie Rodgers, America's Blue Yodeller (also known as 'The Singing Brakeman') sold over 20 million records between 1927 and 1933 and yet was not only virtually unknown in the North, but also in

Oklahoma and Kansas.* Bob Wills, hot fiddling leader of the fourteen-piece western swing band the Texas Playboys, was in great demand for dances in the south west, but meant little in Tennessee. What he did mean they didn't like and he certainly wouldn't have been allowed to perform on the hallowed hillbilly show 'Grand Ole Opry', because he used 'sock rhythms', amplified steel guitar and a drummer – to say nothing of his brass and his saxes.

But we are on the eve of the hillbilly breakthrough. Soon Wills's 'San Antonio Rose' was to be brought to the hit parade by Bing Crosby. No longer was hillbilly music solely plaintive mountain whines made by jew's harps, fiddles and squeeze boxes. Or ex-Elizabethan ballads of unrequited love sung impersonally in a high-pitched screech by bashful Bob. Hillbilly music was getting moving, getting electrified, swinging with stars and tours and radio shows. Jimmie Rodgers stirred Swiss yodelling with blue moans, with Hawaiian hints, with Alley songs, and served this gumbo up in a catchy croon, a little raunchier than Gene Austin's (his pal). He toured his solo twenty-minute act in southern vaudeville, and was so successful that he was able to own a fleet of cars and a big house called 'Blue Yodeller's Paradise'. Thirteen Blue Yodels and sentimental Dixie songs like 'Miss the Mississippi and You' (but it was the latter which were really popular). He wasn't a cowboy but he loved to put on cowboy clothes. So did Bob Wills, who loved the old fiddle breakdowns but also knew the 'St Louis Blues' and the latest swing numbers. Cannily he realized that radio exposure was the key to success so he bought his own air-time slot to play his music and plug 'Playboy Flour' and 'Playboy Bread'. He was a band-leader just like Benny Goodman, except that he gave his cousins jobs and acted as a sort of father to his sidesmen: 'If you have a bunch of good high-bred cattle feedin' in a pasture with a lot of good green grass and plenty of water, you can round 'em up quick. They'll go together and have a lot of life to 'em and that makes it easier for you to handle a whole bunch.' No high-falutin' smart-aleck ways for the country

*However, in the rest of the English-speaking world he was a million-seller.

stars. They kept it down to earth, clanged bow bells, blew train whistles on the air.

It wasn't long, of course, before pop men discovered that there was gold in them thar hills, and by that time the hillmen were less hilly and more in line with regular city slickers.

Really this hillbilly world with its radio shows, tours, stars, legends, etc., was no more than the overground pop world in miniature, hidden in the regions. From the record-sales angle it was no more than our old 'cracker barrel' trade continuing sublimely in the smart-cracker twenties and thirties. How dare it? Weren't we post-ragtime? Together with black music, it led a life of separate development between the World Wars. In the record catalogues this was made quite plain: there was a 'hillbilly' section and a 'race' (black music) section. All the rest was normal.

Actually there wasn't that much difference between hillbilly and race. For example, in the 1922 Paramount Race Series we find Madame Hurd Fairfax's 'They Needed a Songbird in Heaven so God Took Caruso Away', jostling with low-down blues. There was a lot of give and take, a lot of digging each other's music. Southern whites knew much more about black men than their Northern brothers (where they still enjoyed the 'high jinks on the old plantation' myth). Though the poor white 'good ole boy' was separated from the black man by colour he wasn't so much by experience and by music. Just a short slide and a poor white could become a near-nigger. Here is Ruth Sheldon in her 'Life of Bob Wills' telling a story from his childhood:

One afternoon his mother found him on his knees rolling two small rocks on the ground, snapping his fingers and moaning. When she demanded an explanation he said, 'I'm playing like the niggers do.'

'Do you want to be a nigger?' Emma asked him, after telling him that he was doing a wicked thing.

'No,' he said. Before she could speak again he asked, 'Will God forgive me if I ask him to?'

When she assured him that he would, Bob kneeled again on the ground, this time with his hands clasped together. In a few minutes he arose and said consolingly to his mother, 'It's all right now. God forgave me and I won't do it no more.'

Black and white lived extremes. Their world was a wail-vale of sorrow, with heaven as the only reward. *Or* it was just a place for whooping it up here and now. 'Niggers only sing about what they et and what they fucked' opined a redneck Dixie politician/singer jealously, because that's what he liked doing best, maybe some stick-whittling and fishing as well. Georgia Tom wrote the sexy 'It's Tight Like That' and then about-faced and wrote sacred songs. A hellish tug-of-war between body and soul. Get on board the hell-bound express you sinners! Blacks and whites lived lives of black and white and no grey in the South, it seemed. They had much in common, more than they'd admit and they were different from the Northerners and the rest of the world. Southern music was inextricably bound up in Southern life.

However, this is another country and we were dealing with the record business.

The terms 'hillbilly' and 'race' were supposedly supplied by Ralph Peer, talent scout for the Okeh record company in the early twenties. It was he who first opened up this subterranean market by recording black Mamie Smith singing 'Crazy Blues' in 1920. Okeh was amazed when this record sold at the rate of almost 8,000 copies a month for a year or so. Presumably newly migrated Northern blacks bought them, as well as those in the South with enough money (they were expensive, at almost a dollar), but plenty of collegiates also bought copies and enthused. Writer Carl Van Vechten had quite a decent Bessie Smith blues collection by 1925 and loved to turn friends on to them. He wrote an article for *Cavalcade*, a smart magazine, called 'The Black Blues' describing them as 'eloquent with rich idioms, metaphoric phrases, and striking word combinations' and always ending abruptly 'as if the singer suddenly had become too choked for further utterance'.

We ought to note that Mahalia Jackson, black girl and future gospel star, when growing up in the South was forced to sneak Bessie Smith records into her home, for her parents, like many socially hopeful blacks, were ashamed of the blues, which they considered to stink of the shame of Delta life.

A couple of years after 'Crazy Blues' and the opening of the race market, Ralph Peer opened up the hillbilly market by

105

recording a genuine backwoodsman called 'Fiddlin' John Carson' scraping with a zippy plangency on 'The Old Hen Cackled and the Rooster Crowed' and singing in a shrill voice which Peer found 'awful'. Nevertheless it sold briskly and Peer grew to love and respect this music, though Alley denizens considered it no more than hayseed comedy. One can't blame them; rubes were still vaudeville figures of fun and the real rustics actually called themselves 'hillbillies'. Musically this mountain music seemed out of metre, out of tune and prehistoric.

They couldn't complain about New York-based Vernon Dalhart (real name Marion Slaughter), an early hillbilly best-seller. Though he sang of such hokey events as the John T. Scopes Trial, and the death of Rudolph Valentino ('There's a New Star in Heaven Tonight'), he sang correctly and was backed by real crisp in-tune guitar picking. His authentic Texas background was spoiled, however, by Grand Opera experience and a 1914 appearance in *HMS Pinafore*.

In the early days hillbillies had to come to New York to get recorded; Victor executives were shaken by the sudden appearance in their offices of a Confederate soldier and a cowboy in full range kit, both demanding recording facilities pronto. Pretty soon the standard procedure was for talent scouts to venture down into the back of beyond (lugging heavy recording equipment) and cut the folk on the spot, in the field. The results were sold in specially erected tents, or converted store fronts. At the end of a busy day the weary salesman would spin a Caruso to get rid of customers.

Though neither race nor hillbilly have much to do with this chapter, it has struck me that they were both *old-fashioned* and *avant-garde*. Old fashioned because the race records with their simple sex – plumbers plugged holes, milkmen pulled titties, millers ground mamas – harkened back to the frank coon songs; and hillbillies loved to record old Alley tear-jerkers like 'Mother was a Lady' and 'The Letter Edged in Black', whilst even blues-man Furry Lewis liked to perform his version of 'Let Me Call You Sweetheart' (and this at a time when the general public laughed at these songs in parody, 'That Daring Young Man on the Flying Trapeze', and pastiche, 'No! No! A Thousand Times No!').

106

Avant-garde because boogie woogie and the hard riffing Kansas City bands presaged things to come. And both hillbilly and race were soaked in gospel, making an unveiled assault on the emotions, removing the cushions from passion. When country and western music and rhythm and blues broke through in the early fifties it was as if they had been hibernating during the long winter of the well-made pop.

Radio

Can you remember way back in earlier chapters I mentioned Ed Marks, the button salesman who became a song publisher and one of the founders of Tin Pan Alley back in the 1890s? In 1935, looking out on stormy weather from his memoirs, he wrote that, though times were rough, 'song is a tough intangible. Having survived prohibition, it may even weather radio, the most disastrous of all mechanical developments which have so altered our Tin Pan Alley.'

Radio, a blathering cretin in a decorous box, was gobbling up songs crazily, creating a hit in seven days and killing her off in sixty! Radio was no respecter of song, consuming her in bulk, making every man-made work sound machine-made. From the start radio had relied on song but was loath to pay her makers anything. 'All we're broadcasting is *electrical energy*,' claimed the radio boys. A Dill Bill and a Duffy Bill, lobbied by radio interests, attempted to break ASCAP (the song artists' very own society, which was trying desperately to see that its members got their royalties so that they could live the good life like every other God-fearing, hard-working American businessman). Several states passed laws against the battling society. The Supreme Court was involved. Bodyguards were employed. But ASCAP won through.

The Society was demanding and getting a percentage of radio revenue in return for granting a blanket licence for the performance of her members' music on the air. And her members constituted the very finest in American authors and composers: Victor Herbert, George M. Cohan, Irving Berlin, George Gershwin,

Jerome Kern, Rodgers and Hart, Harold Arlen, Arthur Schwartz, Cole Porter, etc. Standards were high and there was little room in the society for the songs of hillbillies and bluesmen. They must learn their craft, study hard to become musical literates. ASCAP's music was America's Music, beloved old favourites of gaslight days and bright new standards of Broadway – so why shouldn't she get four million three hundred thousand dollars from radio in 1939, to be divided between a mere 1,110 writers and 137 publishers? Anyway, Gene Buck, ASCAP president, disliked radio on principle – a frightening machine – and hoped that in time it would fade away and the piano would come back to reign supreme. ASCAP music was good music made by creative artists inspired by American scenes, depicting American emotions and contributing to the civilization of the western world. So was it a crime to make a buck or two?

On the other hand, the National Association of Broadcasters considered that these songsmiths should be only too glad to be 'honoured' by the 'glory' of having their wares 'advertised'. ASCAP was a wicked racket, a monopoly run by greedy men in a guild, they felt. Little local stations were particularly annoyed at having to pay for lush Broadway songs which mostly they didn't even use, because they filled up their air-time with ever popular hillbilly music. Radio men decided that they could do without ASCAP's music if they tapped another source of America's music: they would broadcast out-of-copyright songs – folk music, Stephen Foster, anything before 1884 – and invite upset writers who'd failed to enter the ASCAP club, plus hillbillies, bluesmen, housewives, part-time cleffers even, *the people themselves* – to write for a brand new society which the broadcasters would organize. Broadcast Music Incorporated became a company on 14 October 1939.

The National Association of Broadcasters (NAB) now waited to see what ASCAP would do. Would they come to terms and lower their rates? But would the great radio audience tolerate the loss of their beloved ASCAP music? Battle lines were drawn for THE GREAT POP WAR. How quickly had the broadcasters come to power!

Between the Wars

Less than twenty years and radio was undoubtedly the hit-maker, because 60 million people were supposedly listening to 40 million sets (as opposed to 12 million in 1930) for up to 4 hours at a stretch sometimes, and during the Depression years most of these people would rather give up their ice box and even blankets before parting with their radio set. It was the 'last link with humanity'.

Before the Air Castles beamed mellifluous dreams, radio was just another invention, useful as a telephone, or for air–sea rescue and other sensible things. Today its only actual use is when it tells you which streets are jammed, or who has just taken over the government. A friendly communicastor once agreed to act as alarm clock by shouting, 'Wake up Ian!' at dawn during his radio show, and enabled me to make my plane. That's sensible radio. *Folk radio*.

But the idea of radio as an irrelevancy was soon expressed, by David Sarnoff (later manager of the Radio Corporation of America) in a 1916 memo he wrote to his employers, the American Marconi Company. He had 'in mind a plan of development which would make radio a household utility. The idea is to bring music into the home by wireless. The receiver can be designed in the form of a simple *radio music box* . . .'

After the war Sarnoff's idea became a reality, and from the start music became staple fare probably because it filled time easily. At Lester Spangenburg's home some pianists and banjoists played over the waves, whilst at Lee De Forest's, plugger Mickie Addy accompanied singer Vaughn de Leath in a few songs. She sang soft for fear of bursting the pin in the meter and blowing transmitter tubes – this early 'crooning' drew her an appreciative letter: 'You have inaugurated *a new form of song*, which, no doubt, will become very popular.' That November of 1920, the first station with scheduled programmes, KDKA Pittsburgh, went on the air. Two years later there was a radio craze bringing the number of stations up from 9 to 600. People queued to buy sets. Air-waves were jammed. By 1929 the number of stations had been cut down to 300, but the number of sets had grown by 1,400 per cent!

In the pioneering days of the early twenties performers were

110

terrified of the microphone, that forbidding 'enunciator' clumsy and wire-laden, sometimes disguised with a lamp-shade or placed in a flower pot. But the song-pluggers faced the enunciator boldly. They sang freely at it. They danced around the staid totem fearlessly. Programmers were pleased to have this free entertainment; pluggers were pleased to have a free plug. One of them, Little Jack Little, became so adept at broadcasting that he soon became a star with a band and a revue. Very adept at talking the tune and fondling the mike stand.

A new brand of song, ultra-simple and bland, was pushed. Radiophonic boffins informed songwriters that a range of five notes around the middle of the piano was the most suitable for high quality broadcasting. 'So we simply adjusted ourselves to the cleffing of *ether* material,' an old Alleyman told me. 'Some moonlight here, a touch of roses there, and all painted the colour of a cheap hamburger. You know – beige!'

Not only songs were plugged on the air, of course. From 1922 merchants sponsored programmes; their manner was so smothering as to make everybody concerned part of the family. 'They all chew our gum around the station, from the lowest engineer to the master of ceremonies. Let's hope the folks at home are chewing away too,' said one sponsor. The Happiness Candy Company had its 'Happiness Boys', A & P had its 'A & P Gypsies' and Interwoven had its 'Interwoven Pair'. Sometimes it was hard to tell where the goods ended and the songs began.

Dance bands were in great demand and there was hardly any need for them to stray from their hotel or restaurant engagement. The engineers simply laid on a wire from radio station to engagement, creating what came to be called the 'remote hook-up': 'And now from high atop the luxurious Rainbow Roof we give you the glittering music of . . .' Vincent Lopez takes the cake for being first bandleader to broadcast regularly from a night-spot. One evening in 1921 it was announced over the air that Lopez was speaking and playing from the Pennsylvania Grill, and table reservations poured in. All concerned were very pleased with these dance band remotes; the radio audience got an audio taste of the better life.

Between the Wars

In 1930 statisticians made the staggering declaration that three quarters of the annual radio time was taken up by dance music! That same year J. B. Krannenhorn, a radio spokesman, made an after-dinner speech to the assembled Broadcasters of America in which he summed up the great strides taken by this new air venture. He ended in this way:

'So multitudinous and complicated have been our activities during these nine brief years of commercial broadcasting that our very own historians cannot fathom out how exactly it all began! But, gentlemen, we all of us know and feel the results. True, we have prospered but we have also given them the classics whilst almost simultaneously selling them socks or candy. Who could ask for more in this age of ours? Many of you have fashioned your stations into works of architectural delight—I'm thinking in particular of your red cottage tiles, your ferns and your grand pianos.

'I have in mind the words of David Sarnoff. He said something to the effect that there was an era at hand when the oldest and the newest civilizations will throb together at the same intellectual level and to the same artistic emotions. Well gentlemen, I think we are now in that exciting era!'

Nightly the wires were hooked up and then, from smart hotels deep in the metropolis the music of plenty sang out, filling the night air of the vast continent with a warm cloud which could rain on homes maybe thousands of miles and millions of dollars apart. It fell alike on swank penthouse apartments, on army barracks, on northern fishing boats, on southern mansions and even on tumbledown shacks and sharecropper shanties where families crouched together around the radio momentarily forgetting the starving baby, the spoiled harvest and the hoarse wind outside.

As the Depression closes in with its blanket of darkness so the castles of electric show business stand out bright and twinkly, like lordly havens in the dark Middle Ages, generating songs of solace and rhythms of rest which make for a peace that passes understanding . . .

Passing understanding, too (but full of oral cheerfulness and useful off-the-peg wit), were the tags of the bodyless voices – such steady voices, rich with the fruitiness of a chummy god. 'Howja

112

do! Howja do! Howja do! Hellooooo everybardy! Howja do –
you big ol' radio public! Yowsah! Yowsah Yowsah! Wanna buy
a duck? Heigh Ho, everybody!' The word for the sake of the
word; the song for the sake of the word and the sound.

The first great ace of the air, emerging from that swirl of
voices, was Rudy Vallée. Like other bandleaders he got his radio
hook-up wire and soon he and his 'Connecticut Yankees' playing
at the 'Heigh Ho' Club on East 53rd Street, New York, were
filling the night air. But Vallée was special, a well-educated tryer
with a 'miraculous belief in himself' (as a critic wrote), and certainly not just a stumbling-voiced bandleader, head of an organization. He announced his own numbers – something new – against
a background of soft music; played medleys of just choruses with
no verses – again something new – and each chorus stepped into
a higher key, building up excitement; he broadcast and broadcast
and broadcast whenever he could, wherever he could; he read his
fan mail carefully.

But more than this he brought a gracious sex appeal into pop
music, filling the space left by the death of Rudolph Valentino.
This was achieved through his voice alone – wavy, plaintive, it
seemed to begin somewhere in his head. Then it travelled down his
nose and out. A contemporary journalist hearing him and not
seeing him was quick to recognize this 'radiophonic' first native
genius of the new medium: 'By the divine accident or miracle that
makes art nearer religion than science, the voice that starts its
strange journey at the microphone hardly more than banal fills the
air at its destination with some sort of beauty.' This dripping voice
of lavender and old lace, without a trace of the concentrated pep
so beloved of jazz-age singers and without a trace of the large
larynxed concert style effected by earlier radio singers (such as
Joseph M. White, the silver-masked tenor soloist with the B. F.
Goodrich Silvertown Cord Orchestra), this voice, by 1930, was
a national institution. At midnight, card games stopped and the
women clasped their hands as their menfolk snorted. This first
crooner was not without his male supporters, though, for businessmen in his Maine home town, created a 'Rudy Vallée Square'. And
song-publishers rushed around getting out ancient songs which he

113

might sing on his shows. Out came funny old pieces that Alleymen could have sworn were dead and gone (like 'The Stein Song', a curious marching beer song from 1910). One of Vallée's biggest hits didn't even originate in the Alley, but came instead from the ivied walls of Yale, 'The Whiffenpoof Song'.

In the thirties this first air ace was overtaken by the first air queen – Kate Smith, 'Song Bird of the South', quickly spreading to become 'Radio's Statue of Liberty'. Both Vallée and Smith had a relaxed approach which concealed a high art; both read 'positive think' books (he had *How to Live* and she had *Look Younger and Live Longer*), and both became famous for their straight-faced, rather than their comic, talent although Smith began as a theatre comedienne, and Vallée ended as a film and theatre comedian.

Both were hit-makers, too. But if Vallée was the gentleman lover, Smith was the comfy mother. She was a down-to-earth, homey, football loving, All-American, and a good trencher-woman: she recommended to her fans a Southern dinner of fried chicken, baked squash, peppermint ice cream. Very modern – she didn't read literature and was 'suspicious of anything that required study', loved speedboats and people. Her voice seemed honest and this helped sell her sponsor's product. 'They really are mellow and full of contentment,' wrote in one of her lady fans who had been turned on to the cigars which the singer advertised.

When she sang in that warm log-fire voice about the moon coming over the mountain, radio fans were got at where they lived, underneath all the veneer and make-believe. When she sang that '20 million people are listening to me but I'm singing only to one' she was way off beam. It was estimated to be more like 60 million.

Radio stars like Vallée and Smith needed to have immense skill and tact in order to keep their millions of sweethearts and folks. The medium contributed to making this period the age of the professional, creating art within the strictures of an artistic straight-jacket.

For in the thirties radio was large in audience and small in power centres. Two giant networks – the National Broadcasting Corporation and the Columbia Broadcasting System – held 88 per cent of the total transmitting power, with a third network just nibbling. Shows were pre-packaged for mass consumption and overseen by sponsors, fearful of offending any of their customers in radioland. Sometimes bands and singers were ticked off over tempos or song content. The entertainers took on the aspect of air-travelling salesmen – Paul Whiteman for Kraft Cheese, Ted Weems for Johnson's Wax, Ben Bernie for Pabst Blue Ribbon.

The National Association of Broadcasters set up a code of ethics in 1929. Even General Butler, the former US marine, was rationed to three 'damns' and two 'hells' every ten minutes. Many songs were black-listed. 'How Could Red Riding Hood have been so Very Good and Still Keep the Wolf from the Door?' was on this list (reputed to be the first song banned from radio) and, later, Cole Porter's 'Love For Sale' was permitted only as an instrumental. Many of his theatre songs had to be cleaned up for network broadcasting. Blues of the ethnic variety and hot jazz were frowned upon and not much heard – yet it's doubtful whether the mass audience at that time would have cared for such music. Perhaps the censors were in tune with the majority.

During this heyday of the network air castle Alley publishers found it necessary to employ more pluggers than in the old vaudeville days. Subtler pluggers, too – skilled at 'romancing' a bandleader or singing star with nice meals and honeyed words so that the entertainer would be prevailed upon to put the plugger's song in his arrangement book and air it sometime, hopefully many times. This was very important because the networks were monitored by special survey outfits who published charts based solely on the number of times a song was performed 'live'. Dr Peatman, a Columbia professor, had the most influential Plug Survey and he was known in the trade as 'Allah'. Great 'drives' were organized by the publishers on their current No. 1 Plug and up to 25,000 dollars was spent on getting it high in these survey charts. To a certain extent, then, pop was being made from *inside* the industry and not *outside* – in the real world of real people. This is an important point because most pop styles (e.g., ragtime, jazz, rock 'n' roll) start at grass-roots far from the music industry.

However, the overall result of network radio – the gilded few entertaining the scattered many – was a contribution towards pulling the nation together as one ordinary man. Certainly more people were aware of symphony orchestras and the classics, of what was happening in Europe and Hollywood. There appeared to be fewer rubes and hayseeds. People were on the road to sophisticated modern living. Their stars were pretty regular. (Freaking was left to Frankenstein.) Magazines pictured them making salads in the kitchen of a modest home, or relaxing on the lawn. Even President Roosevelt descended from his White House to deliver 'fireside chats' on the radio.

Talkies

Twenty Million Sweethearts, a 1934 Hollywood musical, certainly was ambivalent towards radio. In the film Dick Powell ably impersonated a drippy radio crooner complete with fluttering eyes and voice. There was also a child-hater who turned out to be 'uncle' on a kiddies show, and a hillbilly band of gum-booted chaps singing 'The Last Round-Up' with Jewish accents. The picture, however, was box-office, and not alone either. Big broadcasts on film were popular – Vallée and Smith were filmed, together with all the other radio idols. Hollywood recognized radio all right, but hated it for stealing glory and audiences, though there were really quite enough people for both of them. Poor Singin' Sam, air favourite, was filmed with his face totally obliterated by a supper-plate microphone!

Song, though, the rivals had in common. The silent cinemas shook with music and song, as pianos and rag bands killed the projector noise; and whilst the film was being mended or the fire doused pluggers led the audience in rousing choruses, keeping them amused. When the flicker houses grew into sumptuous temples of art, pianos and combos were replaced by an orchestra (or a mighty Wurlitzer organ). Appropriate strains pointed up the photoplay, and in the interval recitals were given. Many patrons visited the cinema solely for the beautiful music – and the songs performed by roving pluggers. In the studios, too, music played by small mood ensembles provided actors with just the right inspiration for that certain emotion. John Gilbert used 'Moonlight and Roses' for romantic moments, whilst Ben Lyon called on 'My Buddy' for crying scenes.

117

Between the Wars

Some pictures came with 'theme songs' attached – played endlessly by the theatre orchestra and sometimes of benefit to both Hollywood and the Alley. (For example, 'Charmaine' was associated with the film *What Price Glory?*, and 'Diane' with *Seventh Heaven*. Song and film were hits.)

The Alley was also linked closely to Hollywood as many of the movie pioneers had served apprenticeships in and around her. Jack Warner remembered winning a prize singing 'Here Comes My Daddy Now' at a Brooklyn beer garden contest.

In spite of these song/movie connections, Hollywood failed to take part in the twenties radio craze by acquiring stations through which to plug songs from their films. Probably this was because, as always, the industry was in chaos financially (shares of Famous Players company turned over five times in one year). Only the Warner Brothers acquired a radio station – a second-hand affair on wheels.

Nothing was certain except change, but though talking pictures were possible the industry felt that audiences would never stand for constant jabbering. But Sam Warner gambled with a hunch that music was the answer – they could sell talkies if they 'quit the idea of a talking picture and brought about something the motion picture theatre of the present day really needs – music'. On 25 August 1926 their first Vitaphone short was publicly shown in New York, featuring the New York Philharmonic, some sopranos, a tenor and a world famous violinist. Perhaps popular taste would be improved by this new process. Teachers and students could now watch the finger positions of virtuosos and see how opera singers employed their lips and resonance chambers. Later Vitaphone shorts were more successful: items like *Four Boys and a Ukelele*, *Archie Gottler – His Songs are in Millions of Homes*. The short starring Al Jolson was very, very successful.

Continuing their gamble, Warners' persuaded Al Jolson to star in their *Jazz Singer*, a film with lip-sync. song sequences. Jolson added a stretch of ad-libbing during the filming of one of these songs. Late in 1927 the *Jazz Singer* was released and at once revolutionized the industry. Was the key to success Jolson, the songs, or the talking? At any rate talkies were established, because

118

theatre admissions doubled, and the all-singing picture was considered as important as the all-talking.

Silent stars suddenly burst into song: Mary Pickford, Conrad Nagel, Joan Crawford, Noah Beery had a go. The major studios turned out revues featuring their stars in song and dance, and all hoped to garner a hit song. In the *Hollywood Revue of 1929* (one of the seventy musicals produced that year) Ukulele Ike sang six successive choruses of 'Singin' in the Rain'. The scatter gun spray of songs resulted in hits, but there were hundreds more that fell by the wayside.

Hit hard, first by records then by radio, Tin Pan Alley was tottering. Hollywood now stepped in and took over many publishers. Warner had the cream. Their Music Publisher's Holding Corporation held the copyrights to most of the songs of Victor Herbert, Jerome Kern, Cole Porter, Noel Coward, George Gershwin, Sigmund Romberg, and Rodgers and Hart. As a result Warner Bros. controlled a majority of ASCAP's governing board. Together with the publishing companies of the other major studios Hollywood owned the bulk of America's – the world's – popular music. So that when radio defied ASCAP in 1939 it was really defying Hollywood.

Along with Hollywood's song purchases came the songwriters themselves – those, at any rate, who could make themselves useful all-round craftsmen in this slicker modern era: veteran Fred Fisher wounded by not being called to the West, told MGM's Irving Thalberg, 'When you hire Fred Fisher you are buying Beethoven, Brahms and Schubert.'

An exodus streamed to California, the new promised land. Many made the journey by train, jogging across the continent on an educational trip – passing through those musical town names that they'd written about, possibly nudging the borders of Dixie herself. Sometimes Indians were glimpsed, lonesome and horsed, at tank towns. Hollywood turned out to be a hicky tank town too. A one-horse dump, not the swell and elegant city-by-the-sea that moviegoers were certain it must be.

119

Between the Wars

Ready to welcome the trekkers and already firmly ensconced in movieland (providing sunny, tidy lilts like 'You were Meant for Me' and 'The Wedding of the Painted Doll') was the ex-realtor, ex-tailor and native West Coaster Nacio Herb Brown.

Because songwriters dreamed within the same kind of world as moviemakers, it was felt that they would fit in well. Better, at any rate, than the band of straight prose writers now filling the studios, often talking radical politics in the lunch rooms and thus biting the hand that fed them.

Most studios were at pains to provide comfortable working conditions for the tunesmiths. Steinways were bought by the gross, bungalows were erected, and sometimes spacious lawns, complete with fountains and a bench or two, were provided. 'It's O K, but where is the bum on the bench to make me feel really at home?' asked a songwriter. Quickly the studio complied with his request.

Nevertheless, on the whole they missed the camaraderie of lil' ol' New York with its lunchtime at Lindy's, where the gang all met. Gone was the village atmosphere. Over here on the coast it was all very sunny, the mists swirled, the landscape was lunar – this was the edge of the world – and on rainy mornings rocks tumbled from the hills as the writer drove through a pass en route for the studio. Maybe that was why Nacio Herb Brown wrote such *reveries*! Maybe that was why it seemed so natural to write and shoot about being up on top of a rainbow 'Sweeping the Clouds Away'. Sure, they wrote that kind of stuff in New York, but out here in tremorland they actually believed it!

Suddenly the first musical rush was over. Audiences were tired of all-singing, all-talking, all-dancing pictures. Songwriters – functionless – hung around playing golf, spelling games, practical jokes. Bee-killing was popular.

In 1933, Warner Brothers re-vitalized the musical with *42nd Street*, not just a bag of songs but a tightly-scripted comedy-drama about putting on a show. Musicals continued with the 'back-stage' theme alternating with the 'faraway place' theme for many years. Never-never land was tempered with glimpses of the

120

wheels behind the scenes, so that life was never too fantastic, and never taken too seriously.

The score of *42nd Street* and many other thirties musicals was written by Al Dubin and Harry Warren, two men from Tin Pan Alley who became song kings of Hollywood. Both had written 'heart' songs in the surer past, but in the movies they added the contemporary required edge. 'Shuffle off to Buffalo' typifies sophisticated Hollywood: a nicely coy boy and girl dance in pyjamas on their honeymoon train taking them to Buffalo. They're off and away with 'scanties' and 'panties' for nights of joy. This naughti-but niceness is given a cynical edge by the comments of two worldly dames in an upper berth who sing that 'matrimony is baloney – she'll be wanting alimony in a year or so' because 'when she knows as much as we know she'll be on her way to Reno while he still has dough'. Sweet and sour, romance and reality, all mixed up together.

Dubin and Warren slaved in their office as Busby Berkeley (the dance-director who dramatized their songs) waited on the set with a hundred girls. These girls knitted and sewed quietly but Berkeley's head bulged with ideas – one of these days he'd mix girls kaleidoscopically with Afghan hounds. When he got their songs he set to work – sometimes filming all night long – to glorify them. What the movies could do was to realize in celluloid all those Alley flights of fancy. If the girl spins a 'little world of dreams' in the song, then into that dream went the camera, into a world of feathers, of girls strumming harps made of girls, of girls as petals forming flowers that opened (*Fashion Follies of 1934* with William Powell and Bette Davis).

But frequently the song realizer Berkeley fashioned a playlet that had little to do with the song itself. No indication in the words of 'Lullaby of Broadway' that this was the tale of a party girl who rose at noon and died at night, plunging from the top of a sky-scraper. No indication in the words of 'Pettin' in the Park' that Dick Powell would be called on to attempt the opening of Ruby Keeler's metal corset with a can opener, handed to him by a dwarf baby. But there it all was, in full glory on the screen.

Glorification of the songwriters themselves was to come later when, in the forties, their lives were celebrated in a long series of 'and then I wrote' movie-biographies. For the moment they had to suffer indignities at premières. As they rolled up in their limousines kids would clamber around, peer in and then utter 'That's nobody.'

Actually, the musical works of the *pop somebodies* were educating movie millions during the thirties. Operettas and musical comedies hitherto confined to relatively small and classier audiences were filmed, released and some – particularly those featuring Jeanette McDonald and Nelson Eddy – were very successful. Musical comedy writers had less luck: Cole Porter's score was whittled down to one song ('Night and Day') in the film version of *The Gay Divorce*. Hollywood melody men provided the rest. Rodgers's and Hart's musical film for Al Jolson, *Hallelujah I'm a Bum*, was a box-office flop.

Rodgers and Hart hated Hollywood and longed to return to Broadway. Jerome Kern lived in the hills quite peacefully but guarded his grand piano with busts – one of Wagner and one of Liszt. Only in the films of Fred Astaire and Ginger Rogers did the theatre writers have their subtle works suitably show-cased. Here was not glorification but sophistication and Astaire was acknowledged by the writers as the best interpreter of their songs. Jerome Kern, Irving Berlin, Cole Porter, George Gershwin all wrote for these dancing comedies of manners.

Isaac Goldberg, writing about pop in 1930, prophesied improvement via the tuneful humorists of Broadway:

The musicals of the future will be written, not by ill-prepared tinkers but by the selfsame fellows who keep the capitals of the continent in tuneful humour. What Kern and Gershwin, Friml and Romberg, Youmans and Rodgers are to Broadway, they are becoming for Los Angeles ... When an institution becomes self-critical, when it begins to satirize itself, it is on the way to maturity. This has already happened to our popular songs, the tear-drainers of yesterday call forth only laughter to-day.

Perhaps it was laughter only because big girls and big boys don't cry. The tensions were terrific and the tug-of-war made for songs of matchless craft, which seem to crumble even as you hold the sheet in your hand. Here before me lies 'Thanks for the Memory', by the Hollywood team of Leo Robin and Ralph Rainger, featured in the Paramount Picture called *The Big Broadcast of 1938*. It seems to sum up the whole of the thirties that both attracts and repels ... A tune full of nostalgic meandering – winding down a lane – and words that remember the little things like rainy afternoons, Harlem tunes, motor trips, burning toast, and prunes. Not grand passions, sudden deaths, and blinding tears. These are words that suggest casual wealth: nights in Singapore and sunburns at the shore.

And yet, and yet ... behind the façade of casualness lurk the grand emotions. So clench the briar pipe tight in the mouth as you sing 'We said goodbye with a high-ball; then I got as high as a steeple. But we were intelligent people; *no tears no fuss, hurray for us*' ...

Songs
and Singers

Our 'Thanks for the Memory' couple had travelled 'far and wide together'. Thanks to records, talkies and expertise, American songs, like Universal Pictures' aeroplane trademark, circled the globe. Many settled down as *standards*, spreading the thrill of American life and rivalling local culture. For instance, take Germany and 'Yes, We Have No Bananas', monster hit of 1923. Dropping into the Germany of the Depression and pushing hard as 'Ja, Wir Haben Keine Bananen Heute', it infuriated Adolf Hitler and other patriots because they realized that this was anti-Aryan propaganda, devised by aliens.

After Hitler came to power in 1933 the threat was gradually removed. On the eve of World War Two native songs topped Germany's Hit Parade:

> The world belongs to the strong!
> The sun shines on them alone!
> We are on the march and nothing shall stop us!
> The old are trembling! The weak are faltering!
> But we, the young, march on to Victory.

America was, at that time, 'somewhere over the rainbow' (Harburg and Arlen) and 'didn't know what time it was' (Rodgers and Hart). These exquisite songs had, perhaps, encouraged Europeans to believe that America was highly romantic and highly spineless, concerned only with such trivialities as love affairs – the selfish isolation of 'you 'n' me'.

America *was* popular music all right, but not through musical innovations. Waltzes, novelties, girl songs – all were re-vamped to suit the times, but were at heart the same old song. Even the hot coon re-appeared in such jazzy numbers as 'Red Hot Henry

124

Brown' and 'Dapper Dan – The Sheik of Alabam'. The 1909 nonsense of 'Yip-I-Addy-I-Ay' turned into the pulse of the jazz age's 'Doodle Doo Doo', 'Hoddle-Dee-Dee-Dee-Doo-Doo', and of course the famous 'vo-do-de-o' piece, 'Crazy Words, Crazy Tune'. A little self-consciously Dada, or gaga, perhaps, but suitable accompaniment for the popular pastimes of flag-pole sitting and gold-fish swallowing – and hearkening back to the very dawn of music when dance tunes consisted of irrational be-bop-a-lulas – 'HA HA WO WO HE YA HA HA YA HEI HEI HEI'.

There's just time to extricate some topics from the massive turnover of songs used by band, radio, movie, record and ukelele at this time.

First, the *new girl* in first flush of liberation. In mid-passage. Between libs. In the ragtime chapter she'd become visible – smoking, dancing, ragging – but after the war (armed with her vote but minus her corset) she determined to join the males as a jolly, lively pal. 'The chairs in the parlor all miss you; the pictures all frown on the wall' because she'd moved to a kitchenette apartment and was asking 'Who wants a baby?', anxious to try out her education from the school of Theda Bara, screen vamp of 1914 (who sucked her 'fool' men of their life-force). And at the school of novelist Elinor Glyn, who had taught naive but blooming American girls about the art of love. And at the school of Florenz Ziegfeld, the showman, who had glorified girls of hidden ripeness into alluring creatures dressed in clinging satin, legs sheathed in silk.

Militant freed girls set examples. Dorothy Parker said 'I hate men'; Texas Guinan (night club organizer) labelled them 'suckers', 'big butter and egg men'; Mae West and Joan Crawford forged through them leaving a trail of exhausted males. Songs were quick to recognize the girl-*friend* or good pal, ideal for 'steady company' (as Lorenz Hart put it in the Rodgers and Hart song 'The Girl Friend'), a 'smiling all the while Tom-boy' (as Oscar Hammerstein described 'Sunny') – just 'five foot two eyes of blue', scampering about like Clara Bow, the bustless IT girl

125

or being awful cutie-pie like Helen Kane, the 'Boop-Boop-A-Doop' girl.

So boyish was she with her flat chest, choir-boy face and short hair *and* so girlish were the boys with patent-leather hair, trousers as wide as skirts and sissy-high voices, that a bunch of veteran Alleymen, remembering happy back-slappy days, were absolutely forced to write of 'Masculine Women and Feminine Men'. Today, said this song, one didn't know who is who or even what's what when brother just loves his permanent wave and Sister Susie, instead of sewing shirts for soldiers, was actually learning to shave.

The old coon shouter had turned from Negro life to 1920s jazz age life. Sophie Tucker and co., became *red hot mommas* whilst the older men were dissolved just thinking of their 'Mammy', but Al Jolson's rock of ages was his *mammy*, and though he loved that play-girl she spurned him as a 'Singing Fool'. Altogether, the men were on the retreat during the jazz age, fighting a losing battle against the monstrous regiment of new women! 'Hula Lou' was a girl who couldn't be screwed. 'Red Hot Momma' could part a bald-headed man's hair in the middle. And 'Hard-Hearted Hannah', was discovered on the sea-shore actually *pouring water on a drowning man*.

But though these new girls (jolly or tough or frenzied whirlers to the sax shriek and the trombone wail) might boast that they 'got more sweeties than a dog's got fleas', in the end they usually became the prisoners of love for one man. 'What wouldn't I do for that man?' even though he's 'Mean To Me'. He is, quite simply, 'The Man I Love' and 'I'm Feathering a Nest' into which he can settle in 1929, after the death of the jazz age, 'When I'm Housekeeping for You', doing little chores such as 'Cooking Breakfast for the One I Love'.

Flaming Mamie, you see, was a 'new kind of old-fashioned girl' and not that trendy party-loving 'Glad Rag Doll' who was 'Just a Girl That Men Forget', ending up as a discarded toy and 'The Lonesomest Girl in Town'.

Militant flappers found themselves eventually safe and sound from the storms of life in 'The Little White House in Honeymoon

Lane', where butterflies were flirting and behind a kitchen curtain she cooked and looked out of the window when shadows fell to hear her husband's whistle as he returned 'Home In Pasadena', to that cottage 'Halfway To Heaven'. Gene Austin sold millions of records by saying that it *was* Heaven: 'My Blue Heaven' where 'Molly and me and baby makes three'.

The flapper cycle and the domesticity cycle. From hubble-bubble to cosy nookeries. Yet all through this period, as our liberated girl travelled from parlour to kitchenette to final haven of cottage, the old girl remained steady, had excellent sales: smash hits included decent 'Charmaine', 'Diane', 'Ramona', 'Marie'.

These songs – at least those that were hits – were not merely the products of fertile imaginations in Tin Pan Alley; they were inner and outer reality made into luscious slices of words and music: popular song – more powerful than all your bombs. Of course they weren't potent lying there in sheet music or even played as dance music. Admittedly dancing was the absolute base of all pop music (and, indeed, *all* music) but running a close second was *singing*. Ragtime, jazz, swing, rock 'n' roll, whatever – all these forms appeared to come into pop as instrumental music (ragtime on the piano, jazz on the band, etc.) but quickly became singable (Sophie Tucker, Irving Berlin's songs, etc.). Serious rag and jazz lovers frowned on these singers. You can't sing classic ragtime, you can't sing jazz, they said. But, of course, the truth is that the singing, humming, talking, grunting, sneezing, crying, shouting comes first and the instrumental music is but an imitation of this human activity. *All pop is human activity.* Directly it becomes mere music it is quite pointless. *Pop music has little to do with music.* But that little can be lovely and is just enough to elevate revolting real life into delightful pop. Singers, then, telling their stories in song, were the essence of popular music. Conversationalists was what they were, I suppose, except that they put it better than most of us because they had cheek, songwriters and an accompanying band.

A remarkable group of 'torch' singers gave life to the songs which I was discussing. They appeared in cabarets, night clubs,

Broadway shows, but millions could share their sorrows and joys more intimately because of electric recording and radio. It was as if you were actually in bed with them and they were murmuring into your ear. You could hear even the flutter of their hearts. You could feel the tears. Well, anyway, you could certainly hear them take a breath. Radio experts boasted that the eavesdropping microphone could 'record the swish of a powder puff as it passes over the nose of some fair lady'.

Queen of the torch singers was Helen Morgan. She sat on a piano with her eyes drooped, clutching a handkerchief and singing in a voice that sounded as if she'd seen and had it all. Somebody said her voice was like a composite of 'all the ruined women of the world'. Hidden in the piano was a microphone. Her runner up was Ruth Etting, 'The Sweetheart of Columbia Records' and the 'happy singer of sad songs'. Her eyelids drooped, too. Even through the cigarette smoke and sin something of her country childhood spent in the wheatlands of Nebraska shone through. In slow-motion she put a graceful hand to her chest, a smile to her sad face and sang like an angelic dive-bomber.

Both Morgan and Etting considered themselves as story-tellers and their song stories echoed the toughness of their lives. Helen Morgan died penniless – although she'd starred in The Ziegfeld Follies, the smash Broadway musical *Showboat* and a superb early talkie musical *Applause* – in a tiny room in a Chicago hospital. Etting, another Ziegfeld star, was married to mobster 'Colonel' Snyder (better known as the 'Gimp'). He loved her in his violent way and shot her arranger in Hollywood out of jealousy. It was altogether a tough battle for the new girl. Many of Ziegfeld's discoveries were casualties in the man/woman battle: Jessica Reed went through five husbands, but died in a public ward; Olive Thomas was poisoned in Paris; Imogene 'Bubbles' Wilson, suffered beatings from her comedian lover, died at 42 alone in her Hollywood bungalow; Allyn King committed suicide; Helen Walsh was burned to death on a yacht.

Compared with the torch singers, and their Earth-Mother Sophie Tucker, the men singers appeared rather molly-coddled. In 1929 'crooning', as exemplified by Rudy Vallée and his dripping voice, was all the rage. But Jack Smith (the 'whispering' baritone), Gene Austin (the mellow high-voiced Texas tenor), Johnny Marvin (a ukelele man) and Nick Lucas (the guitarist radio troubadour) anticipated Vallée and set a trend for crooners who looked anguished yet made hardly a sound when they sang. 'Was it singing?' many asked. The record labels marked the crooners as baritones, tenors, etc., just as they'd marked Jolson as a comedian, not a singer. But compared with this murmuring, Jolson was Caruso and Sophie Tucker was Dame Nellie Melba.

Al Jolson, Irving Kaufman, Harry Richman, Eddie Cantor, sang in a hearty semi-concert hall style that could be heard at the back of the theatre. They rolled their *rrrr*s and contorted words in the accepted European operatic manner, but they had also been influenced by the American minstrel tradition. When Jolson sang a coon song he sang in an American coon accent and inserted bits of scatting like 'da dada'. This was in the tradition of Ben Harney, the ragtime pioneer, and Eddie Leonard the great minstrel. From his Jewish background he brought the rabbinical wail (the Hebrew blues) and from himself he brought an emotional power that burst out of the frame of popular song and singing. The words and the tune just weren't enough. He had to break off and recite, even *orate*. In 'My Mammy' he starts pleading in words that weren't in the sheet: 'Oh God! I hope I didn't make you wait. Mammy don't you know me? I'm your little baby!' And he further illustrated his songs by getting down on one knee, by beating his hands together, and by running out into the audience on his specially constructed runway. Gilbert Seldes described this little figure singing 'Row Row Row': 'he would bounce upon the runway, propel himself by imaginary oars over the heads of the audience, draw equally imaginary slivers from the seat of his trousers and infuse into the song something wild, roaring and insanely funny'.

But by the thirties his melodramatic belly singing was made redundant by the heady piping of these crooners, clutching for dear life to that microphone. Jolson said 'It's a sad day when Jolie needs a mike to sing into' and hurled the instrument to the studio floor at the end of his last radio show for Chevrolet in 1932. Not for

129

him this business of making a 'hot mush in the mouth'. And yet crooning, as done by Bing Crosby, wasn't such a break as it seemed. Crosby's first big influence was Al Jolson and he brought Jolie's whistling and talking and play-acting into his crooning, as well as his scoops and swoops. He also brought a more manly baritone (like Jolson's) into a world of high-pitched crooners. Vallée sounded drippy compared with Crosby.

Like most college boys of the jazz age (Crosby had been at Gonzaga University, Washington State) he'd been a nut for real hot jazz. He'd roomed with Bix Beiderbecke, played sock cymbal on stage with the rhythm boys and generally jazzed it up. He'd sowed wild oats, got into a spot of trouble with the police. But in the thirties he studied the techniques of the microphone and utilized electricity. And he sang all kinds of pop songs. He recorded 'Adeste Fideles'. Like all good pop singers he *was* as he sang. Women loved the soft caress of his voice and their men approved of his taste in sloppy sports clothes and his keen interest in sports. Like all good singers, too, he had an art but he kept it concealed, admitting that 'it's not difficult to imitate me, because most people who've ever sung in a kitchen quartet or in a showerbath sing like me'. But somewhere in private he'd practised and practised a new song until he had worked out the phrasing of the words so that the result seemed effortless and quite natural. But to return to song trends . . .

In the late twenties college life became a heavily worked subject, with campus frolics replacing Dixie capers. The raccoon-coated, hip-flask touting, siss-boom-bahing collegiate was the noisy hero of many a song, show and movie. This was no trend devised by Tin Pan Alley but a crazy-mirror reflection of a new goal and a new myth. Further education, scorned in the nineteenth century, had gradually become a 'social necessity'. In the twenties college pointed the way to the Better Life. Some college men were knowledgeable men, but the majority appeared to rank Latin and Greek below how to make the football team (Scott Fitzgerald's failure to do this at Princeton is said to have encouraged his drinking problem). There were other studies in how to mix a decent cocktail, and how to get into Sigma Chi fraternity. Much of Rudy Vallée's popularity was due to his obvious Ivy League background. The ideal was to wear the appearance of a gentleman of easy culture, aware of British authors like Aldous Huxley, yet amused by vaudeville, movies, comics, and the latest songs and dances. The thing was to *cry* at a slapstick comedy, and to *laugh* at heart-wrenching melodrama. To write a term paper in praise of the poetry of Ella Wheeler Wilcox.

Songs echoed college values. In 'The Varsity Drag' a professor cries out his first lesson which is to go down on the heels, up on the toes. After only a little instruction all undergraduates would be doing this newer than new drag dance. Meanwhile, out on the sports fields of America roamed the 'All-American Girl', cheerleading lustily, following every team, with 'Football' as her middle name.

'Doin' the Raccoon' showed that all the world could become collegiate by simply putting on a raccoon coat. No need to actually go to college. All that was necessary was the uniform and Joe Doe became Joe College, American hero. Campus was the Last Frontier.

Oilskin slickers were popular campus kit, too – but as well as looking outlandish they kept off the rain. Generally Americans, at this time, were trying to be less hayseed and more up-to-date. While sons were at college, wives were spending leisure time at 'educational clubs' discussing Greek sculpture, learning 'How We Reach the Sub-Conscious Mind'. Those poorer Americans, whose sons and wives weren't at college or club, wished that they were. Magazines showed how to lay a dinner table; movies pictured suave William Powell demonstrating the gentleman. Only in B picture westerns was the city-slicker type, with his patent-leather hair and tooth-brush moustache, *suspect*.

Pop underwent a literary period with such titles as 'A Farewell to Arms' (inspired by the Ernest Hemingway novel) and 'Strange Interlude' (inspired by the Eugene O'Neill play).

In this progressive setting some subtler song-jewels, written by a select group from the musical theatre, were able to break through via radio, record and movie, and take their places on the newly established Hit Parade (a radio top-ten show which began in 1935). Chief of these composers were *Jerome Kern*, father of American musical comedy song; *Richard Rodgers* and his lyricist *Lorenz Hart*, both Columbia University graduates; *George Gershwin*, apprentice of the Alley and subsequent concert-hall artiste; *Cole Porter*, playboy and member of the international set; and *Irving Berlin*, only real link with the old Alley. By sheer dogged talent he managed to join the ranks of these composing angels – the only member who wasn't musically schooled.

Together with other theatre writers – E. Y. Harburg, Harold Arlen, Vincent Youmans, Vernon Duke, Arthur Schwartz and Howard Dietz – these educated men fashioned words and music which was made to last, conceived in the conservatory of an America still slangy but getting better, getting civilized, getting modern, getting up-to-date, getting out of Victorian wallow, getting out of babbitry, getting out of crude jazz. These were *theatre* composers – mingling tastefully street with salon, traditional music with Alley vernacular and conjuring-trickery. *Carrying the whole thing off ever so lightly.*

Of course, their theatre was more theatre-theatre than vo-do-deo theatre. Between 1924 and 1925 there were forty-six musicals on Broadway, and most of them were simply variations on the gals and gags theme of burlesque and revue: George White's Scandals, Earl Carroll's Vanities and Ziegfeld's Follies. 'See New York and Ziegfeld girls AND DIE' ran the slogan. And though theatre composers might not care for such shows they contributed songs to them. At one time or another Ziegfeld's Follies had music by Gershwin, Berlin, Kern and even the operetta composers Rudolf Friml and Sigmund Romberg.

From about 1910 musical theatre had developed into several types. Apart from the glamour shows like 'The Follies', there was also *Revue* (fast, smart, topical and wittier than vaudeville); *Extravaganza* (fond of spectacles such as motor buses driven on to the stage); *Imported European Operetta* (the sort of show which had princes and princesses disguised as gypsies); *American/European Operetta* (the shows of Victor Herbert, Rudolph Friml and Sigmund Romberg); and George M. Cohan.

132

None of these types disappeared completely during the adulthood of American musical theatre. They were not progressive, nor very daring but they gave satisfaction. Romberg's *Desert Song* (1926) and Friml's *Rose Marie* (1924), packed with lusty, sledgehammer tunes, never became passé and are still very much in demand.

Whatever the form or content of the show – three-ring circus or translation from the French – audiences judged by whether the tunes were any good. The success of the show depended on the songs. In the twenties, with more musicals than ever on Broadway, the Alley rightly considered 'The Great White Way' of theatreland to be song hit headquarters of the world.

So that, providing that songs were catchy and lively, it mattered not that they had little connection with the plot. Two happy-go-lucky songsters dominated Broadway until the late teen years: George M. Cohan with his punchy, jingoistic shows and their hurdy-gurdy tunes, and Dublin-born Victor Herbert, the cellist with the German accent and sunny disposition who desired only to write shows that contained immensely popular songs. This he did frequently – 'Ah! Sweet Mystery of Life' is still reaping in large royalties.

Neither Cohan nor Herbert had any desire to innovate. Herbert simply enjoyed living fully. His contract stipulated that, during theatre work, his dressing room was to be furnished with an ice-box stocked with beer.

But Jerome Kern, who had been loosening up European operetta imports with his graceful tunes, wanted to make the American musical more integrated, and not just an assembly of catchy tunes. 'Songs must be suited to the action and the mood of the play,' he said. From 1915–17 Kern wrote the music for a series of situation comedies about American life – honeymoon couples and hotel clerks instead of royalty – which were presented at the small Princess Theatre in New York. Book and lyrics for these pioneering American musical comedies were by two Englishmen, Guy Bolton and P. G. Wodehouse (a descendant of the Earl of Kimberley). Critics and audiences liked the unpretentious little shows in which actors sang as they might 'in your own home after dinner', and there were no noble loves of earth-shattering dimensions, supported by a vast orchestra.

'Life should be a perfect expression of melody and harmony rendered into deeds' Victor Herbert had said happily. But Jerome Kern was bursting not only with lilting melodies in the tradition of Leslie Stuart ('Lily Of Laguna', 'Tell Me Pretty Maiden') and the Edwardian English operetta composers, but also with a burning desire: 'I am trying to do something for the future of American music, which today has no class whatsoever and is mere barbaric mouthing,' he told the *New York Times* in 1920.

His work seemed to tower above that of his contemporaries, inspiring embryonic artists who might otherwise have gone into the concert world or dabbled in fringe theatre. George Gershwin became his earnest disciple after hearing 'They Didn't Believe Me', a loose-limbed song Kern had contributed to a 1914 British operetta import; Richard Rodgers, as an adolescent, saw *Very Good Eddie*, the Kern–Bolton–Wodehouse musical, many times. 'If you were at all sensitive to music, Kern had to be your idol. You had to worship Kern,' he said in later years. At about the same time Cole Porter at Yale and Lorenz Hart at Columbia were applying their intellect to the micro-art of popular song, determined to improve it.

In 1927 Kern realized his vision in *Showboat*, based on the novel by Edna Ferber, and with a libretto by Oscar Hammerstein, Jnr. The setting was Old South, but not Dixie and mammy. This was an evocation of American heritage – Mississippi gamblers, darkies on the levee, and music in the style of the period ('After the Ball' was played at one point).

Meanwhile, George Gershwin, fired by what he called 'the artistic mission of popular music', had been pushing serious themes throughout the twenties. For George White's Scandals he had contributed a Negro opera *Blue Monday*, which contained flattened thirds. Then there had been 'Rhapsody In Blue', specially composed for Paul Whiteman's 'Experiment in Modern Music'. The production in 1935 of *Porgy and Bess*, his Negro folk opera, marked the climax of a restless search for artistic satisfaction. This wasn't darky stuff but the music of the real Negro,

134

observed in the field itself (Gershwin had spent months down amongst the Gullah Negroes of South Carolina – one night he took part in a ring-shout himself, whooping naturally). Field effects were transcribed into black dots, supported by sumptuous harmonies, and the result was excellent Gershwin.

During the Depression, whilst Hollywood brightened the night by painting the clouds with sunshine songs, the musical theatre tackled subjects of current concern: war was indicted by George and Ira Gershwin (aided by Morrie Ryskind) in *Strike Up the Band*. Even ex-Alleyman Irving Berlin dealt with police and political corruption in *Face the Music*.

The musical theatre had grown up since the jingle-jangle innocence of Victor Herbert and George M. Cohan.

Just as those talkie musicals circled the globe, so did these serious theatre musicals – settling in loftier places. *Porgy* became the first American work to play in the sacred halls of La Scala Opera House, Milan. When movie tunesmith Harry Warren visited Paris he was interviewed at his hotel by an enthusiastic French radio announcer clad in a long raincoat. But this reception could not match that of *Porgy*: the wife of its author, DuBose Heyward, described how 'whenever I saw (the play) in Paris I had a strong-arm man to pull me through this great crowd of people who just wouldn't go home. They thought somebody might drop dead and they would get a seat.'

British royalty attended the musicals, especially those starring Fred and Adele Astaire. Major 'Fruity' Metcalfe invited the couple to dine with the Prince of Wales (later Edward VIII). That was the start of a close friendship. The Prince received copies of the latest show tunes long before they were released in Britain; he irritated his father by murmuring Irving Berlin's 'A Pretty Girl is Like a Melody' in and around the Palace. No night out at a hotel, night club, expensive restaurant, or hunt ball, was complete without a dance to one of those show tunes.

In the good old days of the Alley, Harry Von Tilzer – maker of a thousand hits – could frequently be heard laying down the dictum that 'nothing is too simple for the popular song'. His million-seller 'Rufus Rastus Johnson Brown' had a range of but five notes. Why, even a baby could sing it! But in the advanced new days of the theatre men there were tunes that ranged hither and thither, rambling cunningly from key to key. Gershwin played piano so brilliantly that Ravel asked to hear him play – *as his birthday present*. 'Zong writing iss a question of zounds not zense,' opined Fred Fisher, but Lorenz Hart – a relative of the German poet Heine – loathed songwriters who had 'small intellectual equipment and less courage'. He wrote to fellow lyricist Ira Gershwin: 'It is a pleasure to live at a time when light amusement is at last losing its brutally cretin aspect, and such delicacies as your jingles prove that songs can be both popular and intelligent.'

Few theatre men wrote songs that weren't part of a score. Rodgers and Hart wrote but one: 'Blue Moon'. When Nick ('Love Letters in the Sand') Kenny asked Rodgers for a contribution to his *How to Write, Sing and Sell Popular Songs*, the composer explained that he wrote to capture a 'feeling' in a given 'situation', rather than capture the public taste, '. . . and if the individual song attains popularity its success becomes excess profit'.

Yet though musical theatre reached the high plateau of art, most shows were remembered for a hit song: 'Summertime' from *Porgy and Bess*, 'Ol' Man River' from *Showboat*. And it would seem that the lighter shows existed solely for their songs. Nobody cared much about the plot of *No No Nanette!* but its 'Tea for Two' became a pop perennial.

An Alley tunesmith, sitting at that cigarette-marked piano, figuring out what the next trend would be, forging another thirty-two bar job, shuffling around the standard middle bits (so standardized that the chord sequences were labelled 'sears roebuck', 'montgomery ward', 'woolworths', etc.), trying to think of new ways to say the old truths . . . An Alley tunesmith could only marvel at Jerome Kern, the Gershwins, Rodgers and Hart, Cole Porter, and fellow Alleyman, Irving Berlin.

Definitely they had *class*. Harms Music, which published most of them (including Noel Coward, wonder kid from Britain – home of civilization, where the tweed came from) had *class* and *style*. Max Dreyfus, an errand boy long ago, was the boss. He dressed well, disliked ribaldry, liked to hear Schumann after dinner and lunched his writers at the Astor. His editor was Albert Sirmay, a genuine doctor of music from Hungary.

But much more than class, style, art and world-wide acclaim . . . *these song jewellers could really write songs.*

An Alleyman had to bow his head in silent worship at, say, Kern's 'Smoke Gets in Your Eyes'. He has this rising and falling lovely lyrical melody, but halfway through – when we get to the sears roebuck middle part – he changes key from three flats to five sharps! Beautiful – but how is he going to get back? Well, he does – and very smoothly too, but I can't possibly give it away in words. Porter was good at key change surprises, too. You never knew what key he was in. Major, minor, schmeemer! Some of his tunes wormed all over the place – like 'Night and Day'. They say he got the idea from hearing a Mohammedan priest calling in his flock near Marrakesh (you don't get that sort of lead sitting in an Alley office). A weird tune: forty-eight bars and a sixteen-bar verse with the same note forty-six times. Never mind – after a few hearings the tune got under your skin.

Porter dared to stand outside his form and poke fun at his own music. In 'It's De-Lovely' the singer decides to skip the verse because it seemed 'the Tin Pantithesis of melody'. You had to have plenty of nerve to do that – and plenty of ability to get away with it. You had to have mastered the idiom.

However, they knew their Tin Pan Alley, and grew to love and respect her. Rodgers and Hart, the smart pair with the choppy melodies, eventually came out with a real old-fashioned *waltz* in 'Lover'. A *torch song* in 'Ten Cents a Dance'. A *ballad of domestic bliss* in 'Blue Room' (where 'every day's a holiday because you're married to me'). Even globe-trotting Cole Porter went domestic with 'You'd be So Nice to Come Home to'.

And such lyrics! Such rhymes! Interior, feminine, triple, false, flatulent . . . 'This city' with 'electricity' . . . 'Heine' with 'China' . . . 'hero' with 'queer romance' . . .

Such references, too! Shakespeare, Strauss, Mickey Mouse, British Museum, Franklin D. Roosevelt, etc. There had to be much hard grind behind such light music – plenty of swinking in the kitchen to produce these soufflés. All very well to admire professionally – but were they *pop* popular songs as well?

Yes, show tunes by the song jewellers weren't just beautiful works to be admired in trade circles. Cut off from their shows, many were spread into the homes of millions by radio. Number one song in the very first Radio Hit Parade (1935) was Kern's 'Lovely to Look At', followed by his 'I Won't Dance', followed by Gershwin's 'Soon'. Rodgers and Hart supplied a couple of veterans with movie songs: George M. Cohan in *The Phantom President* and Al Jolson in *Hallelujah I'm a Bum*.

Clearly, some of this *adult*erated style was acceptable to the general public. The more romantic songs found a home in the heart. Many proposals of marriage were prompted by the strains of Kern's 'Who – stole my heart away?' Dancing or sitting or dreaming, a young couple were *using* Rodgers's and Hart's 'Manhattan' – not so much aware of the tricky rhymes and slinky, ambivalent harmonies, as willingly carried away into the afternoon of the melody. The words of the song jewellers expressed those little things that 'he' wanted to say to 'her' so very chicly: 'YOU do something to ME' ... 'I'VE got a crush on YOU' ... 'I get a kick out of YOU' ... 'YOU took advantage of ME' ...

Mushiness was averted because love was no more than 'Nice Work If You Can Get It' – as flip as that. After all, you were both up-to-date romantic realists so a trip to the moon on wings of gossamer could naturally, inevitably, end up as 'Just One of Those Things'.

And all the while that people were enjoying the songs at home, at dance halls, in movie theatres, on the radio, a *select few* – that intercontinental transworld first-night audience who helped create the lore of the world reflected by the song jewellers – were living it up somewhere in Paris, London and New York, last bastions of the civilized world.

Cafe society dated back to before the Great War but in the twenties and thirties it was at full swing. 'It is to be deplored that face-contortionists and night club warblers can mingle equally with Generals and Ministers,' wrote Major d'Arcy Pellago in 1928.

Now through the front door instead of the back marched the entertainers to move freely in the same circles as the old society. Hostess Elsa Maxwell, daughter of a small-town insurance salesman, had mingled, at one time or another, with Winston Churchill, Franklin Delano Roosevelt, Einstein, Scott Fitzgerald, Cole Porter, Noel Coward, Kitchener, Hitler and Mussolini. Cole Porter was on whispering terms with the Prince of Wales; Irving Berlin married the daughter of millionaire Clarence Mackay, who had once entertained the Prince at his Long Island chateau; George Gershwin received a photo from the Duke of Kent signed 'From George to George'; Jerome Kern had connections with the 'Round Table' of literary wits who held court at New York's Algonquin Hotel.

Of all the theatre men only Cole Porter truly seemed to have been born into cafe society, to be the perfect smart cracker gentleman. He had a million dollars and a beautiful wife (so sophisticated that she didn't know how to open a door). At one time he ran a house in Paris and a palace in Venice (where he speedboated on the canals and entertained up to 350 guests aboard his floating night club). He wore gold garters and had visited India, China, Japan, Cambodia but he liked the music of Bali best. As he floated down the Rhine in a boat he composed 'You're the Top', one of his greatest hits.

Before Yale and the world he had been an Indiana farm boy. As the thirties drew on and he grew older so he regretted the passing of simpler times. He spoke of writing songs with more common appeal and 'less of the brittle, bright poesy with which I've been associated'. In 1940 he produced the chummy 'Let's be Buddies' and the Jolsonesque 'My Mother Would Love You'. Perhaps all through the clever years he had been waiting for the times to change. Certainly he always despised the drones of cafe society, just as writer Nathaniel West, at Greenwich Village parties, despised poet e. e. cummings's squatting on the floor shouting four-letter words, or critic Edmund Wilson's gargling and gesticulating.

Perhaps they were all watching each other in disgust – making notes for future works. And just *maybe* that whole cafe society

139

with its junketings enjoyed by night owls in dinner jackets, eyelids lowered, blasé countenance, had been invented by Noel Coward, a real British Englishman and yet another Harms music writer. When he first appeared in London and New York in the early twenties he was the epitome of the *bright* but jaded *young thing* presiding over the decay of gracious living. He had written a hit play about drugs and immorality. He looked like the play, taking phone calls as he sat breakfasting in bed wrapped in a Chinese dressing gown. 'Reality' was needed in contemporary theatre, he told the press. Sex was 'the fundamental root of human nature'. Undergraduates adored him, the general public was outraged. Many of his songs became hits. Where had he come from? From the theatre. Where did he live? All over the place. How did he find time to write all those plays, revues and songs? He tossed them off at weekends, in taxis – he said.

His songs charted a progress towards a more permanent yesterday before the Great War, when British musical comedy flourished. Carriages at eight for tidy, beautifully constructed songs of grace by Lionel Monckton, Paul Rubens, Ivan Caryll and Leslie Stuart. Tunes matched the coy, skittish girls and the dashing men of the plays. In the jazz age, separated by an unbridgeable chasm, Coward warned the 'Poor Little Rich Girl' (his first hit song) of the dangers in that wild typhoon life where 'virtue was a stranger'. 'Dance Little Lady' continued in this moralistic manner in the tradition of Harry Von Tilzer's 'She's Only a Bird in a Gilded Cage'. After the dancing to the 'wicked moan' of saxes syncopating nerves with 'nigger melodies', dawn would show that the lady was 'living in a world of lies'. World weary, high above the mountains and sea, repose could be found in 'A Room with a View'.

'Someday I'll Find You', chokingly yearning for a past littered with things left undone, could almost have been Edwardian except for the occasional crushed chord throttling too much romanticism. '20th Century Blues' nailed the chaos and confusion of his age to a 'slow blues tempo'. Decent English people – mothers, majors, sun-dried bureaucrats, and aristocrats were mocked with affection in his comedy songs: 'Don't Put Your Daughter on the Stage,

Mrs Worthington', 'Mad Dogs and Englishmen', 'The Stately Homes of England'.

Behind the facetiousness lay a seriousness. All the theatre men were disciplinarians: Coward worked from 7 a.m. till 1 p.m.; Porter kept to a strict timetable and composed as he sat between bores at dinner parties; Kern spent hours on a single key change. They worked with the piano, stopping the clock as they fiddled with their tunes. A shame, then, that their tunes were used by dancers, consumed by dance bands, swing bands, jazz bands, to be made into fox-trots, re-arranged into hot items, improvised upon by crack saxists and slurped out by crooners. All subtlety was lost and grammar was outraged. Except for George Gershwin the song jewellers disliked the rhythm-merchants, especially swing bands. Rodgers found his melodies got lost, and Kern felt they made all pieces sound alike. Cole Porter sent Frank Sinatra a telegram asking why he sang his songs if he didn't like the way that they were written.

Swing

Show-tune writers didn't appreciate the excitement generated by a stream-lined big band at work on their work. If it wasn't some arranger re-voicing, adding his very own slabs of dissonance and rivalling their original gem, it was some he-man suited jazz soloist of the day carried away, *sent*, CREATING ON THE SPOT. Sometimes this instant creation became a mass affair called a *jam session* (not in the dictionary). One such session was described by a radio announcer in the excited chromatic note of a sportscaster at a horse race; at some sweaty dive dozens of swing stars were jamming – expressing themselves all over 'Ah! Sweet Mystery of Life', that lovely melody by Victor Herbert. Suddenly the announcer's tone zoomed up several notes. A dozen saxists had burst in, some still wearing their overcoats and hats, to join the big blow. Phrases that had taken the great operetta composer weeks to construct at the piano were twisted and tortured to death in one night of swing fever.

On the whole the swingers weren't song craftsmen. If they did compose in solitude their numbers were generally club sandwiches of riffs – those stammer phrases building up to a climax, like 'In the Mood', a Glenn Miller favourite. Big bands set show tunes down as solid runways from which their instrumentalists could take off on flights of fancy. Artie Shaw ('King of the Clarinet' and hard on the heels of Benny Goodman, 'King of Swing') certainly increased the royalties of all the major show-tune writers, even if he did swing away. Porter's 'Begin the Beguine' (originally part of a flop musical) became a best-selling record by Artie Shaw. Between 1938 and 1939 he and his band recorded 'A Room with a View'

142

(Coward), 'My Heart Stood Still' (Rodgers and Hart), 'Suppertime' (Irving Berlin) as well as 'Vilia' from the old *Merry Widow*.

Swing was king from 1936 till approximately 1940, and played by the big band, *the* new pop unit. High school bands mushroomed but Benny Goodman advised swing students in his book *Kingdom of Swing* not to attempt improvising. Leave that to disciplined big bandsmen, fourteen in gangster suits – Clark Kent figures led by a businessman. Benny Goodman and Glenn Miller wore glasses but the big band was number one stage attraction by 1940. And 'swing' was the word, just as 'jazz' had been the word, just as 'ragtime' had been the word. *Life*, a new magazine of candid camera 'reality' pictures, did spreads on swing; *Time* numbered the jitterbuggers and dealt out some odd facts; *House Beautiful* issued a guide to 'Basic Swinglish'. Hollywood had Gene Krupa's drumsticks on fire, but Artie Shaw refused to say 'Hi ya jive hounds I'll dig ya an' I'll plant ya' in *Dancing Co-Ed*. The new profession of sociology talked of swing's 'restless frenzy' and 'mass hypnotic effect'.

What was swing? Bandleader Chick Webb explained to *Time*: 'Swing is like lovin' a special girl and you don't see her for a year and then she comes back – it's something inside you'. Maybe so – an inner need, an emotion. But here was swing all around. Still it was mass without politics! Nobody really objected.

Thousands of high school kids queueing from 6 a.m. outside New York's Paramount Theatre so that they can get into Benny Goodman's 10.30 a.m. performance. He's scheduled for five shows that day. The band waits behind the screen until the B movie is over. Constant noise from the kids during the movie *and* during the the band show. Jiving in the aisles. One boy jumped from a box. It's like the medieval Children's Crusade commented *Time* on the 200,000 fans who filled Chicago's Soldier's Field Stadium to hear a string of swing bands. During the 'Carnival of Swing' at Randall's Island, New York where 25 bands played before 23,000, police and firemen had to be called in to protect musicians from 'destruction by admiration'.

But it was out-door healthy fun. Hardly a soul got hurt. And all that crazy lingo – 'jive talk' – was screwy but nice. Alligators, crocodiles and killer-dillers cut rugs, spanked skins in a groove somewhere in the big apple. 'Jeepers Creepers' – its composer Harry Warren didn't know it was a way of saying 'Jesus Christ'. Webster's dictionary was getting to be useless. What was needed was a jive-talk guide for songwriters.

For the first time instrumentalists were becoming influentialists. Crowds gathered around the bandstands observing finger movements and embouchures, rooting for their hero, cheering his solo. Band members were known by name, changes in personnel were noted; so and so wasn't playing like he played on the record. As if they were football players. Next thing these kids would be cheering songwriters, or even film editors! Writer Irving Kolodin observed that these youngsters 'comprise a generation more sensitive to musical values than any that have gone before them. In contrast to their elders, who valued dance music as an undertone to conversation, the youngsters of today have a respect for the men who play it, an appreciation of their status as individuals and in many cases a critical valuation of their performance on any given occasion.'

Benny Goodman went further than Paul Whiteman. His band played Carnegie Hall, far more prestigious than Aeolian Hall. There they gave a short and amusing history of how jazz had progressed from its naive beginnings to the stream-lined music of today. Count Basie joined in a jam, 'Loch Lomond' was swung, and finally clarinettist Goodman wailed on top of Gene Krupa's jungle beats in 'Sing, Sing, Sing'. Krupa sweated, his hair fell over his face. Kids shagged and trucked. At last jazz had triumphed! No longer were there any concessions to the classical music of Europe as there were in the Whiteman concert with its 'symphonic jazz'. Swing players had grown up in the jazz age. Jazz, syncopation, beat, africanism, whatever it was – this was their language and it was as American as apple pie. Jazz was swing and now magazines published potted histories of this extraordinary art form which had developed so fast.

But there were a number of jazz experts who agreed that swing wasn't jazz. As mutually suspicious as yachtsmen, they agreed on little. Some said jazz was white, others said it was all black. Some said it had died with Bix Beiderbecke in 1931, others that it was very much alive and kicking down in New Orleans in its original collective form. Jelly Roll Morton settled the matter for himself by claiming to be the inventor of jazz *and* swing.

Europeans tended to be the most assured about what jazz was and wasn't. Hughes Panassie in *Le jazz hot* wrote that he would give a 'precise idea'. The BBC christened 'swing' and broadcast a programme from the St Regis Hotel, New York, major-domoed by Alistair Cooke. (Amongst the jazzers were Hot Lips Page, W. C. Handy and Mezz Mezzrow.) Hot Clubs consisting of dedicated hot record collectors dotted Holland, Germany, France and England. Quite soon American versions appeared sporting raccoon-coated enthusiasts clutching cases of 78s which they had listened to clandestinely during the catacomb days of the so-called jazz age and the dark nights of the Depression. Their Hot Record Society issued only the best in true jazz, printing in the personnel and dates on the record label. 'We will choose to reprint discs that are distinguished both by greatness and by rarity, leaving the corn to the hillbillies.' John Hammond, Jr, was instrumental in championing the cause of jazz. He organized recording dates and concerts and acted as patron to Benny Goodman and Count Basie before swing had become an Age. His 'From Spirituals to Swing' concert amazed New York sophisticates with its new sounds from old sources. A gospel group consisting of a carpenter, two truck drivers and a tobacco factory hand demonstrated the rugged beauty of old-time religious music. Two ex-taxi drivers, Albert Ammons and Meade Lux Lewis, plus friend Pete Johnson, performed some authentic *boogie-woogie* piano. Thrillingly, off from the rigid instrument and into the concert hall billowed this music, imitating the rattle and whoo-whoooo of a railroad train, reminding the audience of the wanderer who lay not far inside every American.

Other braver white Americans didn't need the concert hall for they had been getting out and about and into black music for years. They would tell any kid hep-cat that even Chicago jazz was tame compared with the jumping stuff you could hear in Kansas City, wide-open as an aged hooker and overlorded by Boss

Prendergast. The spare ribs were the juiciest, the broads were the lovingest and (next in life's needs) the music was the swingingest. Northern know-how and Southern grits met in this mid-west railroad centre to cook the surging riffs and rock-easy rhythm of a pioneer swing band like Bennie Moten's – 'The Hottest Band This Side of Hades'. Hell, he didn't need any *King of Swing* and all that jive! He was playing for dancing and those riffs were no more than modern versions of those holy roller calls and responses which you could hear in any down home Baptist Church. When the horn player got up from the band congregation to cut loose on some crazy licks he was just feeling the spirit move him to bear witness to God – except that God wasn't supposed to be there.

And Moten wasn't just a riffer either – he played fine ragtime piano, but by 1930 it was necessary to get low-down and forget that happy two beat jive. His band played the Savoy Ballroom, Harlem in 1932 and when he died a few years later Count Basie took over. Harlem was full of big-band-arranged jazz, had been for years: Fletcher Henderson, Andy Kirk, Cab Calloway, and Jimmie Lunceford played at the Savoy and the Roseland. Dancers creating the next dance step sensation right there on the floor (inspired by crazy licks from the screaming Teddy Hill Band) were watched by brave white enthusiasts.

Of course, that was in darkest Harlem. There were all kinds of delicacies – 'queer joints' and places like the 'Dunbar Palace', but you had to really penetrate. British jazz enthusiast Spike Hughes found his way into the Dunbar and noted that all the patrons wore coats and hats and that many were asleep at tables. Fashionable Harlem, though, was easy to find. The Cotton Club, white-owned and whites only, catered for your carriage trade – the barons, earls, party-lovers and rich socialites who liked slumming. Duke Ellington's band supplied suitable jungly music and the story was spread that his 'Mooche' number, with its grunts and cries, had been a major cause of the national rise in crimes of rape.

If, claimed the black music enthusiast, the Harlem bands had been booked by the big agencies, broadcast on radio networks, recorded by major record companies, then they would have enjoyed rightful glory. Black bands were left to be exploited by

146

crooked operators. Their leaders were managed by gangleaders. So were their major clubs like the Grand Terrace, Chicago. After Louis Armstrong dared to change managers he was cornered in a phone box by a thug who proceeded to burn the trumpeter's moustache with a fat cigar.

Then there was racial prejudice. In the South it was hard for a touring black band to find room and board. Fats Waller's Cadillac was stoned. In the North, black bands had beat but no romantic assets. Billie Holliday, the singer, had to conceal her yellowness by blacking up when she appeared with the more African-toned Count Basie band.

The cards were stacked against real jazz, black or white, being allowed to become popular, it seemed.

The kids, the jitterbuggers, the fans, didn't care whether swing was jazz, whether it was black, white or European. Swing was 1936, 1937, 1938. Swing was peckin' and truckin' and doing the Susie Q, in baggy pants and a sweater, with your *chick*. Swing was jive-talk, was following the bands around from town to town as *band chick*, was smoking a *reefer* with some of the *cats*. Where did that arranger guy get that *hep* bow-tie? And that girl vocalist – she had some good tips on eyebrow pencil and mascara.

The Great Depression was lifting. Liquor had been legal since 1933. Entertainment was thriving. No need to talk doctrine with lefties anymore. The Thomas Edison Company had set the mood of the New Deal years when they put up a sign: 'Roosevelt has done his part. Now you do something. Give a party, see a show. Buy something. Build a house, take a trip, sing a song, get married. This old world is starting to move.' So Gene Krupa bamming away on 'Drum Boogie' was just the job. Boogie-woogie, music of the future! Why couldn't teachers be like Benny Goodman? At this point in time the twenties seemed hopelessly old-fashioned – all that vo-do-deo-do and those mickey mouse bands which they loved in the Mid West. 1928 was 100 years ago, not 10.

But by the end of 1939 the dust had settled. Sweetness complemented swing in the precision music of Glenn Miller and his orchestra, suddenly the most popular band in the USA, possibly in the world. It was estimated that one in three of every juke-box request was for a Miller record. His two biggest hits epitomized his honeyed and fizzy style: 'Moonlight Serenade' and 'In the Mood'. Live the band looked sharp. He looked personable and saxist Tex Beneke looked smooth and singer Ray Eberle looked dreamy. You could listen to the dynamics of the band, watch 'The Modernaires' vocal group come out with creamy close harmonies, as you both glided around the dance floor. Glenn Miller was the tops for every occasion. How could those show tune writers not dig this luscious organization? Maybe this was jazz but Mom and Dad liked it too.

Surely this swinging, but also romantic-sounding, organization represented the very tops in modern music. Glenn Miller, studious in his spectacles, had been reared on the type of small ensemble jazz played by the ODJB. He played a hot trombone for the Ben Pollack Band (which also included Benny Goodman) in the twenties. Then he went on to arrange for the sweeter band of Ray Noble. But all the while he was blueprinting his idea for his own sound. It had taken a few years to finally make it but here, as 1940 rolled in, was that dream sound actually alive and ticking precisely, as accurate as the very finest clock. It was made out of a mixture of saxes topped with a clarinet and was easily identifiable as 'the Miller Sound'. 600 big bands were touring about and doing boffo business playing live and exciting so that special sound was ultra-important: Shep Fields and his Rippling Rhythm, Gray Gordon with his Tic-Toc music, Guy Lombardo's quavering saxes. But Glenn Miller was different. He made jazz. He was musicianly. He represented the climax of forty years of popular music – from the crudities of ragtime through the Mickey-Mouse-ness of early dance music and the undisciplined jazz bands to the sleek but swingy all-purpose music of Glenn Miller. Who could ask for anything more?

An important part of any big band was its vocalists – some trade people suggested that they were what made the band. Miller kept saxist Tex Beneke and female equivalent Marian Hutton for the bouncy numbers whilst Ray Eberle and Pat Friday took care of the smoochy ones. They all welded together (plus two others) to form the juicy Modernaires vocal group. Even the Swing King Goodman had vocalists, and music fans shook their heads. No such thing as jazz singing! Still the crowds loved them. They humanized the whole shoot. There was Ella Fitzgerald with Chick Webb, Perry Como with Ted Weems, Peggy Lee with Benny Goodman, Kay Starr with Charlie Barnet, Jo Stafford with Tommy Dorsey, Anita O'Day with Gene Krupa, and Frank Sinatra with Harry James and then Tommy Dorsey. Back in the twenties vocals were few and far between. The boys in the band chirped up with a refrain for fun in the middle of a number. When Bing Crosby was just one of the Rhythm Boys with the Paul Whiteman band he had to pretend that he was a musician by fiddling with a rubber violin or a rubber-strung guitar. After all, Whiteman's was an orchestra with all the instruments shiningly apparent. As Whiteman's band developed into a vaudeville show, he collected all kinds of acts in his orchestra cum vaudeville show – bicycle pump players, concertos, bits of Victor Herbert, jazz – and this Rhythm Boys vocal group was one such act that he collected. A little later he featured the sister of Rhythm Boy Al Rinker, a hefty girl called Mildred Bailey. What he was doing – consciously or unconsciously – was pioneering band vocalists. He had picked two singers who were to have enormous influence on popular singing. Crosby became the model for Perry Como, Frank Sinatra, Dean Martin and thousands more. Bailey greatly influenced Billie Holliday, Ella Fitzgerald, and Peggy Lee.

Crosby's fame as a solo singer enabled him to cut loose from the strict tempos and one-chorus rationing of band singing. But the other big band singers had to muck in as part of the swinging team – rather junior actually because they got paid less than the instrumentalists. The finest compliment that could be paid them was to be told by a sideman that they used their voice 'like a horn'. Peggy Lee said that she learned more about music from bandsmen than any one else. 'They taught me discipline and how to train.' Sinatra trained to breathe like Tommy Dorsey's trombone. He took underwater lessons towards this. Yet the most unique of all vocalists, Louis Armstrong (who hit the pop world with his performance of 'Ain't Misbehavin''), wasn't emulating his horn.

Rather his horn was emulating him. Count Basie exhorted his band, 'Say it this way!' rather than 'Play it this way'.

But, no matter, it was a good time for musicians, and vocalists were more than crooners in 1940. They were technicians and fellow hornsmen. Never before had there been so much live music around. Never before had there been such clever, witty sophisticated tunes. Never before had there been such a million-dollar business as Pop with its tentacles of radio, talkies, juke boxes. From all angles it was a wonderful, wonderful, wonderful, marvellous time. De-lovely!

Part Three
Britain

Invasion

The Normans invaded Britain in 1066 and the Americans around 1912, with ragtime. It was a peaceful operation and there was little resistance. The siren song was insidious! American entertainment, of course, wasn't new: back in the nineteenth century minstrels had been very well received, settling down to become traditional family fare (especially at the seaside and later on radio and television). Coon songs of a gentler, more pastoral kind had been written in Britain (notably 'Lily of Laguna' by Lancashire organist Leslie Stuart, and 'Oklahoma Rose', by Trinity College, Dublin banjoist Percy French). Cakewalking had been done by royalty. Ragtime piano was found to be charming: the Duchess of Westminster hired Vic Filmer to play 'Temptation Rag' in the nursery at her children's party. So the Afro-American influence was fairly well-established before the invasion of 1912.

However, this latest city ragtime was slicker and smarter. At the London Hippodrome were a bunch of snappy young Yankees in dark suits billed as 'The American Ragtime Octette' who jerked and gesticulated their way through such songs as 'Waiting for the Robert E. Lee', 'Ragging the Baby to Sleep' and 'Hitchy Koo'. This last song became an especial favourite with the islanders. London was held in thrall. An American visitor rushed home to tell the Alleymen about a famous London pub where he'd been greeted by a parrot squawking 'Hitchy Koo, old dear'. No sooner had the Octette burst when in sailed Ethel Levey, rag mistress and ex-wife of George M. Cohan, together with her troupe for the revue *Hello Ragtime*. The strangeness of songs like 'Snooky Ookums' was softened by the inclusion in the show of impersonations of Winston Churchill and F. E. Smith. Miss Levey herself took the anglicizing further by marrying English aviator Claude Graham White.

Hello Ragtime was a great success. Rupert Brooke took parties to it time and time again. Ragtime acts landed swiftly with banjos, saxes and energy: the Hedges Bros and Jacobsen, Joe Jordan and his piano as well as The Versatile Four. To *The Times* ragtime was unmistakably American: 'It is the music of the hustler and the feverishly active speculator.' But to audiences it was *exciting*. Acceptance by Londoners was understandable – they were always pushovers for anything strange, foreign or apparently barbaric. Acceptance in the provinces and up North was more surprising. Up North, especially, they were supposed to prefer more provincial stuff – cloth-capped comics singing of a world recognizable to factory hands (the frightful made funny). But ragtimers did well on music-hall bills which they shared with local favourites such as Jack ('I'm Shy Mary Ellen, I'm Shy') Pleasants and George ('I'm coughing better tonight') Formby (the elder). Yorkshire lad J. B. Priestley was attracted and terrified by ragtimers 'shining with sweat' and 'drumming us into another kind of life in which anything might happen'.*

Many music hall artists, still singing the rounds with their 'special material' songs on a wealth of subjects from boiled beef and carrots to an engagement with the Seventh Royal Fusiliers, resented this intrusion by foreign wildmen. Ragtime was 'bloody noise'. But ragtime would soon pass and go home, just like those Italian jugglers and Swiss yodellers, they trusted.

Ragtime was to be followed by jazz. The music was accompanied by the new dance styles. Dance bands on American lines appeared. Sleek Alley tunes dominated. Crooning in American accents became the rule. Britain was in danger of becoming Little America. Rudyard Kipling, a lover of the old halls, complained in vain about this 'imported heathendom', adding that 'one doesn't feel very national when one is hummed at nasally by an alien'. The

---

*The weirdest thing *did* happen, much later. Whilst visiting Latin America in the late 1950s he was mobbed by teenagers who'd mis-read his name as E L V I S Priestley.

poet T. S. Eliot, having escaped his native America, found that his new haven of England had been polluted. In *The Waste Land* he asked 'Is there nothing in your head but "O O O O that Shake-speherian Rag – It's so elegant So intelligent"?'* But these warnings of impending cultural drowning were ignored by the general public.

Why did British pop fall so easily? Why did we exchange the particularity of 'Let's All Go down the Strand' for the international whoop of 'Hitchy Koo'?

The conquest wasn't total. Local songs about local life continued to be written and even to hit. Native artists singing in their own accents arose and countered the Yankees especially in the North (e.g. Gracie Fields and George Formby Junior).

But before ragtime the British scene had been a thriving, bustling one with hundreds of music halls needing hundreds of songs. Indeed, both American ballad and American vaudeville were directly inspired by the British example. Henry Russell, the first big ballad-monger, was British. Many music hall stars appeared in vaudeville and became as famous in America as in Britain: Vesta Victoria with her 'There Was I Waiting at the Church', Albert Chevalier with 'My Old Dutch' and Harry Lauder with 'I Love a Lassie'.

Alleymen readily admitted that British comic songs were wittier and that British musical comedy songs were more tuneful. In New York saloons singing waiters had constant requests for 'The Man Who Broke the Bank at Monte Carlo', 'Poor John', 'Daddy Wouldn't Buy Me a Bow Wow', etc. There's little doubt that Irving Berlin (who worked as a singing waiter) was influenced by these artful songs.

But British music hall rapidly became catch-all. Perhaps, way way back in the early nineteenth century real working-class singers

*It is not generally known that Eliot was mis-quoting from a pop song called 'That Shakespearian Rag' published in 1912 by the Edward Marks Music Corp. and written by Gene Buck, Herman Ruby and David Stamper. The chorus goes 'That Shakespearian Rag, most intelligent, very elegant . . .' James Joyce, too, was fond of unannounced quoting from pop songs. This is a line which might be pursued by Eng. Lit. students with time on their hands.

had sung real working-class songs at real working-class audiences. But even in the days of pub entertainment, before the halls proper, we have W. G. Ross posing as Sam Hall, murderous chimney-sweep, whilst Sam Collins, real-life ex-sweep, sang comic songs of Irish life. It wasn't long before a bright businessman turned this rough and ready city entertainment into an industry. Charles Morton, 'Father of the Halls', converted his Lambeth pub into a music hall and in 1861 completed the Oxford Music Hall (Oxford Street, London) at a cost of £35,000. Around 1890 a number of Northern businessmen established chains of Empires and Hippo-dromes for the regions; Mr Stoll took Liverpool, Mr Moss took Manchester and Edinburgh and Mr Thornton took Leeds. That time till 1914 is known as the 'Golden Age of the Music Hall' when all of Britain was dotted with these ornate palaces operating twice nightly and getting more refined and international with the years. By the 1900s music hall was 'Variety', was like vaudeville. A typical bill would still feature your landladies, charwomen with bosoms and feathers, and heavy swells, all poking away at the upper classes. But it *could* also feature Sarah Bernhardt, Beerbohm Tree, coon singers and midgets underwater swallowing ping pong balls. Audiences weren't confined to the working class. The number of interlopers indicate that the halls were classless or anyway class-full; Winston Churchill, Rudyard Kipling, General Booth of the Salvation Army, painter Walter Sickert, T. S. Eliot, Sturminster Newton, Melbury Bubb, all frequented the halls. My grandfather, a squire, was removed from the Empire, Leicester Square for putting up an umbrella in the stalls. He returned a few minutes later wearing the doorman's gold-braided uniform. Music hall was simply Britain's first mass entertainment institution and directly something tastier like films or radio, came along music hall had to step aside. It never died out: halls lasted right up till rock 'n' roll. Visual rock 'n' roll was spread via tours of the old halls. But by 1914 the palmy days were over.

Perhaps it's truer to say that real music hall wasn't a collection of gilded buildings but a collection of remarkable individuals who, as the twentieth century raced on, became frozen in splendid iso-lation, relics of a richer age. Their names sat in boxes on the music hall bills, their eccentric personalities were held in the open prison of the stage. In real life they would have been quite insufferable. Marie Lloyd, Little Tich, Dan Leno, Gus Elen – all were exaggerated creatures, gorgeous and glorious, who *just* passed as people. Some, like T. E. Dunville, Mark Sheridan and Dan Leno went mad. Others, like Gus Elen, a genuine coster with an authentic Dickensian cockney accent, survived into the thirties when they enjoyed a revival, were filmed and broadcast and seemed positively lunar. A few, born after the golden years, provided comedy relief from the Americanization process (e.g., Frank Randle with his travesty jitterbug, who set fire to a hotel where he hadn't received satisfaction, who liked to take his teeth out at the start of his act and chuck them at the stalls).

Some of the best of the old music hall stars were incomprehensible outside of Britain. Marie Lloyd flopped miserably in America – she looked fat, elderly and without glamour. She was 'Our Marie' – of London. Even Sheffield didn't twig to her. How could American audiences fully appreciate Gus Elen's song about the cockney garden he'd manufactured in his slum backyard (by planting cabbages and turnip tops that people hadn't bought off his barrow)? It was so very local.

> Oh, it really is a werry pretty garden
> And Chingford to the Eastwards could be seen,
> Wiv a ladder and some glasses you could see to 'Ackney
>   Marshes
> If it wasn't for the 'ouses in between.

Music hall was often very insular, too, which didn't make for decent exports. Marie Lloyd had a song that went:

> I'd like to go again to Paris on the Seine
> For Paris is a proper pantomime,
> And if they'd only shift the 'Ackney Road
> And plant it over there
> I'd like to live in Paris all the time.

In other words, Paris would be all right if it was London.

Not only were many of the music hall songs local and insular, but they were also written to order for the stars themselves. Fred Gilbert, for instance, sold singer Charles Coborn his 'Man Who Broke the Bank at Monte Carlo' for one guinea. Nobody else but Ella Shields was allowed to sing publicly 'Burlington Bertie from Bow'. The stars were legally protected. So busy were the songwriters with this made-to-measure writing that they neglected the general all-purpose song. Everybody could love and understand the US Alley song 'You Made Me Love You' but who, except parochial Britishers could be receptive to 'Lips That Touch Kippers Shall Never Touch Mine' or 'I'm Going Back to Himazaz – Him As 'As the Pub Next Door'?*

The main trouble was that the songwriters as a whole were rambling bohemian types, here today, gone tomorrow, buried later by the parish. Joe Tabrar, writer of 'Daddy Wouldn't Buy Me a Bow Wow', a huge hit in America as well as in Britain, used to dash off songs on a shirt front, or on the paper that his pigs' trotters had been wrapped in. Then he'd sell them to an act for no more than a couple of quid.

Publishers made on slick Alley lines were slow to develop in Britain. By the end of the Great War there was certainly a Tin Pan Alley in London, around Charing Cross Road, Francis Day and Hunter, Bert Feldman's, Lawrence Wright, and Herman Darewski being the most notable publishers. But they had nothing like the complicated sales techniques of the Big Alley, nor had they the writers. And most of their big sellers came from America, even as far back as the 1890s. It's surprising how many songs associated with pure British music hall, those deathless songs sung tearfully at closing-time in pubs, turn out to have been written by American Alleymen. Here are a few: 'Down At The Old Bull and Bush' (written originally as 'Under the Anheuser Bush', by our old friend Harry Von Tilzer), 'Nellie Dean', 'Goodbye Dolly Gray', 'The

*Even so, Britain produced a number of standard hits in the ragtime years: 'Little Grey Home in The West', 'Somewhere a Voice is Calling' (1911 both), 'Destiny Waltz' (1912), 'It's a Long Way to Tipperary', 'The Sunshine of Your Smile' (1914), 'Pack Up Your Troubles in Your Old Kit Bag' (1915), 'A Broken Doll' (1916), 'Roses of Picardy' (1916), 'McNamara's Band' (1917).

Honeysuckle and the Bee'. On the other hand British songwriters never really got off the ground with ragtime. Ivan Caryll made a fine attempt with his 'Ragtime Temple Bells', but it was left to American Nat D. Ayer (who came over to London during the ragtime invasion) to handle British themes in ragtime – 'I'm Going Back to Dear Old Shepherd's Bush', 'That Ragtime Suffragette'. He also created the imperishable 'If You Were the Only Girl in the World'.

The main problem for British writers was that there was no native music idiom. Tunes like 'Joshuah' and 'When the Summer Comes Again' were good and catchy but not pure *British*. True, bits of native hymn harmony were to be found in many a tune (listen to 'My Old Dutch') but there were also great chunks from Italian and German music. Regional differences were apparent only in the words: 'I Belong to Glasgow', 'My Girl's a Yorkshire Girl', 'I Live in Trafalgar Square'. Their tunes could have been French, Dutch, German. Of course, American Alley ballad, with the same musical roots as music hall song, was no different. But America, the fleshy virgin, had living on its body hillbillies, ex-slaves, and immigrants. Hiding in arm-pits and other hidden regions, 'free' to nurture their own sounds and to fill the Afro-American folk fund. Unfortunately the country folk in Britain (who left the plough to tend the loom or push the pen in the Industrial Revolution and in the cities) left their folk music behind. Much of it withered and died, despite the efforts of Cecil Sharp, and others. *There was no Welsh hillbilly, no Cornish ragtime, no Highland jazz.* What did exist was a body of brilliant songs written by bohemian songwriters (quite unsuited to the rush of the twentieth century) for mad stars who had the effrontery to survive the Great War and to live on in a world of popmass. 'Fighting the Menace' was the slogan from the 1920s onwards. Fighting those slick, rhythmic dance melodies from over the sea.

Nevertheless, though the heyday of the halls was over the spirit marched on. English singers puzzled Americans. Humour was all very well in its place but sex was serious! The key word was *soul* and the British were suspected of not having it because they didn't waggle it about as a 'flasher' might his genitals.

Britain

But of course the giants of British pop knew that pop, like all artistic pursuits, was not that important. They knew that a hot meal, a glass of beer and a few cheery friends round a warm hearth were worth more than all the songs, pictures, films, poems, books, plays, happenings in the whole world.

Occupation

'BUNK-A-DOODLE-I-DO' MAN COMMITS SUICIDE AS
JAZZ SWEEPS BRITAIN

In 1923 Paul Whiteman and his Orchestra appeared at the
London Hippodrome in a revue, *Brighter London*. Next year T. E.
Dunville, eccentric/comic singer and pre-war idol of the halls,
drowned himself in the Thames, somewhere near Reading. He and
his 'Bunk-A-Doodle-I-Do' and 'Dinky Doo' songs had been
suffering the boos and eggs of modern audiences. Like so many
of those fantastic creatures who had stalked the halls before World
War One and the Great American Pop Push, Dunville in the
twenties appeared a grotesque anachronism.

As the comic floated towards the sea, crowds of young people
hurried down near-by lanes in the opposite direction. They were
heading for the Assembly Rooms where a dance was to be held –
music provided by 'The Reading Reveller Jazz Maniacs'. The entire land was in the grip of the Jazz Dance. Spruce dance bands were
everywhere: at the Savoy Hotel, London; at the Gleneagles Hotel,
Scotland. Even the Royal Automobile Club sported one, which
made some records. Lancashire lad Jack Hylton, with pierrot and
panto experience, was fast becoming the leading dance band name,
a star of the halls. The year after Dunville's death he and his band
appeared at the great Alhambra Music Hall, Leicester Square.
And in a lonely Suffolk village a collection of middle-class Morris
dancers were stoned out by rustics yelling 'Give us Whiteman,
give us Hylton. Give us Jazz.'

Britain

Was 'Yes! We Have No Bananas' any better than Dunville's 'Dinky Doo'? No, but 'Bananas' sold better! Times were tough – Britain was becoming a dumping ground for American songs (as well as American films). Where were the Jerome Kerns and Irving Berlins of Britain? Some said that her budding writers had been knocked out in the war. One who had survived was Lawrence Wright, lord of Britain's Alley, a publisher, a hit-writer, and a character. He had 'arrived' some years before the war, working his way from a music stall in Leicester Market to a little shop in Denmark Street, London. Before long he owned the entire block and the street became known as 'Tin Pan Alley', Britain. At first he was a one-man business, building the shelves, making the furniture, sleeping on a folding couch in the basement, writing most of the stuff he published. In 1911 he had his first hit with 'Don't Go Down the Mine Daddy'. During the war he did his bit in the Royal Naval Air Service (Ivor Novello was a brother officer) and contributed 'Are We Downhearted? No!' to the war effort. Another piece, 'Love Come from Your Hiding Place', proved that Wright was a genuine, all-round, complete Alleyman.

Shortly after the Armistice he announced to the world that his firm had secured the services of the World's Greatest Songwriter, Horatio Nicholls. Only those in the trade knew that Nicholls and Wright were one and the same. With this and several other stunning names he set about writing a series of songs closely modelled on current US winners. Mostly they challenged those imports published by his deadly rival Bert Feldman. For instance, when the latter secured the US smash 'Beautiful Ohio' Wright produced 'Wyoming Lullaby'. He roamed over other American spots, coming up with 'Omaha' and 'The Whispering Pines of Nevada'. In the immediate post-war years the East became popular, so 'Hindustan' and 'The Sheik of Araby' were rushed in from America. Wright came up to their par with 'Sahara' and 'Baghdad'. Tolchard Evans, another British songwriter, made a bold and partly successful bid to romanticize the British place-name with 'Sunset down in Somerset', 'The Road to Loch Lomond', 'Dreamy Devon'. In order to fight the US menace writers had to come up with very different songs, sometimes dreadful, or else join the enemy as Wright had done. Thus 'When You're Walking Down High Street Africa on the Way to Timbuctoo', and the song campaign to encourage people to 'Eat More Fish'. The publishers of the latter received through the post a month-old rock-salmon stinking to high heaven pinned with a note from an unsatisfied customer.

Wright adopted American plug methods at a time when the real Alley was dropping them, becoming more sophisticated. He put ads in the national press. He had staff members cruising round London aboard a camel advertising 'Sahara'. He went into the field himself, making regular forays up North to Blackpool where he established song shops along the Golden Mile. One summer he persuaded Jack Hylton and his band to be aeroplaned over the seaside resort performing the Wright publication 'Me and Jane in a Plane', as employees threw copies down at gaping holiday-makers. Several bandsmen were sick but the song became another solid Wright hit.

He allied with light music and local authorities in his special conducting tours of coastal towns, disguised as Horatio Nicholls and travelling in his Phantom Rolls (furnished with wireless, gramophone and composing table). In this very car he wrote 'Among My Souvenirs' (now a world standard) extracting the tune from a mandolin as the Rolls creamed past mill and factory on its way to a Nicholls Concert. On arrival at these functions the composer was warmly greeted by light-music-loving crowds and the mayor's hand. Later that night, after dinner, he'd conduct the local orchestra in medleys of his greatest hits.

Yes! The seaside at holiday time was proving to be the very finest sales area. Clarence Green was plugger king, cutting an impressive figure what with his tall cowboy hat, Oxford bags and gleaming co-respondent shoes. He addressed everyone as 'old man'. For Wright he arranged 'Wyoming Nights' in the Brighton Assembly Rooms. The show consisted of Green striking up on the opening notes and beckoning the audience to sing along. 'Omaha Nights' followed. Then a spot of bother with guv'nor Wright, and Green found himself with a rival firm running 'Whispering Nights' (but these affairs, usually held in rough pubs, quickly deteriorated into what Denmark Street men called 'Shouting Orgies').

All summer long, motor coaches and excursion trains transported millions of trippers to the seaside, together with their ukuleles, their community song books, their portable grams. After the war more and more people from the working class were able to enjoy summer holidays.

Nature lovers complained of orange peel and kippers. C. E. M. Joad, later to become known to radio millions as the popular philosopher of the *Brains Trust*, noticed dust and a stench. Amusement arcades broadcast the city sound of American-made pintables and dodgem cars. Yet also at the seaside there was more peculiarly British entertainment than you'd find anywhere else. On the beach were the Little Chapel of the Sand with its luring hymns,* bands of strolling players on Long Vac. from the Varsity singing their own special material, poking fun at foreigners and parvenus, Pierrots in white costumes dotted with pom-poms, and Nigger minstrels. The beach was alive to the sound of entertainment, and had been for many decades. Some said the shows had been more genteel and more gentle before the war. Now the bluer concert party was becoming the norm.

Beach concert parties consisted of sketches, songs and music. The performers vagabonded around from resort to resort carrying their tent, some props and costumes. A change of character meant a change of hat. The world was a wooden platform on the sand and everyone did everything . . . 'Hello everybody, we're here once more, here to entertain you by the old sea-shore, with the RAMSGATE RAMBLERS SUMMER SHOWWWW!' Scarborough was amongst the best beaches, but the corporation knew that too and had been known to charge £600 for a season's

---

*One of the most popular of their hymns had the lines:

'Do not fear the thunder
 Or the earthquake's shock,
You'll be safe for ever
 If you build on the Rock!'

Seaside pranksters would dig elaborate tunnels specially timed to reach the Sand Chapel gospeller's feet on the words 'earthquake's shock'. Suddenly he would swiftly sink from view.

patch of sand. The 'Fol De Rols', one of the longest lasting parties had started there in 1911. It was still active well into the forties and at one time or another its cast included Jack Warner, Richard Murdoch, Arthur Askey and Eric Barker. Concert party was a remarkable training ground for entertainers: Tommy Handley, Max Miller, Bud Flanagan, Elsie and Doris Waters, Naunton Wayne.

Material was mild and chuckly, no breast-beating. Husbands enjoyed mild thought-flirtations with the pretty soubrette who sang outdoor drawing-room ballads of the 'Glorious Devon' or 'Floral Dance' type. The piano tinkled away, its music mingling with the chink-chunk of spade in sand, click of knitting needle, cry of bather. Sloped nicely in deck-chairs, savouring the memory of a lunch topped off with roly-poly pudding and treacle, the audience didn't need to be told about life. Deep down they knew that Edith was potty and Father was broke, but there was no need to make a song and dance out of it. They could cope with life quite well without Art's artists, its instruction, its finger-pointing. Also, here on the sand they could relax away from the bam-bam-bam of twentieth century pop. I, too, feel quite relaxed . . .

Jazz reached Britain in 1919 as a revue turn. The Original Dixieland Jazz Band were presented at the London Hippodrome in *Joy Bells*. They were sensational and lasted one night – because the star of the revue, George Robey (a stalwart of the music hall) issued an ultimatum: 'Either the band goes or I go.' The band went. They played the Palladium, the Royal Palace (and the King laughed), the Victory Peace Ball, Rector's Night Club. They opened the brand new Hammersmith Palais de Danse. Then they went away. But, as in America, they had got a minority hooked, and by the middle twenties this minority, mostly Oxford and Cambridge undergraduates, had outgrown the ODJB. They were a bit of a joke. Real jazz buffs were on to harder stuff, the real thing and coloured! The only way they could get at the stuff was on record. Rich undergrads sailed to America during vacation and came back with suitcases bulging with 78s. Louis Armstrong, Bessie Smith, Duke Ellington – these esoteric names became pass-words to this tight little beleaguered community. Like a Freemason handshake. The jazz buff was a social outcast, always in danger of having his collection smashed by rugger hearties. He sat in his college room as the gramophone shot Miff Mole trombone licks out the ivied window which, winging across the quadrangle, caused aged dons (dreaming of Rupert Brooke) to hurrumph on their walk.

Philip Larkin, the poet, remembers those days of jazz: 'their rips, slurs and distortions were something we understood perfectly. This was something we had found ourselves, that wasn't taught at school, and having found it we made it bear all the enthusiasm directed at more established arts. There was nothing odd about it. It was happening to boys all over Europe and America.' Eventually record companies began issuing hot American jazz. In fact, jazz on record came to have a better deal in Britain than in America. In the thirties those who couldn't afford to go rummaging in America could always search the junk shops of Britain. B. M. Lytton Edwards describes a 'voyage of disc-covery' in the early thirties: 'We began at Croydon and finished at Watford, via Greenwich, visiting every record shop en route. Our jaunt came to a glorious end on my finding the right kind of shop. It was a miracle I did because Rex was moaning about a cup of tea.' Once they journeyed as far as Dublin, where they were offered a hot 'Danny Boy' by Scout Teddy James. Sad to have found no rare items they retired to a nearby tea-shop. On inspecting their teapot stand closely they discovered that it was, in fact, a 78 and a good one, by the Mound City Bluesblowers. Collecting hot records was a lonely, private passion and many buffs felt that by owning rare records they owned jazz herself. But for others the joy of junking and armchair listening (with the occasional strut around the room shouting 'Oh Yeagh!' at a blue slur) wasn't enough. They had to make jazz themselves: Spanish–American Fred Elizalde, a Cambridge undergraduate, cut some fine jazz records in the twenties with his Cambridge Undergraduates, a band that included saxist Maurice Allom, later a Test cricketer.

The most celebrated Varsity man to actually get into jazz was Spike Hughes. Native dance music of the late twenties was, he felt, the laughing stock of the world and he wanted to do something about it and have a good time as well. The spell of Horatio Nicholls had not trapped him: he wore a tie coloured in blue harmonies which showed that he was a member of the 'Anti-Shepherd of the Hills' Club (the title of a song by Nicholls/ Wright). He made a series of records with his 'Decca-Dents' band that were widely acclaimed in Europe, and soon he was voted Number One European bassist. He wrote a 'Harlem Symphony' and a jazz ballet and he worshipped Duke Ellington. In 1933 he reached the climax of his jazz life when he went to America, met the Irving Mills stable of Negro jazz musicians, toured picturesque Harlem and recorded his own pieces with an all-coloured orchestra containing such jazz giants as Chu Berry and Coleman Hawkins. Hughes was so shattered he didn't dare play his bass until the end when they all had a jam session.

After that he gave up jazz playing and stuck to reviewing hot records for the music paper *Melody Maker* under the pseudonym 'Mike'. His reviews were fierce: 'Local boys copy all that's worst in white jazz. Thank God my soul is filled with race prejudice.' But his missionary zeal was offset by his loathing of jazzers who made jazz a 'very important matter'. To him it was no more than good dance music. The fondest memory he had of his European jazz band tours was that dinner at Leyden University: hand-picked claret and 'conversation refreshingly removed from the world of hot jazz'. The Boat Race was discussed.

In 1944, he renounced jazz publicly in the *Melody Maker* as ' ... music for the young and those with the enthusiasms and blindness of the perpetual undergraduate. At my time of life to get excited over jazz is like a schoolgirl having a crush on a male film star.' England made him, England claimed him. Where were the songs about England? he asked in the fifties. Recently he wrote a book about Glyndebourne.

Melody Maker, founded in 1926 and still going strong, was the very first paper devoted to popular music. Lawrence Wright was the founder and Edgar Jackson, public school and Cambridge, was the first editor. Jazzmen and dancemen fought it out inside, sax tips were given, a banjo expert described the peculiarities of the diminished 7th, a hot violin chorus was written out note for note and there was dance band news from all over the country. Pop music was dance music – the 1934 Columbia record catalogue listed 800 dance titles – and in Britain this Afro-American idiom was kneaded and pummelled ever so gently into a shape decidedly national, jazzers notwithstanding.

It was the ambition of all the bands to get into the 'Society Set', to play tip-top London hotels, restaurants and night clubs. To play hunt balls and private parties.

The select few included Carroll Gibbons and Roy Fox (both actual Americans), Ray Noble (who soon graduated to America), Lew Stone, Harry Roy, and Ambrose. The latter was a Londoner and his first name was Bert, but all this was off the record. On the bandstand in evening dress with his fiddle tucked underneath his arm, he was a splendidly autocratic figure, reeking of mystique. Even titled customers approached him nervously with their requests, always tipping in pounds. One night, it was alleged, an aristocrat slipped him a measly ten bob for 'Body and Soul'. The leader crumpled the note and tossed it away with disdain, still keeping the beat going with his foot. The Mayfair Hotel couldn't afford his high price so he left. Calls to the Palace; Oxbridge colleges competing for his services; in the summer he takes his orchestra to play at Monte Carlo.

During the Depression employment for dance musicians increased dramatically. Players in society bands made an average of £18 a week. But it was hard work and here is a typical working day of a sax band-boy playing in a West End orchestra:

Up at noon. Off to the hotel for rehearsal with arranger (1.30 to 3.45). Then change into blue blazer and yellow slacks for tea dance (4.15 till 6 p.m.). Change back into off-duty rig (i.e. wasp-waist suit and pointed shoes). Quick bite at Lyons. Glance at *Melody Maker* and get into argument with hot jazz trumpeter Leo about merits of dirty tone. Change into evening dress for 9.30 start at hotel. Guv'nor arrives in swallow tails, carrying rolled umbrella, and fresh from golf course. He starts us off on a quickstep arrangement from Noel Coward's latest, with an up-and-down movement of his elbow. This is made from thigh to shoulder [rather than the reverse which is normal] and confuses the novice 2nd trumpet who comes in late and fluffs his phrase. The leader has his back to us and is nodding to guests, but out of the corner of his mouth he tells the erring trumpeter, 'Your pay's docked and I'll see you afterwards!' Our bass player is able to sleep on the stand whilst plonking out a steady drone note. I watch romances blossom on the floor. A case of whisky is sent up to our leader by a young blood requesting 'Tiger Rag'. After some reels, a 'John Peel', and many Happy Birthdays to You it is time for 'Good-night Ladies' and the end of work (around 2 a.m.). And so to bed.

But not for all. A few of the band-boys hare it down to an all-night club and blow their hearts out on jazz, egged on by a raffish crowd who keep calling for faster tunes and longer drum solos.

Mayfair, it appeared, was everywhere. Even palais and dance hall bands wore a kind of evening dress (Fair-Isle jumpers could occasionally be seen peeping from inside a dinner jacket). Up North in Sunderland, the Bon Repos restaurant featured a little band of pianist and drummer, plus French dishes. But one diner was startled to hear his order of 'sweetbreads' translated by the Maître D to the waiter as 'One plate of *ram's knackers* and make it sharp!'

Right up in Scotland at the exclusive Gleneagles Hotel, where every suite had a grand piano, was a band under the direction of Henry Hall. He'd had a thorough musical education at the Trinity College of Music, followed by two years with the Salvation Army's music department. A job as a relief pianist at the Midland Hotel had introduced him to dance music; after some difficulty in mastering the rhythm he'd settled into that life and did well. By 1931 he was not only in charge of the Gleneagles band but also the thirty-two bands kept by the London, Midland and Scottish Railway. He pressured the BBC into hooking-up with his Gleneagles dances back in the mid twenties, when band remotes from anywhere outside of London were unheard of. His music caught on; listeners inquired about 'that band without vocals from somewhere in Scotland'. In 1923 Hall was invited to form a brand new BBC Dance Orchestra, to replace the resident Jack Payne and His Band, who were going to tour in variety. Hall threw up his hotel position and joined the BBC.

As in America, radio (called 'wireless' over here) quickly became a national habit. By 1939 sets were to be found in nine out of every ten homes. Unlike America, broadcasting became a state monopoly, under the paternalistic guidance of John Reith, a Scotch Calvinist with high ideals and a tremendous sense of destiny. Answering a message from the wind in the trees near Ben Lomond, he became manager of the British Broadcasting Company in 1922 and Director-General in 1926, when the company became a corporation with a board of governors appointed by the Prime Minister. His message was a mission; his mission was a message: he would broadcast the British way of life and 'all that was best in every department of human knowledge, endeavour and achievement'. And dance music and variety would have its place, could be beneficial. But in the early free-wheeling days there were several BBC bands and rumours about publishers paying £1 for their tune to be played from the London studios, and ten bob from the Midlands studios, flew around. They said that bandleaders collected their 'readies' at the end of each month on the steps of Savoy Hill. There was no question of Henry Hall stooping to this sort of thing. His nick-name was H.R.H. His Salvation Army training had burned into him as high a set of ideals as the Director-General himself. He brought the decorum and taste of the Gleneagles to the BBC. He stressed melody; he popularized 'The Teddy Bears' Picnic'; he had a 'Guest Night' in which music hall artists did their turns (he'd always been a fan of music hall). He and the BBC got on well together. The news was read in evening dress and in a clipped upper-class accent, similar to Hall's.

But popular music and variety were severely rationed on the BBC, although polls showed that they were the most popular fare. Many listeners tuned into Radio Luxembourg for its culture-free programmes such as 'Littlewood's Pools Broadcast' with records by Gracie Fields, George Formby, Billy Cotton. Journalist Godfrey Winn, a keen ear for popular tastes, called for less of 'The Foundations of Music' or 'The Treaty of Versailles and After', and more of the programmes that might 'open magic casements wide on faery lands forlorn'.

In Europe broadcasts by dance bands, rather than Reith's culture, came to represent all that was best about Britain. A Swiss civil servant in a letter to a famous broadcasting bandleader wrote: 'If I told you about the magic of your band, which is such a strength to us in these terrible times when dictators walk the land, it would sound unbelievable ... Yours Pierre LeFanu'. Band leaders should have been the official ambassadors in Europe because they were in reality: Lew Stone was better known to the Dutch than Lord Halifax. Henry Hall, visiting Germany in 1939, was given a greater reception than Prime Minister Chamberlain ever received. Jack Hylton was awarded the Légion d'Honneur by the French government.

Many British bands roamed Europe. And most of the big names appeared at the halls at home. Indeed, they kept them in business. They mixed the latest US hits with rollicking G B comedy songs and carried their own scenery, props and costumes to dramatize them. For example, Jack Hylton's boys, dressed as sailors, sank on stage at the end of 'He Played his Ukulele as the Ship Went Down'; Jack Payne's Royal Command Performance of 'The World is Waiting for the Sunrise' showed a sun rising behind the band (this was effected by a mechanic behind a curtain pulling on wires attached to a washing-up bowl which was fitted out with an electric light).

Sometimes the show misfired; during a version of 'The Old Dun Cow Caught Fire' by a prominent Dorset band some paper hats of the band-boys actually did catch fire. Soon the stage was ablaze. As stage-hands ran around with buckets to douse the flaming players, the audience – thinking it was all part of the act – applauded.

Of course, throughout the golden years of these dance bands there was the Great Depression. They didn't reflect social conditions, but if people had wanted songs about the sack and bands consisting of men in overalls they would have got them. The fact is that most people only realized the hugeness of the Depression afterwards. At the time they read about it in the papers and glimpsed it on the newsreel, but it seemed remote. The coal fire blazed and the wireless crackled. There were more tramps about. The majority were the new Englishmen, who lived in ribbon houses and saved for a baby car. Even shop assistants called themselves middle-class. The millions of unemployed were mostly in the North and in Wales (areas which preserved the older England) and they kept quiet except for the occasional protest march. They might have passed unnoticed had it not been for the visits of the Prince of Wales and the sociological trip of writer George Orwell. The latter reported on the monotony and drabness of life in the coal areas of Lancashire and Yorkshire, a 'lunar landscape' of slag-heaps, scrap iron, fouled canals, paths of cindery mud 'criss-crossed by the print of clogs'. He discovered revolting slums in Wigan – rooms where 'all the furniture seemed to be made of packing cases and barrel staves'. The people had given up hope; an old mother sat on a tub that served as a lavatory and looked at him blankly from a 'yellow cretinous face'. Orwell found that the working class were silent and servile. But if pop music didn't reflect all this, at least it was popular. The time for social and political commitment to intertwine with mass entertainment had not yet arrived. No regiment of dance band-boys marched off to the Spanish Civil War. No dance or jazz bands accompanied the Jarrow marchers. Nobody considered that *that* was a function of entertainers.

A warm, cheap place to be on a cold, wet Depression day was *at the pictures*. 'I have seen young people find ready-made happiness in a cinema. The comfortable surroundings have a refining effect on the mind,' noted a Lancashire judge. By the end of the thirties almost half the population went to the pictures once a week and, for the most part, what they saw on the screen suited the attractive and appealing surroundings: glossy, well-made American movies. Since the war Hollywood had established domination, through art and industry, of the screen, as the US Alley had of pop. Hollywood snapped up talent; Hollywood sound-tracks had the best fidelity; Hollywood dumped its culture in a can.

Some said audiences would never accept those accents and all that 'OK, big boy!', 'Beat it, kid!', 'You're swell, baby!' But audiences were used to slangy Alley songs and they took to all-singing, all-talking Hollywood straight away. Indeed, there were signs that some of the working class actually preferred the American screen life-style; gangster lingo and suits and hats and slouch were adopted by the British crook crowd (Tottenham Court Road supplied these little Caesars with their outfits). At some 'cap and muffler' cinemas in the Midlands and North, West End theatre accents were hooted at, whilst James Cagney's pistol drawl was taken in awed silence.

But the glamour of the far West was tempered by the good humour of home-grown personalities. Despite an absence of slickness, sexiness and American accents, certain regional musical acts were as box-office as Powell and Keeler, Astaire and Rogers. Representing Mayfair on the screen was Jack Buchanan, a star from the musical comedy stage and a debonair yet coltish chap with a legion of lady fans from all classes. Actually he could have been quite sexy but he preferred to be a light comedian (after wooing her with a tune in the canoe he loses balance and they both splosh into the lake). His songs (by Hollywood writers) were amiable, e.g., 'This'll Make You Whistle', 'Everything Stops for Tea'. He crooned through the intimate amplification of his nose and he performed wonderful gangly dances in a style so languid that it seemed he might suddenly flop on to a couch with a 'Hang it all!' and fall asleep. He was the Last of the Silly Asses, an extremely handsome Bertie Wooster thriving on pranks and puppy love and bubbly, and without any visible means of support. Off the screen he was a shrewd businessman and a fine craftsman, (known to take all night rehearsing a single shrug of the shoulders).

Representing northern regions were Gracie Fields and George Formby Junior, two ordinary people as down to earth as Buchanan was up in the air. Buchanan, as the 'typical' Englisher, could be considered a star in America but Fields meant little there and Formby meant nothing. But typical Englishmen were on the wane and the northern couple were, in a sense, ahead of their time: 'They assault graceful living. They roll in vulgarity and commonness. They shout, they elbow, they show off their warts,' wrote Col. Weston Jarvis in his diary. But they were Queen and King of the British box-office – Fields from 1934–38, Formby from 1938–45. Everybody, except Mayfair sophisticates and a few colonels, loved this northern couple – the equivalents of Deep

South red-necks because the North was to southern England what the South was to northern America. US South and GB North housed 'the real, honest, people-people.'

Like Buchanan the northern couple owed little to ragtime, jazz and the blues. Gracie Fields could sing operatic in a beefy voice with dainty bits and ah-ah-ah-ah staccato climbs to the highest rafters. When she sang comic, as in 'The Biggest Aspidistra in the World', she used her natural north-country accent. She never let the sentiment go slushy and at danger points in 'Sally', her greatest hit, she pulled funny faces, and went all mock-posh. The film *Sing As We Go*, set in the industrial North during the Depression, had her leading laid-off workers out of the mill to the jaunty title song. She *was* Britain, she was *an example*, 'capturing the spirit of good humour and optimism that alone has prevented the depressed and dispossessed in smitten industrial areas from succumbing to the tragedy surrounding them' (*Birmingham Mail*). Once upon a time she had been 'Our Gracie' of the North, but now she was 'Everybody's Gracie' who could tackle anything from 'In the Woodshed She Said She Would' to 'Ave Maria' and yet still remain a mill lass from Rochdale, Lancashire, where they left their doors unlatched, and where her mother had told her never to give way to emotion in public.

George Formby was her spiritual husband. He came from nearby, from Wigan. His father had been a master of the halls with his killing cough and his songs about an older, more tragic Lancashire. Formby, Jnr, by contrast, was cheery and sunny, with a Cheshire-cat grin. When Beryl, who was to become his wife, first saw his act she thought it the worst she'd ever seen, and Formby himself never thought he was very good – but he knew he had something that they seemed to want. Today there is a George Formby Society with its own musical director. His records still sell very well and I have almost all of them.

He didn't croon, he sang as he talked and jazz was something to laugh at ('John Willie's Jazz Band' came from 'pitch black coal mines down in Wiganland' rather than Dixieland). Instead of thirties sex innuendo backed by cocktail chords, he strummed a banjo-ukulele and was healthily filthy, like a blues. His was a universal secret language: girls chased his member as he chased theirs – *his* was a 'Little Stick of Blackpool Rock' and *hers* was 'Auntie Maggie's Remedy'. He showed that even ugly bodies might entwine in love-making – you didn't have to be dreamy – and that cammy knicks, jumpers, drawers, loony asylums, corpses in bed, and window cleaners could be popular subjects in modern popular songs. The tunes kept the spirit of ragtime alive, bouncing along and played jagged by his dance-band accompaniments (very often Jack Hylton's boys). After he made the Big Time – the Southern Time – Ealing Studios took him up, their producers racking their brains to find a way to integrate ukelele songs into tight plots. The fact was that people came to see 'Our George' do those songs and to hell with the plot. Ealing thought that he was all right (biggest box-office draw), but he was no kinematic challenge.

The BBC was embarrassed by some of his song lines. They asked him to clean his own windows as well as those in 'When I'm Cleaning Windows', his famous number. He was very shocked and replied that he'd always appealed to a family audience, which was true. He was normal and natural and never sent up his subjects. He liked parti-coloured jumpers – bought lots of them – and he hated jokes about Wigan. Up North families queued from dawn to catch him live on stage. Both he and Gracie Fields disliked filming. Both looked straight into and right through the camera, with a longing to crash the lens, burst the screen and fall into the stalls shouting 'It's me!'

They brought technique to amateurism. Few hobby singers could reach the notes which Fields hit squarely; uke players marvelled at Formby's high-speed syncopated strum (he was the best ukulele-banjo player in the world). Thus the audience didn't just sit and watch the screen. An enormous number were *doing*, despite the increase in mechanical entertainment, but they didn't get canned. For instance, as well as thousands of uke players there were thousands of accordionists.

The 'squeeze box' piano accordion was first popularized here in the twenties by an Italian variety act called The Macari Bros. One of the brothers later formed an accordion band called 'Macari's Dutch Serenaders', a curious mixture with an Italian leader and accordionists in Dutch garb, playing music hall songs and light classics with plenty of twiddly bits. In the thirties the American Arthur Tracey – squeeze box, clean tramp costume and 'Marta – Rambling Rose of the Wildwood' – was quite a success over here. But by this time the country was full of Macaris and Traceys, and *Melody Maker* was full of ads for accordions, many described as richly bejewelled and with scenes wrought in ivory. Newspapers carried reports of gangs raiding music stores for accordions; many were nicked from cars and snatched from the platforms of buses. An all-girl accordion band was the sensation of the Rotary Circuit, until forced to disband after several members damaged their bosoms with the bellows during quick marches. The *Accordion Times* appeared and had a decent circulation, lasting into the forties (when it was merged with the *Musical Express*). Players were urged by its editor – 'Let us resolve to concentrate on the written note and give up ear music. Let us attend to leaky bellows, polish up the ivory and keep the chrome clean. And let us do all this on a Sunday.' But danceband pros and British Alleymen resented the accordionists with their enthusiasm and their know-how. One pro wit defined a gentleman as one who 'knows how to play an accordion but doesn't'.

Though there were part-time singers who sang as unaffectedly as Gracie Fields or the teenage Vera Lynn (her first record, 'Up the Wooden Hill to Bedfordshire', came out in 1936) there were many, many more who took to crooning. The Ayrshire Crosby, the Cardiff Crosby, the Penzance, Seaford and Whitby Crosbies. Child crooners: ten-year-old crooner Johnny Green was prevented from appearing in cabaret by the London County Council. Bathrooms echoed to 'boo bubber boo boos', but for public appearances equipment was necessary. Not many could afford microphone, amplifier and loudspeakers, but a megaphone was within average pocket range. A new transparent model, devised by a bachelor of science, was on sale from 1932. The ads claimed that none of the vocalist's personality was lost and that 'under the limes the singer assumes an almost ethereal appearance'. Would-be crooners were urged by experts to suppress their regional accents and listen carefully to our own Al Bowlly, who had apprenticed himself to Crosby and developed some of the latter's 'indefinable soul'. Beginners must pay careful attention to diction, avoid sloppiness. The 're' of 'remember' should be distinct (with, perhaps, a Scotch roll). Common faults were 'mammory' for 'memory', and 'ter-morrer' for 'too-morrow'.

Crooners, ukulelers, accordionists – but not everybody could sing or play. Millions wanted to participate in the new urban folk music of Great Britain. So they danced. And not 'Old English Folk' but 'Jazz Modern', with modifications. America anglicized yet again.

During the twenties certain bodies had tried to revive the old Morris dances but had met with resistance (see page 161). However, they continued to try over the next ten years and in the thirties they were joined by an odd bunch from Hampstead, many of whom wore beards, avoided meat and were vaguely left-wing. Armed with flagons of dandelion wine, loaves of nut-bread, portable antlers and a May-pole, these revivalists would board excursion trains at spring weekends and jump off at remote villages. The May-pole would be set up, antlers fixed to brows, lutes struck, picnic spread and a medieval afternoon would begin. But one Saturday, near Aldeburgh (Suffolk), a fed-up squire packed his local dance band into a lorry and drove them – bandsmen tearing away at a hot number – clean through one such Morris group, squashing antlers, lutes, loaves, wine jugs and a few left-wingers.

Ballroom dancers and their teachers (millions of authentic urban folk) were unaware of these modern medievals. Anyway they wouldn't have had time for them because ballroom dancers and teachers were hard at work fashioning what came to be known and admired throughout the world as 'The English Style'. Ragtime, jazz and tango dances had thrown social dancing into confusion. The Edwardian dance professors retired hurt. In an attempt to get new dancers and dances into line the Imperial Society of Dance Teachers, in 1924, invited five teachers of American jazz dancing to cut the chaos down to but four basic steps: waltz, fox-trot, quick-step and tango. Most of the more eccentric animal

177

dances were eliminated. Others were modified. For example, the full charleston (solo and done in one spot and full of high kicks and waving of arms) was anti-social. Passers-by were frequently hit or kicked or both. And a great band of charlestoners could cause nasty traffic jams on the parquet. So the flat charleston was arranged, a scissor step interpolated into the regulation quickstep (which was a British invention too).

One of the five teachers called in to advise the Imperial Society about taming jazz dance was Victor Silvester. He was to become the leading figure in fashioning the English Style. He knew nothing of 'old-tyme' or animal dancing when he was quite suddenly pitched into the foxtrot scene at a Harrods tea dance in 1919. He had chanced there, but the instructress offered him a job as a 'professional partner' (i.e. paid to dance with wall-flowers). Dance life proved to be exciting for this son of the Vicar of Wembley – one client offered to set him up with clothes, etc., if only he'd become her 'escort'; another enticed him into her home knowing her mother was out. Escaping from this scarletry he concentrated on learning the new American steps and in 1922 he won the World Ballroom Dance Championship, partnering the daughter of a retired colonel.

Six years later, whilst recovering from an illness he wrote *Modern Ballroom Dancing*. This instruction book sold very briskly over the next decades till by 1955 it had been through fifty-five editions. Meanwhile, Silvester's fame had spread even as far as Japan where his name was household and more: a Tokyo university student likened him to the Messiah.

He started a West End dance school in the early thirties and, in running it, discovered that most so-called dance records were in quite unsuitable tempos. So he filled a gap by forming his own band, one that stuck strictly to the melody and to a metronomic beat. By 1955 (the year of 'Rock around the Clock') his records had sold more than 27 million copies. *In other words, he'd sold more records than any other British dance band and, for that matter, any other British pop person.* He was Head Man.

Unlike what happened in America, our ballrooms became less dancehalls and more social clubs, or even villages – with aspirations. The phrase *Palais de Danse* had come from Paris (centre of social dancing until the rag wave) trailing the refinement of serviettes. The first big ballroom was the Hammersmith Palais de Danse, opened in 1919. It had a sprung maple floor and forty instructresses. The Prince of Wales visited it (he's all over my story). After a short slump in the late twenties (the Hammersmith Palais went over to ice-skating temporarily) ballrooms entered their golden age. Like cinemas there were chains – for example, Associated Dance Halls owned Locarnos in Streatham and Glasgow, plus the Palace, Edinburgh and the Ritz, Manchester. More people spent more time each week at the palais than at the cinema. The palais was a de luxe village. Surrounding the green (dance floor), under the brilliant blue electric sky and glinting silvery moon, tucked away behind fluted pillar-trees were little shops selling all kinds of things. A sax-shaped cigarette-lighter, personal stationery, finest confectionery.

Countless marriages were launched from the parquet green or hatched in nearby shady booths. Potential husbands could be assessed: if he waves to friends as he dances, if he gives displays of tricky steps, if he brags about past conquests – he's a bad prospect. If he sits on his heels he's stubborn, if he's springy he's childish. Clammy hands means sexiness; cheek to cheekers show no depth of character. But if he keeps an even keel then he'll be balanced in all things and thus a good prospect.

Apart from this function the palais also encouraged *togetherness*. There were wheelbarrow races and basket balancing, but no marathons. Community dances came to be an important part of palais life in the late thirties. Everyone could join in these, even the most unappetizing of wall-flowers. First invented was the palais glide – you all formed a chorus line, linked arms and then stepped along with high kicks, to the tune of 'Poor Little Angeline'. Next came the Lambeth walk, a Cockney swagger with hitch-hike thumb movements and shouts of 'oi', adapted by a Streatham Locarno instructress from the dance routine performed in the 1937 hit London musical *Me and My Girl*. The Duke and Duchess of Kent did it. King George VI and his Queen entered into the spirit of things by helping to popularize the dance 'Under the Spreading Chestnut Tree'. More energetic and less royal was the bottom-banging 'Hands, Knees and Boomps-a-Daisy' invented by Annette Mills (sister of screen actor John Mills), and introduced by her at a tango contest at Dorchester House in 1939. Although democracy had been helped by these 'all together' steps 'Boomps-a-Daisy', though big at the palais, was not done at the Palace and was shunned by upper-class adults. They did allow their children to do it at parties, however.

Togetherness – pre-Woodstock – was a feature of late thirties life in Britain, a far less sinister version of the rallies and youth movements which were happening in Hitler's Germany. Togetherness, without militarism but with youth, was fostered by Ralph Reader, a Canadian, in his annual Gang Shows. The first was staged at London's Scala Theatre in 1932 and the idea caught on at once. Within a few years there were gang shows all over Britain and the Empire (and other parts of the world including Indo-China). Reader's cast was composed entirely of scouts and scoutmasters. He wrote the whole thing. His songs were bright and breezy, thick with ozone and whiffing of camp-fire camaraderie. Very catchy indeed.* 'We're Riding Along on the Crest of the Wave' became his greatest hit. In the finale of the Gang Show film made in 1938 Reader took the verse, dressed in naval uniform and making much use of an outstretched arms gesture, and in the chorus was joined by sea scouts in shorts and jerseys plus tap-dancing cadets. It also contained a popular feature from the stage shows – boys dressed up as girls, some of them looking extremely convincing. Critical reception was cool, the *Kine Weekly* commenting that the film 'should amuse those who find humour in boys masquerading as girls. Second feature for unsophisticated youngsters.'

As well as scout camp togetherness there was also holiday camp togetherness. Billy Butlin, born in South Africa and with Canadian experience, opened his first camp at Skegness in 1936. Over the camp entrance was carved 'Our true intent is all for your delight.'

* Ray Davies of the Kinks and protest singer Phil Ochs are among today's admirers of Reader songs (especially 'Children of the New Regime', which begins 'We pedal up hill and we pedal down dale'.)

Inside Redcoats (in bright blazers and white flannels) and loud-speakers jollied campers along, organizing their day with ping-pong, swimming, knobbly knees contests, community sing-songs, etc. Meals were communal. The best in entertainment was purchased: Len Hutton bowled to Gracie Fields; Monty Mantovani and his orchestra were regulars. A few observers feared that too much regimentation might lead to Fascism but this was far-fetched. 'Sieg Heil' was a war-cry but 'are you enjoying yourself?' a caterer's cry and a genuine question – answered by one and all, 'YES WE ARE!!'

Meanwhile, the songwriters . . .

Before we return to them I must mention that in the hobby-filled thirties, Denmark Street Alleymen were challenged by a host of amateurs, hoping for that sudden hit, followed by a pound paradise, magical like a pools win. Their manuscripts silted up music trade letter boxes. Experts warned them off. N.W.5 is advised not to write about London because 'there is no obvious music in words like "Leicester Square" as there is in "Tennessee" or "Texas"' (before the war, before rag and jazz there was plenty of music in names like Leicester Square, Tipperary, Glasgow, Piccadilly, the Strand). An Irish amateur from Youghal is told that his charming line 'Everyman with a happy wife and babies laughing as much as they like' isn't sophisticated enough. And McL. of Sligo is told that he's eccentric or just plain wrong with his line 'I can see your eye in a tear' (the poor devil was a quarter of a century too early).

Meanwhile, the songwriters. For these 'pros' life was hard and getting harder. Hollywood songs on stage and screen and bandstand. American writers, like Rodgers and Hart, Harry Woods, Sam Coslow, Sigler, Goodhart and Hoffman hired to provide songs for our own Jessie Matthews and Jack Buchanan – while our own men were still selling songs to artists and publishers for a few quid, were lining up at publishers' doors on Friday evening for an 'advance', a hand-out; then tapping each other for loans in Peck's Wine House (their favourite haunt) with 'Hello, old sport! Can you lend me a half-crown?' 'Funny, I was just about to ask you the same thing!' One music hall writer was reduced to pawning his underwear.

There were exceptions, however. Noel Coward, but he was never a pop man really. Jimmy Kennedy (graduate of Trinity College, Dublin) put words to the tunes of Austrian Will Grosz and the result was a string of world hits: 'Isle Of Capri', 'Harbour Lights', 'Red Sails in the Sunset'. Kennedy also collaborated with Michael Carr to produce Mexican songs like 'South of the Border'. Holt Marvell and Jack Strachey wrote 'These Foolish Things', equal to the best of the song-jewellers.

The older tradition of sturdy ballad was kept alive by Tolchard Evans, Bob Hargreaves and my great-uncle Stanley J. Damerell (real name Jack Stevens and a fine stump speaker; he once delivered a speech in a busy high street for a bet). They wrote that eternal money-spinner 'Lady Of Spain', as well as 'If' and 'Unless'. But they also did comedy songs like 'Let's All Sing like the Birdies Sing', throw-backs to music hall days. Dance-band leaders thought this was crazy but the public took to the stuff. Carroll Gibbons, American society bandleader of whispering cornet fame, was magnanimous enough to call up Evans at dawn and admit 'O K, brother – you win!'

Sometimes Evans and co. wrote with Ralph Butler. This man with the ripe apple face, sunny beam, and general look of a gentleman farmer, jotted words on odd envelopes for such hits as 'I'm Happy When I'm Hiking', 'Horsey Horsey', 'We All Went up up up up up the Mountain' and 'There's a Good Time Coming' – but actually he was swimming against the tide. He was the last self-contained man. He kept his life in an attaché case which was forever flying open, scattering inland revenue forms, lyrics, false teeth and sandwiches. He admitted to no fixed address and his main expression was 'They're coming!' Mass America was the enemy as he saw it, so he nailed her, calling her pop songs 'lugubrious lamentations of a disappointed lover'. Life was bad enough as it was without these dirges, what with the tax man hounding him and all those records, radios, movies, and tin-openers that he didn't understand – the whole incomprehensibility of this century! Still, he kept up appearances, lifting his battered trilby and smoothing down his cardigan over his waistcoat, before starting a sales-pitch to an upstart publisher. Once he'd got the required cash advance on royalties he'd scamper off to his mysterious farm deep in the country where he would read Anatole France or Voltaire, and write songs about animals.

Amongst the things in his attaché case was a book called *Constant Reminders*. Here are a few: 'Don't fear corn', 'Be excited if you want to succeed', 'Be careful of showing ideas to other writers'.

He showed the right ones to Noel Gay, who shared his optimistic outlook on life as portrayed in song. Gay's tunes were real whistlers ('Leaning on a Lamp-post', 'The King's Horses', 'The Lambeth Walk') and together they celebrated the out-doors with 'Round the Marble Arch' and 'Run Rabbit Run'.

Bud Flanagan wrote about the open air as well. His real name was Weintrop and he'd been born in Russia. He once walked from Barnet to Glasgow for a job in a revue. Someone threw a meat-pie at him during a twenties show – but it missed and the gravy ran down the cinema screen behind him. He let undergrads pull him off stage and into their theatre box in order to de-bag him. But he accepted all this because he saw himself as a public servant.

Chesney Allen, very dapper, was his partner and they appeared on the halls and in films as a couple of genial tramps – thirties hippies – singing of their nomadic life spent sleeping 'Underneath the Arches', wandering the countryside and admiring the rainbow with its divine colour harmonies. All of this was 'free', and at the end of the record Flanagan breaks the spell with a pun: 'Free? Free! Four! Oi!!'. This was Variety, taking your emotions for a switch-back ride.

When war broke out in 1939 switch-backing was out. Pop was told to grow up and become responsible. Pop was to take its place in society. *Don't you know there's a war on?* But in 1939 the war was 'phoney', or so it seemed. The rude awakening came one night when Flanagan and Allen were singing Butler and Gay's 'Run Rabbit Run' at a London theatre. The lyric was pure Butler-land: it's Friday and the farmers are out in the fields banging at rabbits for rabbit-pie.

But the song had a current affairs meaning too – for a German bomber had just recently dropped a bomb somewhere in the Shetland Islands killing one rabbit. And Bud Flanagan was waving the corpse as he sang 'Run Rabbit Run'. Suddenly a voice from the stalls interrupted loud and clear with 'RUBBISH! YOU'LL SOON FIND THAT HITLER WILL DO MORE DAMAGE THAN KILL RABBITS WITH HIS BOMBS!!'

Naturalization

I am on dangerous ground in the People's War. They say 'McNamara's Band' wafts them back to boot polish and blanco in a Scotch barrack room, that 'Sierra Sue' is the Blitz; they say we sang this, no we didn't, we sang that, and *you* can stay out of it because *you* weren't in it, but I *was* – born 10 July 1941 and first-remembered tune 'I Do Like to be Beside the Seaside'. So from now on this story will become increasingly vague and personal.

1939. Another war, another demand for stuff like 'When We've Wound Up the Watch on the Rhine'. Current affairs in pop! But no. 'Run Rabbit Run' was one casualty in the head-on crash with reality. Others were 'God Bless You Mr Chamberlain' and 'We're Going to Hang Out the Washing on the Siegfried Line'. Neither were there many songs for the march because this was the first all-mechanized war. Nor were there 'bird's eye view' songs except for 'There'll Always be an England', our answer to 'God Bless America'.

A job to be done jiffily, without heroics and with home on the front line; a series of anecdotes. War songs there weren't but songs there were and they came from anywhere, mostly full of solace or jolly: 'Lili Marlene' from Germany, and 'Roll out the Barrel' from Czechoslovakia – both *the* big war hits. Plenty of singing as well – not careful crooning but full-throated and all together. In the factories girls sang along to *Music While You Work*, BBC radio's twice-daily instrumental programme, and in the intervals they made their own concerts of work songs, just as nineteenth-century slaves had done on chain gangs and plantations in the old South. For 'Day Of Jubilo' or 'John Henry' substitute 'I've Got

185

Sixpence' or 'That Lovely Weekend'. Down in the air-raid shelters sing-songs were the order of the day, but rarely were the works of Cole Porter and the other song-jewellers heard. Too complex, too clever, too flip, too singular. Instead it was 'Hey Little Hen!', 'She'll Be Coming Round the Mountain', 'Down Forget-Me-Not Lane' – just right to boost morale. Round War Office corridors boomed war leader Winston Churchill's version of 'Roll out the Barrel' if things were going well, but during the dark days of 1940, when Britain stood alone with her back to the wall, he stuck grimly to 'Keep Right on to the End of the Road'.

So everyone mucked in and pulled together. Railings came down, dance pumps were put away, Churchill wore a siren suit and Mayfair went up the spout, distasteful. The People's War was the climax of pre-war togetherness, the whole Gang alone against the Axis. In 1940 Jack Buchanan found himself stranded on the road with a failed show called *Top Hat and Tails*, but it wasn't long before he was out entertaining the troops, together with Gracie Fields and George Formby (first entertainer into France, armed with ukulele and dartboard). On the screen Old Mother Riley visited war workers and tracked down food racketeers; Flanagan and Allen beat up Goebbels, winged over Germany in a bomber squadron, singing choruses of 'Flying through the Rain' over their cockpit radio, with which crews joined in. Over the air waves as well came the reassuring voice of Vera Lynn (the Forces Sweetheart), clear and bell-like and without the trace of an American accent, singing requests and passing messages between separated couples. It was common knowledge that she darned her husband's socks backstage.

Dance halls were full to capacity, servicemen with hobnail boots bashing the parquet and civilians no longer having to dress up in best clothes and dance pumps. Informality and more simple community dances – the conga (a snakey line, hands on hips of the person in front, guided by a leader upstairs and downstairs and in and out the toilets), the hokey cokey (a sort of ring-shout done to the indoor field-holler of 'Oh! the hokey cokey! That's what it's all about!') And the RAF's 'Do You Know the Muffin Man' dance (all over the mess, with tankards of ale balanced on your head).

A woman I know was dancing with a GI in 1944 when he dropped his clutch, shook his head and said, 'The trouble with you Limeys is you don't know how to reeelaxaayvouz!!' The Americans were here, and with them athletic jitterbug dancing, boogie-woogie and millions of Glenn Miller records. To many local girls they looked more appetizing than our servicemen; a typical fraternizer was a Shrewsbury dance-hall girl who with her mid-Atlantic twang, mouth full of gum, and sweaters three sizes too small was quickly dubbed 'Yankee Dot'. Traditionally, jealous local males muttered that the Yanks were 'over-fed, over-sexed and over-here'.

After Victory in 1945 the Team broke up, the Labour Party took over. Belts were tightened a few more notches – had we really *won* the war? – but mass entertainment enjoyed a short boom. Alas! just an Indian summer before grim winter, followed suddenly by a strange spring of *rock 'n' roll*, 1955 (at last, modern times).

Only ten years and everything was topsy-turvy, ass over tit! Gone was the old crowd of the golden years – the silly asses in top hat and tails, with their laughing gels; the palais millions, the mums and dads and lads and lassies. Gone, at any rate, from the centre of our stage. Gone home?

After Victory, it had been prophesied, things would return to what they used to be, pre-war. Pre-war! Word drenched in betterness; better quality EVERYTHING in those days. Even the late war itself sounded better (Winston Churchill re-recorded his war-time broadcasts for the new LP market), felt warm – looked back at from frigid Austerity Britain. And if you looked back, as a senior citizen, from Rock 'n' Roll, '55, or from Beatles, '63, or from Pot-Pop '70, war and pre-war increasingly appeared glorious, glamorous and gone.

'Peace is declared' wrote novelist Angela Thirkell, on behalf of the upper middle classes, which included the Mayfair tails set, patrons of the big society dance bands. Mayfairers now beat a retreat from socialist levelling into walled county estates, ringed with signs reading 'Trespassers Will be Prosecuted'. There they could continue to dress for dinner, to dress madly, to be colourful, far from drab everyday Britain where everybody read *Everybody's*

187

and 'progressive' *Picture Post* (crammed with ads showing model girls looking like Princess Elizabeth – and she who looked like any old shop-girl!).

Those few Mayfairers remaining Up West, looking a bit soggy, had to be content now to follow trends, not set them. 'Common types', lavishly dressed, filled the old West End night haunts. For example, 'spivs' and 'wide boys', younger cousins of the thirties razor gang louts, with beautifully manicured fingernails, neat pin-striped gangster suits and snap-brim hats. Very elegant, very well-stocked with nylons, etc., and the latest US records. 'Psssst! Wan' the very latest Frankie Sinatra, wanna Frankie Laine, Dinah Shore, Teresa Brewer, Phil Harris, Doris Day, Rosemary Clooney?'

Of course, this was the age of the singer, and especially the ballad belter, feverish: Frankie Laine and Johnnie Ray. Pretty soon you could obtain all these artists easily on British-pressed 78s, from any high-street shop. The lights were on again; there was hope and it was blowing hot from across the Atlantic. During this hiatus period we had a fine collection of home-grown crooners and croonettes, very good likenesses indeed and hard at work recording their own versions of the current US hits. We had Lita Roza, Dickie Valentine, Alma Cogan, Ronnie Hilton, Tony Brent, Joan Regan, Dennis Lotis.

We had others who fitted no especial category, but filled a bill nicely, pleasing all ages: Anne Shelton (clear diction, English accent, stentorian voice); David Whitfield (the ex-bricklayer with an operatic voice); Eddie Calvert (the Man with the Golden Trumpet); Ronnie Ronalde (whistler); Winifred Atwell and Her Other Piano. Like all true variety artistes, these sat isolated in their poster compartments. Without roots, on shifting whispering sands. Without the hard rock of rock 'n' roll.

I bought their records. They helped form me. Although I am a rocker I can't truthfully say that I discovered pop via rock 'n' roll, and that all this earlier stuff was 'moon-june crap' of the 'Palais Age'. I was only nine but I was saying 'See the pyramids along the Nile', asking my love to 'Answer Me', telling my friends, 'Enjoy Yourself it's later than you think', narrating the story of the 'Night the Floor Fell In' (runner-up in the 1951 'Write a Tune' contest, and recorded by Billy Cotton and His Band, vocal by Alan Breeze), whistling 'I'm in Favour of Friendship' (The Five Smith Bros.) and marching around the gym shouting 'Somewhere at the End of the Rainbow' (Dick James and the Stargazers, with Malcolm Lockyer and the Barnstormers).

It was a particularly rich time for easy-to-sing tunes. Our comb and paper band at school did well with 'Shrimp Boats is a Comin'', 'Bimbo Bimbo What Ya Gonna Dooeeo?', and 'Where Will the Dimple Be?' Was I worried that these songs didn't reflect my youthful desires? I don't think so.

Music hall was hanging on, getting seedier and grimier. Gracie Fields had gone abroad, and on record restricted herself to songs of a motherly nature, forgetting her earlier brazen, elbowing comedy. George Formby was no longer top of the box office (though in Russia he was second only to Stalin in popularity, and awarded the Order of Lenin). He turned up in the South, in a West End musical, very tidy and very mundane. When he did sing the old naughty songs he exuded the charm of nostalgia: quaint old thirties, northern dole-land, ladies' knickers and loony bins! You could take the whole family *then* but *now*, in the late 40s/early 50s what with all these strip shows and nudie shows and that everlasting tour 'Soldiers in Skirts' (rudely known in the trade as 'Pouffs on Parade') it was all getting too rude. And the comedians, last bastions against American domination, were still going on about the war. Frank Randle, funniest comedian ever, was still filming the Service Farce in 1953.

Dance halls were becoming dangerous places in the early fifties. After the war, in the short boom, even our little Shrewsbury hall had been visited by such name bands as Victor Silvester and Sid Phillips. But now there was only a tiny local band defending themselves against a horde of newcomers – what the older regulars, who took their dancing seriously, termed 'the rough element'. Maybe a mighty dance band of fifteen or so could have fought back and won, but these were few and far between, most of the society bandleaders having entered safer branches of show-business. (Roy Fox and Jack Payne were agents, Ambrose a manager and talent-spotter, Jack Hylton an impresario.) Only for irregular special occasions did they gather a large orchestra together: a hunt ball, a deb party.

So the newcomers had it easy, not only in Shrewsbury but all over the country. Drummers had their bow-ties ripped off, sticks snapped, skins broken. Double basses were razor-slashed. Windows, basins, lavatory bowls were broken. Soon this rough element had a name, *Teddy Boys*, because many of them wore a distinctive costume of long drape jacket (velvet lapelled), drain-pipe trousers, pointed black shoes and thus looked a little like the 'toffs' of Edwardian times. However, the Teds (originally a few working-class lads from South London) certainly didn't sing 'I'm Gilbert the Filbert the Knut with the "K"' or selections from *The Gaiety Girl*, or swill champagne and that. No – they had little to do with England, Edwardian or any time. but they had lots to do with Hollywood, America, especially her B Picture Western country. Horseface Harold – today a regular army sergeant, in 1950 a Ted – told me recently that Teddy style was inspired by city-slicker cowboy movie 'baddies': black greasy hair, long sideburns, frock coat, 'bolo' string tie (called 'bootlace' over here), pointed cowboy boots.

As yet they had no theme music, nothing hard enough for them – except the occasional hillbilly beat record like Tennessee Ernie's 'Shotgun Boogie' with revolver shot snare and masturbating boogie beat, or 'Kiss Me Big' with bash sex lines like:

> When our lips meet just under mah nose
> Don't turn me loose till it curls mah toes.

and

> I wanna be kissed, I wanna be grabbed
> I wanna stand and quiver like I've been stabbed.

The girls were better served. They had Johnnie Ray, and they loved to lie all day in the upstairs bedroom of the terraced house, on their bed, on their eiderdown, eyes down, dreaming to 'Cry'. Some wore bits of cinema carpet (upon which Ray had trodden) round their neck. All British girls, too. And when there

190

wasn't a Ray around to pull bits of clothing off they found substi-
tutes locally. So it came to be that meek, law-abiding crooners
were chased across dance halls by teenage girls, their stiletto heels
taking great chunks out of the parquet. Dennis Lotis, virile pipe-
smoking crooner from the colonies, became the rope in a tug-of-
war on stage between girl fans and the boys in the Ted Heath band.
Local jazzman Johnny Dankworth was mistaken for Sinatra and
badly mobbed. 'Silly cows' commented our man in the street. So
far it was only silly cows involved.

Denmark St was amused but not unduly worried. 'Good music
and melody will return' vouched Harry ('Sally') Leon, with twenty-
one hits in thirty years and his latest 'You Must Have Heartaches
when You Fall in Love or You Haven't Got a Heart at All'. Ben
Nisbet of Feldman's thought that Johnnie Ray must be a parody
crooner act, not as funny as Tony Hancock's 'Mr Rhythm' sketch
which went something like: 'And now I'd like to do you a lil
toon, a toon we recorded over here and would like to bring to you
over here from over there to over here, our latest record which
would have been a hit but they forgot to put a hole in the middle!!'
Ha! Ha! Ha! It was an old tradition: Frank Randle had travestied
the jitterbug; Gracie Fields and George Formby had sent up
Yankee accents, but a fat lot of good had it done! Ha! Ha! Ha!
What was to come was no laughing matter. Young England,
unprotected by Ralph Reader and his Gang Show, was waiting. In
the winter of 1954 a weird clickety-clickety record was the thrill
of teenage parties, 'Shake Rattle and Roll' by Bill Haley and his
Comets. Then a tough pic called *Blackboard Jungle* featured 'Rock
around the Clock' (again by Haley and the Comets) behind the
opening credits. I bought 'Rock around the Clock' the same day
I bought a LP of the Original Dixieland Jazz Band. Both were
transporting. But *rock 'n' roll* was a magical phrase. Mysteriously,
minorities from all classes, all walks of life (but all young) linked
up to love rock 'n' roll.

In March 1955, around midnight, I wrote in the snow on the
lawn in front of my school: 'ROCK 'N' ROLL IS HERE
TO STAY'. That very same month a demand appeared in green

191

paint on the wall of the ancient Shire Hall, Taunton, Somerset:
'WE WANT BILL HALEY'. Well, we got it. The gleaming
future – far, far from austerity, and far, far, far, far from pre-war.

Gleaming future, lure of America – of old musics for new pur-
poses. That's what pop is all about, and always will be. Que Sera
Serock. I'd lived in Adventureland, USA, for years. Ages ago
I'd gone down the road and away from the oppressiveness of
fifties' life with its galoshes, and trousers riding up fat legs, my
headmaster saying, 'You must give up childish things and prepare
to take your place in our society.' I remember the *Daily Sketch*
had a depressing centre-spread of a beach-girl smiling in a
two-piece bathing costume, and underneath the caption: IT'S
WEDNESDAY AND ALREADY WE'RE HALFWAY
THROUGH THE WEEK SO CHEER UP! I remember
being driven through empty high streets on Saturday afternoons
and passing bunches of youths in freeze-shot on corners, waiting
for something to happen, for animation. Weekends could be
bleak, but I discovered the blues on a record in Seaford. In that
other country I knew all the words of 'Never Trust a Woman' by
age ten, and a garbled version of 'Shotgun Boogie': 'she had a
sixteen gage shoked darn lakka raffle . . . I assed her what she got
she said a foss score tin . . .' I could have sworn that at one stage
in 'Twelfth Street Rag' leader Pee Wee Hunt ordered the band
'Put Your Doowackers on!' The credits, in brackets under the
title, said 'Bowman' as composer and I had a teacher called
Bowman. The music was supported by the pictures or both or vice
versa. It was all the same. On TV Johnny Mack Brown, dressed in
buckskin, was plagued by the Mystery Riders, who sang as they
rode 'We're shadows we come from nowhere' . . . Depression hit
like a wet kipper in the face as I stepped outside afterwards. Pine
trees in Surrey looked like cowboy country but weren't. I changed
my nationality to Canadian, then Red Indian. I told friends to call
me Zane. Life improved. Then there was the blue jean problem,
and you have to be a certain age to remember this: jeans were impossible to get hold of so I simulated a pair by turning up the
bottoms of my pyjamas. More difficult was to actually *look*
American: our faces seemed all over the shop compared with

theirs, scientifically built. This was due to better food, I was told . . .

Anyway, to cut a long story short: rock 'n' roll made fantasy into reality.

Rock 'n' roll hit us in our sleep, suddenly. Rock 'n' roll came to us fully armed 'like Minerva springing from the head of Jove', as Jack Good put it later. Rock 'n' roll came trailing no stormy background. It was Rockabilly without rednecks, R & B without ghettoes. A bundle of purple music for leaden Britain.

From ragtime to rock, a friendly invasion. Over 40 years of peaceful penetration.

Part Four
Our Time

The Road
to Rock

For me, as the writer of this book, it's very convenient to divide up my material into decades – twenties, thirties, forties – as if they had personalities of their own. It's not so very artificial because on New Year's Eve of the new decade people are aware that they're turning over a slab of time and that they're either going to get into change or resist it.

A new World War, which America entered in 1941, coupled with a new decade to make for feeling of Big Change. The music of the golden thirties – 'good music' era of the well-made song with wit and grace, of the creamy big band – lingered on but was still the music of the thirties. Good old days.

But that was *feeling*. In fact, and maybe curiously, a number of changes took place in pop music from 1940–46 which were eventually to revolutionize it and eventually bring in the barbarians: rock 'n' roll, kids and chaos, modern times.

Here are the changes: the B M I – A S C A P war, the renaissance of the record, the appearance of independent record companies, the fall of the big band, the rise of the solo singer, the start of teen frenzy, the spread of hillbilly music. The end of the old Tin Pan Alley.

Now, details: a new war and where were the go-get-'em songs like those of 1917–18 when Alleymen fought the Allemands? It wasn't tackled in the same way because there was no longer a vulgar Alley with windows open on a hot day letting out the jangle of a hundred pounded pianos. The Alley was now 'composers' and 'authors', members of the A S C A P 'country club' and creators of civilized music. Their war contribution consisted of things like

197

'Serenade In Blue', 'The White Cliffs of Dover' and the occasional war song but wit-edged not straight-punched: 'Praise the Lord and Pass the Ammunition'.

Instead the war spirit was fostered by musicians on the fringe of pop – hillbillies who were carrying on the old Alley tradition. Record distributors reported huge sales of Bob Wills's 'White Cross in Okinawa', Roy Acuff's 'Cowards over Pearl Harbor' and Elton Britt's 'There's a Star Spangled Banner Waving Somewhere'.

Surely, thought sophisticated Broadway writers over a highball, this hillbilly stuff was mainly comedy – done by hicks in overalls sucking straws, hee-hawing and dropping store-bought teeth from their mouths for a quick laugh? It *did* have its romantic side and Bing, the old crooner, did ride a western trend in the thirties – 'Empty Saddles in the Old Corral', 'The Last Round-Up' and so on. Of course, *der Bingle* was as much a real cow-poke as the guys in New York who penned such songs. As much a real mountain william as Gene Autry or Tex Ritter, singing stars of B Picture Western movies. Hadn't Cole Porter joked the whole trend out of existence with his lynching song 'Miss Otis Regrets'? And Rodgers and Hart with their 'Way out West on Western Avenue'? To say nothing of Johnny Mercer's story of the fake cowboy in 'I'm an Old Cowhand':

> I know all the songs that the cowboys know
> 'Bout the big corral where the dogies go
> 'Cos I learned them all from the radio
> Yippee Ki O Ki Ay.

During the war millions more people were exposed to the real McCoy hillbilly music and they found that they liked it. Perhaps because its simple foursquare sentiments and tunes were a breath of fresh air after the perfumed thirties songs. In war-time you get down to fundamentals and hillbilly kept it all close to the earth. Even *Time* magazine noticed that there was a 'Bull Market in Corn' (October 1943). How did it spread? Mainly through war migrations. Through people. A two-way traffic was operating: southerners were moving north to work in defence plants and bringing their home music demands with them (Detroit juke operators reported in 1943 that hillbilly records were easily the most popular). And northerners, stationed in Dixie army camps, were bombarded with rural sounds (from 'Grand Ole Opry' radio show tours, from over 600 hillbilly stations).

On the ocean, on troopships country boys found an intrigued new audience for the good ole songs: Ferlin Husky, later a country star, entertained his merchant marine mates with the guitar songs he'd previously sung to kith, kin and neighbours at fish fries and pie suppers and church socials. 'Some of the most enthusiastic people were those who came from parts of the country where this kind of music was almost unknown,' said Husky. In Europe the American Forces Network Radio declared Roy Acuff, king of the hillbillies, to be more popular than Frank Sinatra, ace swooner-crooner. And in the far, far East, at Okinawa US soldiers were charged at by Japs screaming their war-cry: TO HELL WITH ROOSEVELT, BABE RUTH AND ROY ACUFF!! AIEEEEEEE!!' 'Roy Acuff?', a New York songsmith might inquire. Roy Acuff, son of a minister/lawyer, star of the *Grand Ole Opry*. A modern mountain singer in sports clothes, supported by a band in overalls, yo-yoing and balancing his fiddle on his nose and racing straight from that foolery into the sacred, almost metaphysical 'Great Speckled Bird' (about eternal salvation after earthly travail) with tears rolling down his cheeks. Nashville, home of station WSM's *Grand Ole Opry* radio show, was fast becoming the nerve-centre of hillbilly music, and the latter was fast becoming an industry. Fred Rose, ASCAP writer, went down there and worked for WSM, wrote songs under the homey pseudonyms of Floyd and Bart, then teamed up with this Acuff to form Acuff–Rose publishing in 1942. Others followed. In 1945 *Billboard*, already listing the hillbilly hits as 'folk', prophesied about country music that '. . . when the war is over and normalcy returns it will be the field to watch'.

But hillbilly was still a fringe pop music. The centre stage was occupied by the big bands, and for those left intact by the draft the war was better than normalcy. There was a huge demand for entertainment, especially musical. Big bands bulged bigger than ever and held the top of the record charts (a new feature). Here's *Billboard*'s Top Five for 24 January 1942:

1. Chattanooga Choo Choo	*Glenn Miller*
2. Elmer's Tune	*Glenn Miller*
3. This Love of Mine	*Tommy Dorsey*
4. Blues in the Night	*Woody Herman*
5. You Made Me Love You	*Harry James*

Yet after the war there was terrible change and decay. None of the above bands were on the scene by 1947; Miller died in a war-time plane crash, but Herman, James and Dorsey had folded their original bands in late 1946, together with Benny Goodman and many others. The straighter, less jazzy bands like Lawrence Welk's and Guy Lombardo's survived (for a specialist and ageing public) but the Big Band Era, just over a decade, was finished. Why? No one is quite sure but there were lots of immediate reasons: fallen standards in the war due to lack of sidemen and plenty of all-girl orchs, a 20 per cent amusement tax, sky-high-priced bands just after the war and too many bands, the lure of domestic bliss and television, esoteric be-bop with its cult figures and weirdo Chinesey music that you couldn't dance to, Stan Kenton, the domination of the *singer*.

By the war's end the singer was in charge. Backed by the band, no longer just a team member trotting up to the mike with a smile to sing a vocal refrain at the touch of the leader's hand. Why had the vocalist taken over? First of all, he or she had always been a very popular feature of the bands. (Some said vocalists could actually make a band, and that was in the thirties.) Secondly, in the war-time rush and mass a friendly individual crooning old truths was highly prized, especially by women. Thirdly in August 1942 the American Federation of Musicians went on strike against the use of records in juke boxes and on radio stations. Canned music was an 'anaemic substitute for real live music' and records were 'music monsters' and the 'Number One Scab of the business,' said AFM chief James Petrillo. For two years no bands recorded, but singers weren't covered by this union and they made records with just vocal accompaniment. The records sold very well indeed and by the time the bands came back to the studios the singers were in charge.

They also ruled the radio air waves. From February 1943 till the start of 1945 Frank Sinatra, ex-band singer, was to be heard on the radio show *Lucky Strike Hit Parade* breathing ballads softly, a great change from the brassy fast bands which had previously dominated. Sinatra was the most celebrated, the most *sensational* of the solo singers.

'The Voice' reminded a girl of the guy away from her arms in Europe somewhere, and it coaxed 'have yourself a merry little Christmas' (in one long croon) despite the war and all. But he was more than just a radio voice, or an ex-band singer, another crooner. He was a public figure, a skinny, hollow-cheeked person almost hidden by the mike stand – just the bow-tie and shoes sticking out – singing for her alone in the packed Paramount Theatre. Girls were 'swooning' (medieval word for 'faint', revitalized) left, right, and centre, some were screaming, some were answering the words of his ballads, most were in a shivery hush. Detractors – male – jeered that he was 'a fugitive from a blood transfusion'. The guy wasn't even conventionally handsome, like, say, Cary Grant. Now, Crosby was a *regular joe*. He liked sports, and loud sports clothes; he kept horses and he played golf; and he sang *friendly-like*. He could regularize any song. But Sinatra. Well, he called himself *Sinatra*. Italian and proud of it: 'I'm just a kid from Hoboken,' he liked saying, not trying to anglicize up like so many entertainers had done in the past.

He was both traditional and prophetic, emerging from 'good music era' classicism but presaging, in some ways, 'rock age romanticism' – sudden fire and bluntness = great honesty.

Like all crooners he'd listened to and digested the casual artistry of Crosby, and he'd graduated from the cross-country college of band tours – learning team-work, voice discipline, how to work a mike, how to work a room, how to milk maximum drama from a ballad. Those in the know appreciated him – a singer's singer – and rewarded him: *Metronome*, a discerning trade paper, voted him Best Singer of 1942.

In September of that year he'd left the umbrella of Tommy

Our Time

Dorsey's band to strike out alone. On New Year's Eve he was but an added attraction, at New York's Paramount Theatre, on a bill headed by Benny Goodman, the old King of Swing himself, the man who'd set the hep-cats jiving in the aisles back in the thirties. The solo singer stole the show and was retained for eight weeks, breaking the attendance record set by Rudy Vallée in 1924. 'Swoonatra'-ism began. Soon there were 'Sinatraddicts', adolescent bobby-soxers who wrote to him in lipstick: 'I love you so bad it hurts. Do you think I should see a doctor?'

Fan fever: a bishop knocked down in a teen charge towards the singer; the singer almost strangled by two girls who pulled at opposite ends of his bow-tie. Fan fever for a popular singer, not a film star. *Novel.* His cigarette butts, his un-eaten cornflakes became highly-prized items. So did locks of his hair, often plucked from his very head. The hysteria was compared to the Children's Crusade of the Middle Ages.

Curiously, the lyrics of his well-made New York–Hollywood songs were taken in deadly earnest by the fans. 'I'll walk alone,' sang Sinatra, breathing well and correctly. 'I'll walk with you!!!!' – a cry winging across from the back stalls. 'Nobody loves me,' got the quick reply 'Are you kiddin' Frankie!!!!' Sometimes the singer would bust out of his song prison: 'this has too many words' he muttered right in the middle of his air version of Cole Porter's 'Don't Fence Me In'.

'Have you got that new Sinatra song?' asked the girl at the record counter. Not the name of the song necessarily (always the practice in the past, in the Alley days). But, even so, Sinatra's songs were pretty classy. He wouldn't sing that hillbilly nonsense 'Pistol Packin' Mama'; he made out magnificently on Jerome Kern's 'Ol' Man River' – old pros were amazed – but effected a small change: the word 'darky' he excised because he thought it offensive. Was this his idea or that of his press-agent's? Trade people had admired, or envied, 'Swoonatra-ism' and *Billboard* in 1943 had awarded his press agent with a scroll for 'The Most Effective Promotion of a Single Personality'. But the crooner went on to talk publicly on such non-show-biz subjects as racial and religious intolerance, truth, Lincoln, the Paris Peace Conference.

Was this due to press-agentry? Wasn't this a bit out-of-line? The crooner was *involved* in everything he did. This was new, different, weird. He delivered this statement, heralding pop commitment: 'I get an audience involved because I'm involved myself – if the song is a lament at the loss of love, I get an ache in my gut . . . I cry out the loneliness . . . Sentimentality, after all, is an emotion common to all humanity.' When he sang he believed he was honest and when he talked he used words such as 'broads' and 'endsville'. He wore drape suits, pegged pants, bulky sweaters.*

To the teenagers (and his average fan was small-town female, aged fourteen) he was for real, easy to identify with. 'I think he is one of the greatest things that ever happened to teen age America,' ran a girl's entry in a 'Why I Like Sinatra' contest, organized by a Detroit radio station. 'We were kids that never got much attention, but he's made us feel like we're something. He has given us understanding. Something we need. Most adults think we don't need any consideration. We're really human and Frank realizes that. He has given us *sincerity* in return for our *faithfulness*.'†

Just a few years and faithfulness was being heaped on another: a barrel-voiced singer – a 'working stiff' *guy* belter, not a frail crooner – resembling Clark Kent (before he strips to become Superman). He actually wore glasses on stage and persuaded fellow artiste Patti Page to do the same. You had to smash all your Sinatra records in order to join his fan club. 'The Lainettes' spoke everything in unison. In the thirties, as Frankie Lo Vecchio, he'd been advised by bandleader Ted Weems: 'You got a ton of style, kid – but not for ballads.' In 1946, as Frankie Laine he sold two million records of a torchy ballad he'd picked up in a piano bar, 'That's My Desire'. Next year the assembled Disc Jockeys of America voted him 'Most Promising Newcomer', and one of them described him as having 'the virility of a hairy goat and the delicacy of a white flower petal – and BROTHER when

---

*The only detail that made him appear unlike other kids was that he carried his own public address system from date to date.

†Quoted in E. J. Kahn's book *The Voice*. Most of the material I've used on Sinatra comes from this informative book.

you got that you better believe you're IN and I mean but IN!!!'

Laine sold Emotion ('and spell that, please, with a capital E', he asked), barnstorming his way like a melodrama actor through a big country of material. He sang of 'Jezebel', the devil woman without horns; of the travelling salesman they called 'The Rock of Gibraltar' – he even sang 'On the Road to Mandalay' and of 'Roses in Picardy'. He was the rip-roaring westerner of 'Mule Train', the hillbilly of 'Your Cheatin' Heart' and the fundamentalist preacher of 'I Believe' and 'Answer Me, Lord Above'. Words were like T-Bone steak to him, a hungry man; he tore and gnawed, adding dashes of 'h's to 'and's, taking audible breaths, trailing his voice downhill at the end of a phrase attack.

So did Johnnie Ray, but he looked less stable, quivering, sobbing, crying and finally collapsing on the floor – carried away by the emotional content of his smash, slightly old-timey ballad 'Cry' (1951). Ray was no chromium-plated crooner, he really did look like he was suffering for the world and his deaf-aid was perfectly visible. What if he did hit the occasional bum note? The feel was there always. All over the world girls went ape for him, ripping off his suits and mauling this martyr from Oregon, this half-Blackfoot Indian who spoke up for his black mentors (Bessie Smith, Mahalia Jackson, Lavern Baker) and made it quite clear that he believed in God.

For those needing a relaxayvoo from frenzy there was the balm of girl singers: Dinah Shore, Patti Page, Jo Stafford, Doris Day, Rosemary Clooney. Amongst the boys Nat King Cole, with his hickory-smoked voice, was perhaps the most perfect, but he was exceptional in another way because he wasn't of Italian descent. The Italian–Americans dominated this period: apart from Sinatra and Laine there was Perry Como, Mario Lanza, Tony Bennett, Dean Martin, Vic Damone and Al Martino. Of course, they all still remain fully booked, very popular, but why they should have been so prominent at this time is not clear. Yes, Valentino's popularity in the twenties started the Latin trend. Then there was Russ Colombo, crooner rival to Crosby, in the thirties. And they do say that some of the forties Italian–Americans were helped by friendly countrymen, owners of important night clubs, but even if that's true it wouldn't explain why audiences voluntarily took to them. Maybe in and after the war, Americans needed their sunny, bracing lyricism. Also, they had hearty voices and were able to embrace all manner of material.

This was necessary for pop music was becoming a sort of supermarket of songs. Many had been imported from faraway places. From real Paree came 'C'est Si Bon', from real London town came 'I've Got a Lovely Bunch of Coconuts', from real Hawaii came 'Now is the Hour', from real Mexico came 'Cuanto le Gusta', from brand new Israel came 'Tzena Tzena Tzena'. Fewer exotic songs written from cubbyholes in publishing offices deep in New York. Songs about Dixie written by Dixiemen – non-members of the Alley hailing from that middle America which lay somewhere between Lindy's restaurant in New York and the Brown Derby restaurant in Hollywood . . . An actual Tennessean called Pee Wee King wrote 'The Tennessee Waltz', smash by Patti Page, 'The Singing Rage'. An actual hillbilly called Hank Williams wrote 'Jambalaya, on the Bayou', smash by Jo Stafford. There was the avant-garde 'Nature Boy', by a fruit-juice drinking, desert living, long-haired, sandled nature boy called eden ahbez, smash by Nat King Cole. Believe it or not, an honest-to-God *ex*-murderer nick-named Leadbelly (real name: Huddie Ledbetter) was composer/lyricist of 'Goodnight Irene' – smash by The Weavers.

Pop looted the past too, as if aware of hiatus. King of relaxay-voo, Perry Como, fond of gardening and pipe-collecting, was a specialist in revivals (amongst them were 'Lady of Spain', which my uncle wrote together with Bob Hargreaves and Tolchard Evans in 1931, and 1909's 'I Wonder Who's Kissing Her Now?'). Good ole jazz (in its pre-bebop, pre-mechanized swing era when the music was gleeful and outward bound) was successfully remembered by Pee Wee Hunt in 'Twelfth Street Rag' and bubbly Teresa Brewer and the Dixieland All-Stars on 'Music! Music! Music!'. It was simple memory time – 'Dearie, do you remember when . . . ?', 'Give me that old soft shoe . . .', 'I wanna hear it again . . . that old piano roll blues' – for simple melodies and Irving Berlin's 1914 'Play a Simple Melody' was a hit again in 1950.

The remains of the Alley were to be found embattled up in the Brill Building, on 49th and Broadway – watching from their up-town hide-out the strange things happening in the vast world around them. A lucky few had escaped the frightful hurly-burly of instant pop by getting into the safe backwoods of movies and theatre. There they could live at peace amongst grand pianos and crab cocktails dreaming of those literate days before the war.

For war hadn't only taken place in the outer world. There had been a major conflict within the pop industry itself, which had resulted in the storming of the ivory castle of pop. In order to understand this revolution we must zoom back to 1939 and page 109 where we left the radio controllers lined up to do battle with the music controllers. The latter, ASCAP, were saying 'You can't do without our music, so we can charge what we like.' The radio men replying (and *maybe* bluffing) 'Yes we *can* because we'll start our own licensing society and tap other sources of music.' Broadcast Music (BMI) was formed and got to work finding material just in case the ASCAP rates, to be announced sometime before 1941, were too damned high.

1940 and the two giants busied about. At the San Francisco Fair ASCAP threw free concerts (66,000 attended) featuring their greatest writers performing their greatest hits. Announced the ASCAP President: 'There is nothing finer than a song to hang a memory on.' Then forward they came, the heroes of our story so far, magicians who could steal back remembrance of times past and set memory free by just a few notes and few words . . . Yankee Doodle Boy George M. Cohan with his 'Grand Old Flag', struggling widow Carrie Jacobs Bond with her 'End of a Perfect Day', World War One veteran Ernie Burnett with his 'Melancholy Baby', father of the blues, W. C. Handy with his 'St Louis Blues', domesticity expert Walter Donaldson with his 'My Blue Heaven', talkie kings Freed and Brown with their 'Singin' in the Rain', musical comedy master Jerome Kern with his 'Smoke Gets in

Your Eyes'. Then, finally, the real all-American pop man himself: Irving Berlin with his 'God Bless America'.

Meanwhile B M I bustled, receiving gratefully songs from writers who'd failed to make the ASCAP grade, from hillbilly writers, from boogie-woogie boys, from lawyers, mechanics, milkmen, housewives. One love ballad foxtrot was set to the tune of 'The Star-Spangled Banner'. Seventy-five staff arrangers swiftly made 400 arrangements of other non-copyright songs such as 'Jeannie with the Light Brown Hair'. The catalogue built up and then suddenly Alley pioneer publisher Ed Marks left ASCAP and rented his huge collection of oldies to BMI for a cool million. That was wonderful and other publishers were encouraged to join the rebels. But BMI encouraged new publishing ventures too, donating lump sums to go get material. Proudly BMI stated its purpose:

As a nation the United States has long been unduly modest in matters of the arts. At present we are one of the most musical nations in the world. The most vital, most original music being written today is American music. Up to the present time you have been able to hear in public, and to buy for your own use, the music of none but a comparatively small group of writers. The established publishing houses have preferred to deal only with established writers. BMI has dropped the bars and now the new men, the young men, the men you have not known can bring you their songs.

ASCAP's 1941 rates were at last announced: a hundred per cent increase. Radio refused to pay and for almost the whole of 1941 no ASCAP music was aired – none of the nation's best-loved tunes, its heritage. ASCAP tune sleuths, they said, even monitored auto horns to make sure that the toots didn't infringe on one of their copyrights.* Ray Noble swung 'Camptown Races' and generally Stephen Foster had a field day, but he was dead. There was no public outcry of 'Where are our songs?' They were struck dumb. And ASCAP came to terms.

But ASCAP warned America of the possible horrors in store for her. Here is a part of a 1946 ASCAP statement:

Time and world events have placed added obligations upon ASCAP.

*Sharkey, the musical seal, had his radio career cut short, as he only knew one tune and that was an ASCAP one.

Our Time

The struggle in ideologies that we see everywhere throughout the world today is the struggle of the group against the individual. Democracies are the last bulwark of the ego, the last opportunity for man to express himself as 'I'; the last chance of freedom ...

Mechanical advancement is useless if it destroys our world-perception and cuts our link to the infinite. We must look beyond the machine to a broader field of living ...

Years rolled by and veteran songwriters sighed as they looked out on a rapidly changing scene: now a whole bunch of Latin-American numbers – 'Amapola', 'Maria Elena', 'Frenesi', etc. – now a whole lot of hillbilly numbers – 'I Love You So Much it Hurts', 'Hey Good Lookin' ', 'Your Cheatin' Heart'. Kids screaming (it said so in the paper) and disc-jockeys *conducting* them, coaxing them day in day out on the ubiquitous radio. Even the wife was house-cleaning to a little portable radio. The children carried them around to parties, to the beach, all along the street. Half the 'songs' you couldn't even get in sheet music because these amateurs – milk-truck drivers, school teachers, cowboys, etc. – made them up as they went along. They certainly knew nothing about minor sevenths and modulations. The *New York Times* of 28 July 1957 reported that Hank Williams, the hillbilly writer, actually threw a song away if he didn't complete the thing in a half hour. Sometimes you could get a lead sheet and what a sheet! 'Peggy Sue' (by some Texan called Buddy Holly) was only fifteen short lines with her name repeated eighteen times. See, the broadcasters were maybe searching the arm-pits and orifices of America for cheap music to fill their air and keep our expensive good music off. YES! Perhaps BMI pull a big switch which WWWRRRRRRRR turns on great cycles of music. They and the broadcasters and record companies are involved in a monstrous conspiracy to brainwash the nation with *bad sounds* not good, literate *songs*.

Latin-American cycle, hillbilly cycle, rhythm and blues cycle (perfectly natural among coloured people) and now, in the mid fifties, a new sound from under the sun. A brutal, ugly, degenerate, vicious form that fosters a negative and destructive reaction particularly in young people. A rancid aphrodisiac, a vile mixture of all the cycles: ROCK 'N' ROLL. Our vital, organistic living culture (that many of us came over on cattle boats from Europe to build) subverted by –

> Oh boy, oh boy,
> Gettin' me some love tonight.
> Oh boy oh boy oh boy,
> Gonna have me some fun tonight.
> Are you ready? (No no no no)
> Are you ready? (No no no no)
> Are you ready? (No no no no)
> Are you ready? (No no no no)
> Are you ready? (Yes yes)
> Here I come . . .

From 1953 the songmen had tried to do away with this 'conspiracy'. In that year their pressure group the 'Songwriters of America' had filed an anti-trust action accusing BMI of conspiring 'to dominate and control the market for the use and exploitation of musical compositions'. In 1956 there was an investigation by the Anti-Trust Subcommittee of the House Judiciary Committee at which was heard this statement by songwriter Billy Rose ('You've Got To See Momma Every Night', 'Happy Days and Lonely Nights', 'Cooking Breakfast for the One I Love', 'I Got a Code id by Dose'):

Not only are most of the BMI songs junk, but in many cases they are obscene junk pretty much on a level with dirty comic magazines . . . It is the current climate on radio and TV which makes Elvis Presley and his animal posturings possible . . .

When ASCAP's songwriters were permitted to be heard, Al Jolson, Nora Bayes and Eddie Cantor were all big salesmen of songs. Today it is a set of untalented twitchers and twisters whose appeal is largely to the zootsuiter and the juvenile delinquent.

In 1957 the songmen were again in Washington, this time with a proposed bill to divorce the broadcasters from their music holdings. At the hearings Vance Packard, author of *The Hidden Persuaders*, put the conspiracy case:

I feel Americans are being standardized, homogenized, hypnotized and sterilized by all that is going on. I think we are, as a people, losing

209

ground in several key tenets of our American creed cherished by our founding Fathers. In particular, I think of such tenets as respect for the dignity of the individual, freedom from conformity, and freedom of choice . . .

In the process of developing and selling their own product, music, the major broadcasters have found it to their advantage to use their control of the public airways to reshape the musical tastes of Americans to suit their own commercial interests . . . The result of all this manipulation has been . . . a gross degradation in the quality of music, supplied to the public. Our airways have been flooded in recent years with whining guitarists, musical riots put to a switchblade beat, obscure lyrics about hugging, squeezing, and rocking all night long . . . The constant aim of the broadcasters is to obtain music in bulk cheaply. They are so relentless in this resolve that they would be willing, I am convinced, to drive us all back to the dark ages of music, if necessary, in order to achieve their goal. . .

But, later in the hearings, Robert Burton – a vice-president of BMI – answered these charges and explained the modern world. BMI had helped democratize pop music, he said. When he visited Nashville, now one of the music centres of America, he was 'amazed at the number of people who come up and say "Mr Burton, I am John Jones, one of your publishers," and it is exciting. A cab driver in New York the other day said "By the way, are you with BMI?" And I said "Yes". He said "I am one of your publishers." And he is.'

SENATOR POTTER: Cab drivers – I am not surprised.

ROBERT BURTON: . . . Prior to the 1940s much of the recorded music played on stations was on so-called electrical transcriptions especially made for radio broadcasting.

In the 1940s and particularly after World War Two, technological improvements in the making of phonograph records and the reproduction of sound brought about a sweeping revolution in the music publishing business and in the exploitation of music. This revolution is the *prima facie* reason for hits being able to spring up from anywhere, just depending where a particular record happens to catch the public fancy. There isn't a market in the United States today of any size that isn't a place where a song may start. It may start in Portland, Oregon. It may start in Georgia, it may start anywhere.

Non-breakable recordings, possessing high fidelity, were developed. Technological developments, principally the use of tape – and this is a highly important point – made it possible to record music almost any place in the United States, whereas in the 1940s music could only be recorded in elaborate studios, and by the use of expensive recording equipment, which was available in only a few localities.

In the forties, you had to catch an artist in New York, Chicago or California. If he was on the road playing one-nighters, there wasn't a thing you could do about it. Today I doubt there is a town of any size in this country, certainly a town that has even a 250 watt daytime station with tape, that you can't go into and record...

What we are now enjoying in the United States is a new form of publication. It is an *acoustical* type of publication.

SENATOR POTTER: That is an interesting term.

ROBERT BURTON: The invention of the printing press was the beginning of a great era in the world, and the word 'publication' historically and legally derived from the concept of disseminating copies. Back as far as 1908 the Supreme Court said if it wasn't printed it wasn't a copy. But recently two Federal courts have reflected what perhaps is a sociological fact. They have said that the dissemination of phonograph records is now a publication. So I think we have reached a new age, a new era, with a new type of publication.

The bill was dropped – none of these probings came to anything – but the upset continued. In 1959 the songmen started the 'Payola Investigations', accusing disc jockeys of accepting money from record companies in return for plugging their records. 'Payola' was a new-coined word but bribery had always been a part of the pop business. Out of 10,000 DJs working for some 5,000 stations only 255 were found guilty. Congress made a law banning payola. And rock 'n' roll steamed right ahead.

Why the upset from the old-timers. Was it money, money, money? It was a cry from the heart, not from the pocket-book.

Long-held deep beliefs of a civilized way of life were being assaulted by hillbilly songs of fightin', boozin', cheatin'; by rhythm and blues songs about gettin' loaded, wantin' a bow-legged woman and rockin' all night long. But worst of all was assault by rock 'n' roll noise, which when coherent seemed to be solely concerned with sex, violence and our own people. All those years of gradual growing away from crude ragtime and jazz towards a disciplined fine art of reticence (with maybe hints of suggestion) all wiped out by our wives and children leaping about to Chuck Berry on the phonograph!

'Maybe I'm old-fashioned but I never talk about toilet paper,' said an old songwriter, who had escaped from Poland at the dawn of the century. The upset continued but the well-made song survived. In fact ASCAP made much more money from radio and record than she'd ever made in the good old days. Here's the amazing Top Ten of the Rockin' Fifties (computed from how long each record stayed in *Billboard*'s Top Ten):

1.	Mack The Knife	*Bobby Darin*
2.	Vaya con Dios	*Les Paul & Mary Ford*
3.	Because of You	*Tony Bennett*
4.	Unchained Melody	*Al Hibbler*
5.	Melody Of Love	*Billy Vaughan*
6.	You You You	*Ames Brothers*
7.	Battle of New Orleans	*Johnny Horton*
8.	Singin' The Blues	*Guy Mitchell*
9.	Love Me Tender	*Elvis Presley*
10.	Love Letters In The Sand	*Pat Boone*

Not a rocker amongst them! Number 1 is a German song of 1929, number 5 is a 1903 copyright, number 9 is a Civil War song originally called 'Aura Lee' and written by W. Fosdick and Geo. Poulton, and number 10 dates from the thirties.

Yes, the song survived and stayed much the same as ever, dated only by lyrics. But rock 'n' roll wasn't a song. It turned out to be a walk, a talk, a time, a pair of faded jeans. Oh, *everything* – but not a song.

First of all it was a record, the 'new type publication' which had superseded the music sheet. We must now look at the renaissance of the record in order to start our journey into rock 'n' roll. This renaissance had begun, if you recall, at the end of the thirties. By 1942 sales were exceeding the best years of the jazz age, and band-leaders admitted that they'd rather have a record hit than a radio hit. At that time all these hits were produced by just three com-panies – Victor, Columbia and Decca – but from 1942 new com-panies appeared until a decade later there were well over 400. The three 'majors', based in New York, had been joined by three from the regions: Capitol and MGM in Los Angeles; Mercury in Chicago. These Big Six took care of 'overground' pop, but largely neglected race and hillbilly, leaving these 'specialities' to the hundreds of fast-growing 'independent' labels scattered all over the country, e.g., Chess in Chicago, King in Cincinnati, Peacock in Houston, Modern in Los Angeles. New York, however, held the most successful company, a comparative latecomer called Atlantic. The trade recognized that this little record scene was im-portant and *Billboard* gave the two basic music styles politer titles: 'race' became 'rhythm and blues' (R & B) and 'hillbilly' became 'country and western' (C & W). They were given their very own little hit lists and so pop became a recognized segregated scene.

Actually the two basic fringe musics needed new titles for musical reasons as well as economic ones. Since the thirties both had be-come much harder, louder, more urbanized. Millions more blacks had moved from country to city and their musicians brought the old country blues but upped it and jagged it a little, made it *nastier* (in the nicest way). The new/old urban blues was now played in big city bars by guitarists who sported glittering bejewelled guitars, all-electric. They could play them over their heads, behind their backs, and they could make plenty of noise. A relentlessly pounded off-beat supported them, with a piano chinked in treble clusters and an evil saxophone far from Rudy Vallée, making music that could cut through all the chatter, clinking, fighting. OK, it was sometimes a bit out-of-tune and there weren't too many minor sevenths and added eighths but there was plenty of naked excite-ment. Making music of another kind, then, that echoed the sound of the city, as ragtime had done years ago. Making records that trapped the excitement.

And making money. Nothing like what the majors would make, but it was a nice little market and it took only one or two hits to establish a speciality artist for years, whereas in the pop field they were so often flashes in the pan. Typical of the independent companies ('indies') was Chess of Chicago, specializing in very raw R&B made by such bluesmen as Bo Diddley, Howlin' Wolf and Muddy Waters. The rural blues transplanted to the city, electrified and shrieking. Leonard and Phil Chess were Polish Jews and were really into blues – maybe it took them back into the synagogue. Leonard turned his garage into a recording studio and there he fiddled about with bass drums trying to get more thumping bass, right through the heart. He made a crude sort of echo chamber by experimenting with a sewer pipe. He didn't know what he was doing, but he was doing it himself. Sometimes new stars just dropped in off the street to play their blues; sometimes the brothers trudged round funky clubs in search. Once in a while Leonard would pack a hefty tape machine into his auto and make a 5,000-mile swing through the South, recording bluesmen in cornfields and even in a radio station whilst a disc was spinning and the mike was free. He grilled distributors and supplied them with boxes of singles from the boot of his auto.* In Memphis, a blues centre fast rivalling Chicago, he leased a lot of blues tapes from Sam Phillips' Sun Records. An ex-disc jockey and a lawyer, Phillips had both blues *and* country in his catalogue. But he wasn't about to copy the fiddles and steel guitar shit-kickin' country coming out of nearby Nashville. He wanted to combine blues with country and one day he would. 'What I need is a white boy who can sing coloured,' he was always saying. Chess wasn't interested because his field was doing OK specializing.

The indie world was a twilight one. Some of the smaller companies were decidedly shady – in the business for a fast buck, knowledgeable on law, but shaky on music and people. Stories circulated about singers getting paid in jugs of wine, and never seeing a royalty. On the west coast an oooh-waaah-waaah harmony group with an obscure bird name had come off of a smash hit

*He watched customers buying records and noted that it was women who bought the most blues.

years ago but hadn't seen a penny in royalties. One evening the lead singer confronted the indie boss in front of his recording shack (which was right behind a railroad station). Politely he asked for the money. 'No' was the answer so the lead singer produced a sawn-off shot gun and proceeded to blow off the boss's head.

All the indies longed to get out of twilightland and grab a piece of overground pop action. In the early fifties the number one pop company was Columbia, thanks to its 'Artists and Repertoire' chief Mitch Miller. This job was as high as it sounded for now that the record was king these A & R men took over the all-powerful position previously held by Alley publishers. They chose the songs for the singers and they fixed up the orchestral accompaniments. Miller was an expert at all this, honing down his product so that the result was a beautifully machined money-making weapon. By the end of 1951 he had produced twenty-two hits. Songwriters came to him with manuscripts or, better still, demonstration discs, and they had to be prepared to have their work doctored. 'I don't think that the second eight measures should do what they do do. I think you should repeat the first eight measures where you now have a new eight-measure section,' said Miller to show-tune writer Arthur Schwartz. Schwartz took his song away with him and refused to resculpt, but that didn't worry Miller. He found a rich source of material in C & W records. As pure C & W these records didn't arouse anybody much but when Miller got his Tony Bennett to do 'Cold Cold Heart', his Jo Stafford to do 'Jambalaya – on the Bayou' and his Rosemary Clooney to do 'This Ole House' the result was hit records. Maybe the songs were originally salty stories about sin, sex and salvation, full of morality and retribution and guilt – but the Miller magic turned them into healthy pop.

An important part of his magic was the accompaniment. Not standard dance band but odd combinations making for refreshing sounds. For instance, he put French horns with Guy Mitchell, a harpsichord with Rosemary Clooney, a single guitar with Frankie Laine, a vocal group with Johnnie Ray. The song itself was just one part of a whole.

Miller was *producing* records for their own sake, and this was something new because in the past bands and singers merely reproduced in the studio what they'd been performing nightly at public appearances. Miller knew that his record must hook the radio audience from the very first grooves. It must be different, exciting, gimmicky, in order to stand out from the stream of disc-jockey fodder. And the DJ must like the record, as well.

By 1950 the DJ was Number One Big Plug, and therefore a man 'romanced' by record company promotion men. He got 'personalized' sample records and his 'pic' and 'bio' in 'jock. newspapers' specially published by the disc trade. Some people gave him gifts, such as a car, at Christmas or his birthday. If he was in a key city and he really got on a record and *rode* it ('here's a platter by her nibs Miss Georgia Gibbs – a gorgeous hunk of scenery much nicer than mountain greenery!!') chatting it in and out, maybe spinning it fifty times in succession, you might get a *spreader* and then a *national break-out* and a *hit*. This had happened spectacularly in 1947 when an obscure Carolinian jock. had ridden a 1933 record of 'Heartaches' by Ted Weems and his Band right up the charts. A few years later 'Jazzbo' Collins in Salt Lake City had done the same to Art Mooney's slack banjo singalong effort 'I'm Looking over a Four-Leaf Clover'. (This was a modern recording of a 1927 song in a quasi 1927 style.)

Jocks. had first been heard in the early thirties, the result of an economy move by small 'one-lung' stations unable to afford live bands but wishing to simulate network grandeur. Most notable jock. was Al Jarvis of KFWB, Los Angeles, who devised a programme called *Make Believe Ballroom*. For up to six hours he sat alone with his pile of self-bought records and, in a chummy voice, spun them throwing in tit-bits about the artists, some criticism and quite a few commercials. Martin Block, an associate, borrowed his idea and title when he moved to powerhouse beamer WNEW, New York, in 1935. There the show caught on big and by war's end *Make Believe Ballroom* with Martin Block was nationally famous. 'And now, ladies and gentlemen, we go to Stage 2 for the sweetest music this side of heaven' – needle poised over disc – 'I'm talking about Guy Lombardo and his Royal Canadians.'

Soon there were thousands of disc-jockey shows presenting all manner of music in all manner of voices – screamed, sung, rhymed, purred, soft-sold, hard-sold – blanketing their regions twenty-four hours a day. By 1950 it wasn't necessary to 'make believe' that the band was right there in the studio. Records were records and the very bed-rock of radio, along with chunks of news. Television attracted the top sponsors because television was now the family entertainment box. Radio changed its role, became less network and more local. Appealing to a specialist audience consisting largely of housewives, poor people, Negroes, owners of car radios, kids. So well did radio change that in 1959 there were three times as many radio sets as T V sets.

Back in the early fifties it was a gas to just take off and ride around the country digging the beam of gut sounds caught on the car radio. Specially exhilarating were the R & B stations like those around the Delta. 'Don't you worry 'bout nuttin'!' screamed Fat Daddy over a belching, squawking, chicken 'n' gumbo record, as the car pounded along Route 66. 'Hey mama – take out yo false teeth 'cos daddy wanna suck yo gums!!' In L A the beatnik wanderers jumped out the car to drink in the smell of real life in the Negro section. 'What brutal, hot, siren-whining nights they are!' wrote Jack Kerouac, chronicler of the beats, in *On The Road*.

Look! On South Main Street 'booted cops frisked people on practically every corner . . . You could smell the tea, weed, I mean marijuana, floating in the air, together with chili beans and beer. That grand wild sound of bop floated from beer parlors; it mixed medleys with every kind of cowboy and boogie woogie in the American night.' Blacks were really black, black as spades – maybe they drank snake juice. See the rich, swirling circus! Long-haired, broken-down hipsters, old desert rats, nature boys in sandals. No fixed address, just rolling along, moving on. 'Right across the street there was trouble.'*

*Also on the streets at this time was beat poet 'Denver' Rottingumm who, in a moment of mescalin truth, wrote these lines on the myth of the blackman:

> Jazzin' nigger how I love ya
> Even though ya don't exist
> When I kiss yer rockin' botty
> It's M A H cheek that's gettin' kissed.

Our Time

Well, phew! all that wasn't far from the peaceful radio set, but quite far enough. Rebels were definitely in the minority and for millions of young people, reasonably content with life, gut radio was sufficient. They danced, they sang along and they necked in the car. In that very same Los Angeles of Kerouac and danger was Hunter Hancock, a white jock. playing R & B for a black-beamed radio station – and getting tremendous reaction from 'Caucasian kids'. Distribution men were flooded with calls from excited record store owners: 'Hey baby! Your R & B discs are selling POP!' In self-defence the pop stations programmed some R & B to win back those truant kid Caucasians.

The same thing was happening with Poppa Stoppa's show in New Orleans, and Dewey Phillips's *Red Hot and Blues* in Memphis. Gene Noble's R & B show on WLAC, Nashville could be picked up in twenty-two states in the South and Midwest – almost half of the states of the Union.

However, the North was still the storm centre of pop and it was from there that rock 'n' roll came flashing from rhythm 'n' blues, conducted by DJ Alan Freed, first master of rock. Without him there would have been much big beat but no rock 'n' roll.

Rock 'n' Roll

There was something noble and tragic about Alan Freed. He had a loser look. Maybe half-breed. Frizzled hair and scarred face. His father was a Russian–Jewish immigrant and his mother of Welsh Protestant stock and he was raised a Baptist. His early ambition was to front a name band but then the war came and he developed an ear infection which left him hard of hearing. He got into radio in Ohio, in the sticks, after being turned down by the mighty CBS, New York – his Mid-West accent was too 'grating', he'd never make it as an announcer. That's what they said.

But in discovering rock 'n' roll he discovers himself. A terrible car accident, his face in shreds, they look at his fingernails and shake their heads. He pulls through and while doing so realizes that he is only a speck in the universe, but his mission is to champion rock 'n' roll. Right there in the hospital he starts broadcasting, lying on his back, rooting for the beat. 'Anyone who says rock 'n' roll is a passing fad or a flash-in-the-pan trend along the music road has *rocks in the head*, dad!' he said later. A far-seeing remark. Freed lived for rock 'n' roll and he died for her, too – destroyed by the Payola investigations of the late fifties.

His conversion to the beat had come in a flash, suddenly. One day in 1951, whilst hosting a 'good' music radio programme (i.e., Tony Bennett, Al Martino, Peggy Lee, etc.) for WJW, Cleveland, Ohio, he got an excited call from Leo Mintz. Now Mintz was the owner of Cleveland's largest record store and he told Freed to come down and just watch the kids snapping up 'specialty' records by people like Bullmoose Jackson, Peppermint Harris and Eddie 'Cleanhead' Vinson. Freed did and was so impressed that

219

right away he programmed some R & B records for the station. Encouraged by audience response he introduced a show called *Moondog's Rock and Roll Party* – nothing but solid R & B. *Moondog* was Freed in lunar disguise. *Rock and roll* because this was R & B outside of the ghetto, presented for black and white youth – and anyway perhaps 'R & B' had a slight racial stigma attached to it. Mintz and Freed built their phrase 'rock and roll' from certain key words which seemed to crop up time and again in the bouncy side of R & B. For example, *rock* me mama, my daddy *rocks* me with one steady *roll*, all she wants to do is *rock*, let the good times *roll*, good *rockin'* tonight . . .

Actually rolling and rocking wasn't the sole occupation of R & B. True, the perpetual motion was always in there – rolling along like old man river himself – but the style also included a lot of pretty (almost cloying) songs, especially favoured by close-harmony groups. A lot of cooing and slithery harmonizing and ethereal falsetto. Images of angels, dreams, chapels and moonlight. Could this be a shuffle towards the Alley?

Freed and his kids, though, preferred those R & B records that had plenty of thumping great off-beat, boogie riffs, and frog-in-throat sax. No fiddles under any circumstances. On the air Freed loved to join in with the record beat, whopping a telephone directory with his fist (protected by a golf glove) and shouting so hard he had now and then to service his voice with hot tea and honey. He started collecting fans. He started collecting poison-pen letters calling him a 'nigger lover'. Also, there were many peaceable black citizens who found 'moondog music' a bit off-colour, even dirty, and certainly unprogressive.

Freed's attackers were horrified by his abortive 'Moondog Ball' at Cleveland Arena in March 1953. 80,000 racially mixed kids turned up and there was only room for 10,000. Worse still – Cleveland was a segregated city or supposed to be. Coloured people were coming out of the woodwork! The Ball had to be cancelled but nobody asked for their money back and this was curious; they had come together to jostle, to fool around. To celebrate something. Afterwards there was talk of arresting Freed for violation of fire laws and other unnamed things. His later

Cleveland shows weren't dances but reserved-seat concerts at which teenagers saw acts hitherto confined to black audiences: Joe Turner, Fats Domino, the Drifters. By this time the majority of Freed's audience was white.

The news of Freed's success spread. In September 1954 he took up a 25,000 dollar a year job spinning R & B for WINS, a middling New York station. New York, big time city which had once turned him down; full of stations exuding soothing 'good' music. Are they ready for Moondog? Within a few months WINS was top of the radio ratings and all because of Alan Freed and his rock 'n' roll.

Anita Holland, today a California family woman, was a New Jersey teenager at the time and listening regularly to Freed's nightly show:

He started out by saying 'Hi, welcome to Alan Freed and his Moon-dog Music' (then a big howl) 'and his little moon puppies' (this was followed by yapping). He had to change the name of the kind of music because a man named Moondog (who had a record album of weird beatnik poetry music) said that the radio station stole his name. Then they started calling his show *The Big Beat* and kept referring to his music as 'rock 'n' roll' all the time, which we kids thought must be because of the song 'You got to rock with me Henry all night long; roll with me Henry, I don't mean maybe.' Parents got real upset with the words and the song was changed to 'Dance With Me Henry'.

Rock 'n' roll it was from now on. R & B, as a term, took a back seat again. Nevertheless, Freed refused to play the copycat 'cover' versions of R & B hits which were rapidly being turned out by the major pop companies,* and he accused rock-knockers of being racists.

*Making different versions of popular songs was always an established practice – 'St Louis Blues' is reputed to be the world's most-recorded song. Making versions of popular sounds was an extension of this. A striking characteristic of the new practice was that it was always whites 'covering' blacks (although you might say that throughout pop history blacks have been 'covering' whites, not quite making it but producing a great sound instead). Perry Como covered Gene and Eunice's 'Ko Ko Mo', the Crew Cuts covered the Chords' 'Sh-Boom' and the Penguins' 'Earth Angel', Pat Boone covered a whole lot including Ivory Joe Hunter, Little Richard and Fats Domino. The list is long and most of the early covers were the hit versions. LaVern Baker,

Our Time

This is what he did that was really lasting: he took an idiom of only minority appeal and jazzed it up into theatre. He bought the street and plonked it on the stage. And he did quite well out of his rock 'n' roll, but why not? He had to move quickly, though: 'In this business your career is so short you've got to get it from all angles.' So he spread and soon his partners owned more of 'Mr Rock 'n' Roll' than he did, they said. There was a publishing company, a record contract, rock movies, a weekly show for Radio Luxembourg plus rock stage shows throughout the North East.

At the Paramount Theatre, Brooklyn, he broke Sinatra's attendance record. Sharon Leibermann, a manual arts student, was there and afterwards she wrote down her impressions in an exercise book:

---

covered by Georgia Gibbs right down to the crucial arrangement, tried unsuccessfully to get a law passed which gave copyright protection to arrangements.

Why did the covers sell? Was it race prejudice, better distribution or public taste? In fairness to many of the coverers it must be said that their versions very often sounded very different to the black original. For instance, listen to Bill Haley's 'Shake Rattle and Roll' and then to Joe Turner's original and I think you'll see why Haley had the hit. Haley's record was a hybrid and maybe rotten R & B, but it was pure rock 'n' roll!

Randy Wood's Dot Records of Gallatin, Tennessee (operating out of a large mail order store and thus well distributed) made a lot of its money out of cover jobs. But Wood was also fortunate to attract the services of ace promotion man Mickey Addy (one-time early Alley plugger) whose masquerades as a wax-moustached, spur-clicking German baron did much to win over disc jockeys to Dot products. Artists on the label included pleasing crooner Pat Boone, disc jockey Jim Lowe, screen star Tab Hunter, TV child star Gale Storm, professional 'madman' Nervous Norvus and Billy Vaughn and his Orchestra. Vaughn did most of the arrangements and sometimes he imitated an R & B record note for note (with a bit of cleaning and tightening up) and at other times he rocked up old standards, stressing that indescribable (perhaps *just* describable as tango with French connections) lope of a bass pattern first featured by veteran blues and boogie pianist Jimmy Yancey, and dressing it with kazoo-like saxes in rippling thirds. Two of these old songs, 'Love Letters in the Sand' and 'Melody of Love', are in the all-time Top Ten of the Rockin' Fifties.

A couple of Dot hits were really outstanding productions: Leroy Van Dyke's rattling impersonation of 'The Auctioneer' and the mystery of the 'Shifting Whispering Sands Parts 1 and 2', narrated dramatically by Ken Nordene.

Rock 'n' Roll

We were standing in line from dawn and boy was it cold! Kerry and I had brought cheese 'n' jelly sandwiches so we ate them to keep warm. We had a lot of laughs too. Just goofing. Cops on horseback, huge in greatcoats with whirling sticks, kept galloping near us but we numbered thousands and we all booed them. We just made the 10 a.m. show and we stayed till the last one which was around 1 a.m. I guess we saw around 6 movies, all dumb with aging lovers but we had fun booing the smoothy hero and rooting for the bad guys. It was funny because there were these fattish men in the audience dressed alike in bright sport shirts and denims and they tried to join in but we all knew they were cops. Especially when two of them whipped out flashlights to break up a smooching couple. The stage shows with mostly colored singers were the greatest, but Alan Freed was the mostest. He ran on in a Scotch plaid jacket and luminous face to lead the band, shouting 'Go man Go' and wiggling a bit too. Then he blew kisses at us and said 'Hi' with a beckon so we all replied 'Hi'. It was great and later he brought on his wife who's a doll. I really dig Alan because he's not like most older people. He's like a father ought to be. He makes me feel wanted – not like my own father who when he gets home every night just flops into a chair with the paper, switches on the TV and grabs for a beer. If we argue with him he beats us up. But my boy friend could stand up to him any day. My boy friend doesn't say much but he looks real mean. In fact he looks like a cross between Marlon Brando and Sal Mineo.

Teens were a fact because increasing prosperity and parental attention nice and nasty were giving them some money and power. Rock 'n' roll was soon released from Alan Freed (for a short time record companies had actually paid him for the right to use his phrase) and became public domain. Rock 'n' roll was teen music, *their* music, no matter that its parts were from adult sources. All the world, and especially the teens themselves, were becoming very conscious of teen life.

'They taught me rock 'n' roll,' said Bill Haley, kindly uncle leader of the Comets, the dance band that became the world's very first rock 'n' roll group. Did they really teach him rock 'n' roll? No, but he gave the right sound at the right time with the right record company to the right crowd and when he was a big smash he didn't really know what had hit him: 'I'm just a country boy,' he said, bewildered by riots and ripped seats.

223

Haley had been around the fringe music business a long time before rock 'n' roll. A Detroit boy, he had played his guitar at auctions. On medicine shows touring the Mid West. On the radio as the 'Rambling Yodeller'. Eventually he became programme director of an independent Pennsylvania radio station and there he organized hillbilly bands – 'The Four Aces of Western Swing', 'The Saddlemen' – singing with them on the air live. Doing dates within the station's beam and it was a good one. A Northern built-up area, close to New York and success.

His eyes and ears were close to the ground. He was aware of teenagers and the fact that there simply weren't enough leapy bands around for them. Too many crooners and too many bands for tired adults. If an ordinary youngster wanted a lively night he had to sneak out to a hall in a coloured town. This sneaking had been going on since the swing thirties. White youths went 'juking' in Pennsylvania mill towns to learn from jiving black cats the important 'pelvic motion', the latest jive-talk, the whole shebang. They returned home with a bouncy walk, hunching their shoulders and popping their fingers. Then they introduced jitterbugging at the high-school prom.

Haley played high schools. He picked up catch phrases – 'crazy man crazy', 'hot dog buddy buddy' – and he asked the kids what they wanted. Like many western swingers he'd long had an affection for, and an affinity with, boogie/blues/shuffle/beat – that basic trundle which as far as we know dates back to the great boogie-woogie father pianist Jimmy Yancey – and he probably heard it somewhere else, Erewhon.

Around 1950, like other country bands such as Cliffie Stone and Merrill Moore, he started featuring the hard urban boogie with his Saddlemen at clubs and school dates. The new jive went down well and soon he was recording for a local independent company, making his versions of R&B records together with straight country songs. DJs were puzzled by the hybrid music he made on such flip-sides as 'Rock the Joint'. Not country and not R&B, but somewhere in between. Nevertheless, the kids liked the beat and in 1953 Haley's 'Crazy Man Crazy' made the national charts. By this time the Saddlemen had become the Comets, signifying speed, space, way-out. Comets music was tougher than country; made from the trundle boogie of an R & B band like Louis Jordan or Wynonie Harris, slapped along by a Dixieland bass fiddle, punctuated by pan-crash drum shots from a kitchen catastrophe, spiced with morse-code riffs from a western swing electric guitar (aided by steel guitar swipes). And a honky Earl Bostic sax. All topped with Haley's talk-song voice.

His records were clean, brisk and sharp – without either country charm or R & B deep mud-funk. Dreamy love was avoided. Haley, a merry personality, called the dances rather like a square dance master of ceremonies: 'On your marks! Get set!' Through the years he called on dancers to rock the joint, razzle dazzle, do the ABC boogie, rock through the rye, and though at times he may have wearied of being genial rocker-chief, he stuck to his guns and continues to stick.

But back to the early fifties. Most important of all, his records continued to sell. In Autumn 1954 he was in the Top Ten with a domesticated 'Shake Rattle and Roll', pipping Joe Turner's lustier original. 'Rock around the Clock', helped by being in a popular movie, reached the Top Ten in May 1955 and stayed there for five months.

'Clock' has become the anthem of early rock, and its back-stage story is interesting. It had a melody and form similar to 'Rock the Joint' and was written as a novelty foxtrot by two ASCAP members in 1953. They showed it to Haley who thought it was just the job. But the little record company he was contracted to at the time didn't agree and only when he was signed with the mighty Decca in 1954 was he able to record the song. They cut it at the Pythian Temple, New York and they used the guitar solo and shuffle rhythm of 'Rock the Joint'.

'Clock's' lyricist was sixty-three-year-old Max Freedman ('Sioux City Sue', 'Liebestraum', 'Blue Danube Waltz') and its composer was Jimmy DeKnight, who was really James Myers of Myers Music and later became technical adviser on *The Blackboard Jungle*, a social comment movie about delinquency in schools.

It was one of a clutch of movies on the rebel youth theme, a minority occupation spotlighted into fame and fashion by the movies (still the main mass medium). One scene had schoolboys smashing up their teacher's prized 78 jazz record collection.

But the most exciting bit was the title scene because 'Clock' was on the soundtrack and very searing under the delinquency circumstances. *The Blackboard Jungle* was released in February 1955 and by May the song from the movie was in the Top Ten. Hollywood had linked rock 'n' roll with wild, untamed rebel youth, and youth flocked out to see itself on the screen, instead of those toupéed movie stars from the thirties still going through that old soft shoe routine.

Next year when rock 'n' roll had really got under way, Haley and the band were starred in a low-budget quickie for Sam Katzman (producer of the *Jungle Jim* series). It was appropriately called *Rock around the Clock* and it told how Bill and the boys were discovered in Strawberry Springs blowing up a teenage storm and brought to the Big Time where they met Alan Freed and did coast-to-coast TV. Poetically, it was all true.

The movie, which cost only 200,000 dollars to make, grossed a million in its first US year (1956). It was a gathering point for rocking youth and though the contents were fairly quiet the audience was often noisy. Sociologists had to visit the movie twice: the first time to watch the movie, the second time to watch the audience. Katzman, Haley, Freed and co. were riding an unexpected wave! There were disturbances in certain areas where the movie was played, including the Princeton Campus. New York, supposed capital of teen violence, received it fairly quietly.

The farther that the movie roamed from home the wilder the reception. The first reports of European rioting were from Dublin. But the scene had to be described in print before the real-life action began – in Britain the picture played 300 cinemas scattered around the country (including such tough cities as Glasgow and Sheffield) without any trouble. Then, after a performance at the Trocadero in South London, there was some good-natured larking: a few hundred boys and girls danced and chanted 'Mambo Rock' on Tower Bridge, holding up traffic. Some cups and saucers were thrown about, too. Later there were a few ten-shilling fines. One boy was fined £1 for accidentally kicking a policeman.

But the newspapers splashed the story as a riot. 2,000 were on the streets, claimed the *Daily Express*. More stories followed and young people appeared and acted out the drama. At a Croydon cinema there was jiving in front of the screen, and when the manager (in evening dress) protested he was squirted point blank by a youth armed with a fire extinguisher. A mob at Lewisham sang 'Nine little policemen hanging on the wall'. The Rank Organization banned the showing of the picture on Sundays. The King of the Teddy-Boys (Desmond Turrell of Reading) was gaoled. Everybody got involved: Fabian of the Yard and Promenade Concert conductor Malcolm Sargent commented; the *Evening News* film critic was baffled by the picture and went in search of a double brandy, reciting Gray's 'Elegy', but the communist *Daily Worker* found it was a 'direct and refreshing' film, adding that 'the music isn't obscene but the relentless commercialism is'. The manager of the Gaumont, Shepherd's Bush was warned by a young customer: 'Just wait for Friday, mate. We've got the boys from Notting Hill coming, and the boys from White City and Acton. We're gonna tear the place apart.' The Queen, in Scotland, cancelled her screening of *The Caine Mutiny* and commanded a *Clock* print to be sent up by fast train.

Egyptian authorities saw the film as part of Eisenhower's 'Rock Roll Doctrine', designed to sow Middle East trouble by undermining Egyptian morale. Iran banned it as a threat to civilization. In Bombay it ran eleven weeks. Moscow condemned it as fake folk music, but pirated prints circulated underground and made rock 'n' roll as popular as George Formby.

The wildest thing in the picture was the vaudeville routine of the Comets: bassist lying on top of his instrument whilst saxist straddled them both. Later this saxist blew on as he removed his Scotch plaid jacket, revealing braces. Haley watched all, smiling.

But quiet and very popular moments were provided by the dreamy ballads of the Platters, a black vocal group with a smooth, classy and well-rehearsed act. Trained by white lawyer/songwriter Buck Ram (who had once arranged for the Ink Spots, Glenn Miller, Count Basie), they proved that rock 'n' roll could be quite lulling and they went on to win admirers from all walks with their renditions of such good old songs as 'Smoke Gets in Your Eyes' and 'My Prayer'.

Rock 'n' roll was revolt, though, wasn't it? To the industry and to the general public 1956, the year of the *Clock* movies, was the year the sky fell in, the year of ELVIS PRESLEY. Hip-grinding, pelvis-rotating or undulating, mouth-pouting, dreamy, romantic, red-neck, Romeo from *Classics Illustrated*, symptom of a sick society, releaser of repressed desire for strong, biological urges, debaser of the 'method', ex-King of Western Bop, *anything you like*, he eclipsed Haley and Freed and co., to become the world's living loving epitome of rock 'n' roll.

Was he real? On some of the photos he looked artificial, painted under the eyes with lipsticked lips. Had an artist been at work touching up? He looked the ideal male in an action comic. Those who could be mistaken for him were mobbed, e.g., 'Jolly Jack' Priestley, visiting South America and thought to be *Elvis Priestley*. Today his power is still strong. To writer Nick Cohn, speaking for adult millions, he is 'where pop begins and ends'. Elvis is King. John Lennon, however, has finally managed to wrench himself out of Elvis's spell, stating with finality that he doesn't believe in Elvis (or Jesus, Buddha, Beatles and more).

At the start people in show-biz thought 'Elvis Presley' must be a stage name, but rural folk knew it was only too true, a real plough-boy name. *Tacky*. Like Haley he came out of fringe music and was made phenomenal by media exposure. Unlike Haley he came out of the South, that Wild West where so much of our story springs from. He came out of the bush like ragtime and jazz, out of the life-long affair with the black man, out of a heritage near as old as the hills. His home was our first chapter (tearful ballads, brimstone churches, revival meetings and inner feelings hung outside) but he was young and it was the 1950s. So there were electric guitars, recording studios, juke boxes, radios, kids. It seemed odd when he talked of his mammy and of God and said 'Sir'.

He came from Tupelo, Mississippi, the son of poor whites in the poorest state of the Union. In a holy-roller church he heard his first music and it had him swaying and clapping. He watched the demon preacher cutting up down the aisle, jumping on the piano. A land where sin was followed by salvation; great courtesy by sudden bestiality. Bob Wills had almost become a nigger here, then almost an outlaw but finally a star with a song recorded by Bing Crosby.

Presley heard the modern pop and was influenced. He liked crooners Gene Austin and Dean Martin (decades apart), cry-guy Johnnie Ray and all the regulars on *Grand Ole Opry*. He also heard and loved the blues, just like Jimmy Rodgers and Bob Wills before him. Blues drenched the Southland, only it didn't get into the papers. And when the Presleys were dead broke they moved on Memphis, blues centre of the South. But his daddy was looking for work.

Sam Phillips of Sun Records, Memphis, was still looking for his white boy who could sing coloured. He wasn't going to compete with the fiddles and guitars of nearby Nashville. Besides, he felt their kind of country music was getting a bit samey. It wasn't till almost a year after Elvis Presley, of the Crown Electric Company, had first made a private record at Sun (saying that he didn't sound like nobody) that Phillips thought maybe the boy could be used. Sun's studio was a matchbox with, they say, only two mikes but, for certain, plenty of feel, and the engineers could miraculously set up and catch a bulbous, deep and cooking sound with an eery echo. After some tries Elvis and Sam's pick-up group settled into an old blues that Sam liked. Easy gait with an edge of tension, the guitar lolloping along and the slap-bass all rickety like a shack. Elvis was out of crooning, was now high-pitched and seemed in a hurry and very ravenous. The whole thing was lazy but com-bustible – ready for action on a hot night, to make those porches shake and those rocking chairs jump. It was (and still is) an extra-ordinary sound and Phillips got immediate good reaction when local DJ Dewey Phillips played it on his *Red Hot and Blue* R & B show; there were phone calls and telegrams. A lot of people thought Elvis Presley must be coloured.

The record, 'That's Alright Mama' (originally sung by Arthur 'Big Boy' Crudup)* was coupled with 'Blue Moon of Kentucky'

*Crudup, a black left-handed guitarist from Mississippi, grew up on rag-time, country music and blues. He didn't start recording till he was thirty-six (a rocked-up version of an oldish Bill Monroe country waltz) and was released in 1954. It made the charts in a few southern cities. But was Elvis country or was he blues? DJs were puzzled, whilst the next releases started to sell. In 1955 'Baby Let's Play House' reached the national charts as a country hit and *Billboard* received calls from country fans protesting that Presley music was nigger music.

Sam Phillips, despite attacks, was encouraged enough by sales to drop his R & B and collect other boys such as Johnny Cash and Carl Perkins, steering them on to this potentially hot sharecropper blues. Then a powerful DJ set Perkins, Cash and Presley on road tours: three 1949 hire-purchase autos making their way in a motorcade down dusty roads to a schoolhouse-date in a lonely village. Helping set up these dates was (honorary) Colonel Parker, fond of wearing straw hats. As a carnival man in the thirties he'd once sold painted sparrows as canaries. Lately he'd been managing country stars. Now he had hawk-eyes on Presley.

On the early tours Carl Perkins had closed the show because he moved around the most, but quite soon it was discovered that when Presley so much as twitched a leg (due to nervousness perhaps) there was amazing audience reaction and on top of this Presley had smouldering good looks and a husky body. So he came to close each and every show and never took less from then on. Perkins says Presley was a star in those days and forever.

He was now billed as 'The Hillbilly Cat' and quite a sight to see: no cowboy rig-out but rainbow dazzle sports clothes, a satin stripe down his trousers, a drape jacket with collar turned up. Longish hair in a duck tail, with truck driver sideburns. A dangerous Dapper Dan in white-face, very *common*. When he sang the slow songs his voice was deep and virile (like Dean Martin broken up). But on the fast ones he wailed high, threshing his guitar and wiggling his body. A white male who teased publicly! 'Mr Gypsy

---

and by that time he'd run through a batch of rustic jobs such as being a farmer, a levee worker and a water-carrier. In 1942 he made his first record for Victor's 'race' label, on an electrified cello guitar. He had many hits but, strangely enough, he only became professional in 1968.

Rose Lee', muttered a small-potato country singer. There were rumours that bunched hankies were stuffed down the front of the Presley trousers to add to his sex personality, but if this was true it had decent black precedent: the Lindy Hoppers of the 1939 Broadway musical *Hot Mikardo* similarly filled their jock-straps just before show-time.

Anyway, Presley – moving naturally to the music – had to make only one wiggle and the girls got excited. They were reported making 'weird guttural sounds' at his shows. A reporter at the Memphis auditorium saw one girl scratch her arm with her fingernails, leaving red welts. Another confessed: 'I grabbed his hand and he grinned sideways and said "cut me loose". It was *heavenly*. He's the dreamiest thing I laid eyes on.' He was kind of shy so that every moment was extra exciting, like he was straying. Rough but cute, a real sweetmeat, a winning mixture for the times. They tried to tear his clothes off in Jacksonville, Florida.

He was hot all right but he was still a country property. The Country and Western Disc Jockeys voted him Number One 'Up And Comer' at their annual Nashville Convention beano late in 1955. He was on view and he went through his paces very well because he was getting it all into a style. 'He's good,' opined a grizzled old-timer. 'But he *still* ain't ready fer the *Opry*.' However, Colonel Parker, fast becoming Presley's manager, wasn't interested now in *Grand Ole Opry*, showcase mecca for country artists. His boy was for the Big End of Show Business, and next the World!

First of all, though, Sun Records: a nice enough happy-go-lucky outfit but really too small, too local. And Victor, a major label hunting for a rock 'n' roller with only Perry Como doing 'Ko Ko Mo', was interested to the fantastic tune of 40,000 dollars. Parker had coaxed a terrific deal and Phillips agreed. Presley bought his first Cadillac with his advance on royalties. Why did Phillips sell up? The sum was huge (for those days) and Sun, they say, was in the red. Besides, Phillips had other sharecropper rockers such as Cash and Perkins. Early next year Perkins went high on all national charts (R & B, C & W, and pop) with his song of teen-life narcissism, 'Blue Suede Shoes'. Even so, Phillips wasn't sold on

231

rock 'n' roll or Presley. Would it all last? 'In this business,' he said, 'you can't figure an artist's life more than six months in advance.' Blues was a steady little field, so was country, but pop-rock?

However, Presley was Presley and a unique contribution to the twentieth century. He was much more than a country rocker singing his soul: he was an entertainer. When he made his first records for Victor in January 1956 his voice was already more controlled. Breathlessness was now on tap. On 'Heartbreak Hotel' he ranted like a Shakespearean barnstormer, but the backing was tepid, cool jazz almost. Nobody cared too much for that one and it was scheduled as the B side to 'I Was the One'.

Television broke Elvis Presley nationally. The producer of the network TV programme *Stage Show* was looking out for sensations because his ratings were slipping badly. Presley looked to him like a 'guitar-playing Marlon Brando' and 'Heartbreak Hotel' was garish tabloid stuff – a song by a Florida schoolteacher about lovers crying in hotel gloom, and desk clerks all in black. TV melodrama! Good visual potential! Presley was signed for six appearances, peak-time Saturday night.

He followed the mellow big band music of the Dorseys with his old act, now whittled down to a clean T. All at once he staggered millions coast to coast. A rare spectacle – a boy star on TV jumping about, playing the guitar, singing rock 'n' roll. Girls had lusty dreams and boys were inspired to an alternative calling. In togetherness ranch-style homes across the nation, rows were started between parent and child. 'Heartbreak Hotel' was released and went into the charts.

He appeared on the other network variety shows: Milton Berle, Steve Allen (in which he was asked to wear evening dress and to avoid movements) and the great Ed Sullivan (who shot him from the waist up). Even this *face* act gave offence, the *New York Times* critic complaining that he 'injected movements of the tongue and indulged in wordless singing that were singularly distasteful'.

He was making it. *Life* did a spread on him and *Time* said he had a 'frantic quiver as if he had swallowed a jack-hammer'. His records sold so quickly that Victor had to use the pressing plants of rivals Decca, Capitol and MGM. Soon Presley records accounted for almost half Victor's sales. At the end of the year he disappeared into movies, and, except for a spell in the Army, he wasn't seen again 'live in person' till 1969.

Sometimes he was glimpsed in Beverly Hills or at his 'Graceland' home near Memphis. Objects connected with him became marketable: an elderly man was caught stealing leaves from the grounds of Graceland and it was discovered that he had built a tidy business selling them in packages to fans. Colonel Parker, manager proper by now, ordered his release because (it is alleged) he rather admired the man's business flair.

The Presley industry proper turned out Presley lipsticks, bracelets, hats, jeans, shoes, T shirts and a colour pic that glowed for an hour after lights out. Presley statements were never surly, always humble: 'God let me come along at this time,' he said about his success. He never talked politics: 'Writers ask me my opinion about things like Suez. I don't like that.' He loved his parents greatly.

He was a superstar that hardly anybody had seen in flesh and blood. Around the end of 1956 there were rumours that he was dead.

Elvis Presley had three major effects on rock 'n' roll. First, as a successful business operation, Presley and Parker became the inspiration for the coming age of the Teen Idol and Father/Manager. Secondly, as a polite, family-loving all-American boy, Presley pacified millions of worried parents. And thirdly, as a superb rock singer backed by a guitar group, he influenced musically most of the boys who were to be the pop stars of the next decade. Dollar success apart, Presley was, and is, a great artist.

By 1957, with rock 'n' roll everywhere and record sales higher than ever before and Elvis Presley the king of it all, the industry realized that if this music was a passing fad it was taking an awful long time passing. Many insiders felt that *the state of such stuff was surely not accidental*, and (if you remember) a select band of songwriters went to Washington. Amongst them was Oscar Hammerstein II with a particular loathing of 'You Ain't Nothing but a Hound Dog'. Back at home a few game old-liners, tossing aside their lexicons and neglecting the beauties of nature, attempted to come to grips with teen topics. But an analysis of 'Tutti Frutti' at the piano reminded them that they hadn't lived on the street in years and so they sat back into the dignity of age.

Songs for rock 'n' roll records were provided by a wide variety of people ranging from canny adults like Leiber and Stoller ('Hound Dog', 'Charlie Brown', 'Yakety Yak') and Doc Pomus and Mort Shuman ('Teenager in Love', 'Little Sister', etc.) through boy singers like Paul Anka ('Diana', 'It Doesn't Matter Anymore'), Neil Sedaka ('Happy Birthday Sweet Sixteen', 'Stupid Cupid') and Bobby Darin ('Splish Splash', 'Dream Lover') to little old Southern ladies ('Tutti Frutti', 'Long Tall Sally') and even an old Paul Whiteman associate ('At The Hop' by Artie Singer). However, the first to deal directly with teen life had been Chuck Berry, about whom more later.

Rock 'n' roll, though, was still mainly a record, not a song, and the record companies, hoping for another Presley, had signed up likely young rockers. Capitol held a competition and Gene Vincent won. His first record, the panting 'Be Bop a Lula' was an immediate hit. Decca (home of Bill Haley) leased tapes of Buddy Holly and the Crickets from a little company in New Mexico, released them on subsidiary labels and watched them sell. Mercury had the Platters, and did a Southern deal by which they got the incredible Big Bopper (a latter day Ted Lewis, not Dizzy Gillespie) and his 'Chantilly Lace', a smash in the grand tradition of telephone songs. MGM, late in the rush, came up with Conway Twitty, a country boy-cum-rocker who reformed after a string of hits. Victor, of course, had Presley. Columbia, the other major company and only recently master of pop under Artists and Repertoire chief Mitch Miller, came up with virtually nothing. Miller was shocked at the turn that pop had taken and voiced his dislike of market domination by what he called the 'pre-shave crowd' with their 'baby music'.

Most of the hot-rocker records were concocted by the indies. Often hole-in-the-wall shacks with primitive equipment and able to afford only local talent and singers turned down by the majors. But these very limitations could help create weird and wonderful records lacking major label blandness. A few of these indies had been stimulated into existence by the success of rock 'n' roll but many were specialty companies with a new market. Sun is a typical example. Chess, who had leased much blues material from Sun but no Presley, were surprised to find their Chuck Berry, signed as a blues artist in 1955, suddenly emerge as a teen idol.

Berry didn't deal with narrow blues subjects but had a knack for writing and performing witty, clangy songs on 1950s teen topics. In a light voice and with clear enunciation he raved to his guitar about the drag of school ('Ring, ring Goes the Bell') and work life ('Too Much Monkey Business') and the marvellous escape from it all provided by rock 'n' roll and fast cars and following the idols around: 'Sweet Little Sixteen' in hot pursuit of 'Johnny B. Goode'. He sang about how great today is and how dark yesterday was. 'Hail, hail rock and roll! Deliver me from the days of old!'

Two other entertainers who might have otherwise languished in the South were thrown on to the world by indie pop success. Their hits enabled them to appear at concerts, on television and in movies. The effect was to turn them from being quite shy lads into demon preachers of rock 'n' roll. Jerry Lee Lewis and Little Richard outfired Elvis Presley.

They were the most exciting performers since Al Jolson.* They would have been stars of vaudeville and to hell with the material. Lee Lewis of Louisiana started on piano when he was eight and within six months had fashioned his final style. From 1950 he was a professional playing in 'knock down – drag out' clubs of the South. Sam Phillips signed him soon after he'd sold Elvis. 'Whole Lotta Shakin' Goin' On' topped all three charts in 1957. His role was clearly a rocker. In public performance he cut an aristocratic figure (a sort of proud planter) as he sat ramrod-backed, pumping a grand piano with his curls flying. Stroking the keys as if they were feline. Kicking away his stool with grace. Stalking the piano

*Jerry Lee Lewis says that as a kid he listened to Jolson all the time. He still has all his records.

lid as he told about having a chicken in the barn. Rocking southern church services had had their effect on him (he'd even done a spot of preaching in his time).

They'd deeply influenced Little Richard of Georgia and he loved to howl little bits of secularized gospel as he washed dishes in a Greyhound bus station. Through rock 'n' roll success on the indie label Specialty he became 'The Bronze Liberace', whooping the praises of 'Long Tall Sally' and 'Lucille' in a blaze of healing music (which he claimed could make the blind see, the lame walk and the deaf hear) as he stood at his piano dressed in billowing shiny balloon suit, backed by a glittering fat sax band. He travelled with a court and had future plans for an electric suit.

Tempering the wildness of these demons was another pianist/singer from the South: genial Antoine Fats Domino (with some of the spirit of Fats Waller). He had rings on fingers that drummed warm chords, and he sang his catchy songs in a pleasing voice with a Creole accent of great quaintness. As long ago as 1949 he'd been an R & B hit, and now, hardly changing, he was a hero of the young set.

But the outdoor lustiness of original rock was short-lived in popularity. There is more to life than jumping. Fast rock's appeal was more to growing males rather than females in search of romance, with a view to permanence. 'What is a Teenage Boy?' asked the hit record, and answered that he is a crew-cut, black-eyed Huck Finn type who likes to take clocks apart, go fishing, or just plain goof. 'What is a Teenage Girl?' asked the other side of the record: she's the chief customer of the Teen Business. She calls the tune and increasingly it's a love song from a beautiful boy – often Italian–American. The late fifties and early sixties were full of teenage Comos: Bobby Rydell, Frankie Avalon, Fabian, James Darren, Dion.

Meanwhile the music makers were developing rock into good sturdy pop. Violins were rediscovered. Honking saxes became *passé*. Producers were adding Latin touches and thinking of French horns. *Writing little symphonies for the kids*, as Phil Spector put it.

Many of the teen stars were not happy with the thought of

rocking for the rest of their days and wanted to reach out beyond the beat. Bobby Rydell said: 'I love it when the girls start screaming and carrying on after I've sung, it gives me the most wonderful feeling ... But they could murder me and I wouldn't care ... No one can deny the lure of the swinging type of music. But if you ask me my ambition, careerwise, that's easy – I want to grow up to be an all-round entertainer ... like Sinatra'. Dion of the Belmonts described his progress into maturity: 'On the strength of my earnings, I bought an eight-room house for my folks ... I also bought an elegant grey and black Thunderbird; dental capping for two front teeth; an abstract painting by a distinguished artist; a gold wrist-watch for my manager, Sal Bonafede; a load of presents for my old pals in the Bronx; three tuxedos; ten pairs of slacks; seven custom-tailored suits; several pairs of custom-made Italian shoes with elastic on the sides; and ten thousand dollars' worth of expert advice to help me work up a night club act with which I could step into the adult show places.'

For the young performers development into personable all-rounders (with good teeth, nose, hair, act, car, clothes, manager) capable of holding a Las Vegas audience for forty-five minutes was very important. They had to grow up professional, leaving childish things behind. Elvis Presley provided a good model for progress. In his movies he was learning how to time gags and do love clinches.

At the same time, however, the pop world was becoming fascinated with the idea of *permanent teenage*. It had discovered that mothers and fathers were growing to love the beat and were now keen on entering that gay Arcadia twixt twelve and twenty where lovely youth (spick-and-span but still with gangly charm) danced and sang and had a fun thing. Beauty wrought in darkness by a Supreme Being but aided into daylight by the arts of the electronic media for the delight of watchers.

The most popular window was a television dance party called *American Bandstand*. It was on every weekday afternoon, telecast nationally from Philadelphia (urban Arcadia) and statisticians worked out that, on an average day, it was viewed by 20 million teenagers and 20 million adults. The show had started back in

1952 as a time-filler but quickly developed into a casual dance party and found its final form when disc jockey Dick Clark became host in 1956. Within a year it was network and the most important plug for a new record. 'He was the king, and you just had to lip-sync. his show and it was all right,' opined Phil Spector.

Clark was neatly pressed, squeakily clean and quiet. He didn't try to glitter, he just let the kids get on with it because they were the stars of the show. There was a family of 'regulars' – 'The Bandstand Brigade' – and their romances were followed avidly by the viewers. 'Regular' Carmen Jiminez wrote a 'Bandstand Newsletter' for *Sixteen* magazine: 'FREDDIE CANNON and I do not go steady, though I did see a lot of him when he was in Philly . . .' Another 'regular', Carole Scadeferri, revealed that 'CARMEN JIMINEZ and MIKE BALARA have been seen together all over Philadelphia.' Also: 'JOE FUSCO no longer is linked with TERRY CELINI. MARY ANNE CUTT will kill me for revealing this, but the middle name she never admits to having is HANNAH'.

The Bandstand Brigade showed off the very latest dances (pony, stroll, wobble, locomotion, choo-choo, fly, fish, crawl, slop, mashed potato, etc.) in an easy manner far from Broadway. They judged the new releases on the strength of *the beat*. They told Dick Clark which schools they attended. They went steady right on camera. Occasionally singing guests dropped into the party to mime their new record: Jerry Lee Lewis, Bill Haley and the Big Bopper were just plain folk here. Over the years most of the rock stars called by, always pleased to receive an invite. *Bandstand* itself helped make a few stars, such as Fabian and Frankie Avalon, Bobby Rydell and Chubby Checker (the twist king). What Philly did today, America might do tomorrow! Record companies sprouted in that area and for a time it became a major recording centre with its own 'Philly Sound'. Record promotion men renamed the city 'Brotherlylovesville'. Syndicated columnists considered that its TV children were a symbol of all that was good in the younger generation.

What about the 40 million watchers? Fortunately there is written record of early sixties Arcadia by a British observer.

Rock 'n' Roll

L. M. S. Farquhar, the travel writer, happened to be at the Jerry Knox University gathering information for a book about Red Indians:

Having no permanent address and tired of the Y M C A, I eagerly accepted the offer of a room by my friend Dwayne Hickenhacker, a sophomore in the new 'Dry Cleaning' degree course. He lived with his wife and two daughters in a bungaloid home – ranch-style, with patio, he told me – on the leafy outskirts of town.

No sooner had I arrived (my head full of Indians) when I was near keeled over from behind by Dwayne's two daughters. 'They're fresh from school and heading for the den,' said Mrs Hickenhacker as she popped out her cheek for me to kiss.

'Jumping jellybeans we're almost in latesville!' shouted a shapely one, in full make-up, as she flung some text books around me. *I was intrigued*. Mumbling an 'excuse me' to Mrs H I quickly followed the girls down into the den where I found them tangled around easy chairs watching a TV screen as the whirling figures of laughing teenagers took shape.

'Oh just catch a look at Arlene today! She is just FANTABULOUS! And Shari's bando – isn't it the LIVING END ? ?'

'Yuppee. Fasten on to Frank of the keen threads. Shiny, huh? He's dancing with Donna 's' afternoon. Guess he goes ape for pony tails!' I was scribbling madly.

At this moment Mrs H appeared pushing a trolley full of steaming food and frosted drinks. 'Hi, L.M.S.! Just relax and have fun,' so I sat down again and picked up a copy of *Teen World*, fastening on to an article called 'How to Chase a Boy (without his knowing it)'.

Mrs H said: 'Hey Girls! Thought you might like a snack so I whipped up some Twittyburgers!'

'Shuuush!!! Suffering sockertash. Emily mother you must learn to cut out the yak when *Bandstand*'s on the vijj. Anyway, you know how you love it and learn from it. Chubby Checker's just about to give you your next Twist lesson.'

'Oops, sorry girls. Let's see if I can remember last week's lesson. Mmmmm: you go through the gestures of drying your behind with an imaginary bath towel, whilst pretending to grind out a cigarette with one foot. Yikes, where's the rest of me?'

During Mrs H's dance lesson I got her to briefly explain the origins of the Twittyburger. Apparently, it is the invention of singer Conway Twitty and is a self-contained banquet consisting of equal parts of meat patty, melted cheese slice, bacon, grilled pineapple, tomato, lettuce, mustard, chili sauce, jam, peanut butter, pickle and serviette. All housed inside a sesame bun. And very sustaining too!

'I must fill Dwayne in on that latest Twist lesson when he gets home from work,' said a perspiring Mrs H as she waggled to a halt. One and a half hours later *American Bandstand* ended for the day and our family viewing circle seemed at a loose end. We were all pretty flushed from Twittyburgers washed down with flavoured milk, but we heard Mrs H say:

'Kids I went on a shopping expedition 'safternoon so stand by for blast-off! Mary Jane, here's some more real silver cutlery for your hope chest and Terry, I got you a fancy *training brassiere*'. Terry looked not a day over eleven but when I questioned Mrs H about the brassiere she assured me that Terry was already well into double dating, blind dating, and even active sports dating. 'You see we're gung ho on progressive education,' she told me *sotto voce*. Then she said to the whole company:

'Now girls, we've a busy night ahead, haven't we? Remember? It's *family council night* in the living room, followed by your pajama party with the Limbergers. Oh, L.M.S. – I clean forgot to give you your gift from me to you' and she handed me a large tin of personal deodorant.

A few minutes later Dwayne came home, gripped my hand and then strode off to get out of his wash-'n'-dry suit and into 'fun' clothes: tapered trousers and a bright gaucho shirt. 'OK, let's ease into a martini, folks. Ha-bam-boola-dah! Tea and crumpets old boy and how's the Queen in jolly old England?', as he playfully punched me in the stomach.

After dinner we all assembled in the living room, 'at *exactement* 1800 hours as we used to say in the war,' said Dwayne slapping his wrist watch on the word 'hours'. 'COOL IT, DWAYNE', shouted the girls and Mrs H. Family Council began and we all freely discussed war and peace and the nation in general. Then Mrs H put on rhine-stone spectacles and read us an article by Connie Francis, the singer, about 'Come Alive' and 'Positive Think'. I was called on to read out another article, this time by Pat Boone. The gist of it was as follows: 'Be popular with a capital P, have a well-scrubbed face, get plenty of sleep, think positive, be a leader, don't be a tearer-down, play by the local ground rules without too much protest, have fun.'

From a Lazy Susan chair Dwayne commented that I sounded like Winston Churchill in his finest happy hour. I was really getting into my stride – deep trembling voice – when Mrs H suddenly jumped up, clapped her hands and announced: 'IT'S PARENT PROBLEM TIME!'

This was the cue for Terry and Mary Jane to deliver a list of wants. I became a bit bored because most of the demands were concerned with

Rock 'n' Roll

school and shopping details. I made notes about what Terry was wearing and how it all hung. The room swam around me and I felt young again. Suddenly I heard a piercing scream and I shot bolt upright. Mary Jane seemed to be throwing a tantrum. 'I want go Hawaii!' she screamed through tears and next minute she was gone and we heard the roar of a car. As it faded away Dwayne said, 'It's the Oldsmobile. We still got the Ford.'

Now it was Terry's turn. 'You don't understand me,' she shouted. 'Equal rights for teens!' and off she stalked to her room, chucking a pile of 45 rpm records at me on the way. 'That's a NO-NO', admonished Dwayne softly. Silence reigned for a few minutes and then we heard a record about 'Only The Lonely' floating out of Terry's room.

'She's at peace with Roy Orbison,' said Dwayne. 'I feel OK when she plays "Only The Lonely" – safer than "Running Scared". Maybe in a few minutes we'll have "In Dreams" and after that snoozy-woozies, know what I mean?' I didn't, but I later discovered the joy of Roy Orbison, a deep South rock 'n' roller from the same 'school' as Elvis Presley but with a semi-operatic voice and a repertoire of concerto-like songs.

'What say we hit the town?' said Dwayne, getting up and hitching his Capris. 'Coming Marilyn?' Mrs H replied no because she'd better stay and pacify Terry; perhaps slip into a look-alike dress.

So Dwayne and I drove off to New York in the Ford. He took me to a number of 'Twist joints' where we joined the audience of watchers viewing the youngsters as they swayed away. At one storefront cafe Dwayne actually leapt up screaming 'Geronimo', grabbed a teen girl and tried to dance but was quickly restrained. I palled up with a reporter from a showbiz magazine who filled me in on the Twist. Apparently, it's the rage of cafe society and it was all started by a group of jaded Broadwayites who dropped in on a club called the Peppermint Lounge one night and *dug the terpsing*. Soon the place was stiff with the white dinner jackets of the *mature elements* and the resident band – Joey Dee and the Starlighters – became famous. Later they played the swank Metropolitan Museum of Modern Art to an audience which included such V.I.P.s as Warren Beatty and Natalie Wood and the Marquess and Marchioness of Tavistock. Video and disc spread the *terps mania* throughout the western world and even Noel Coward did it.

After five hours' twist viewing Dwayne complained that his war wound was playing up so we retired to a dim-lit piano bar to nurse bourbons and call for 'Melancholy Baby'. This is a strange country and I am dropping my Indian studies to follow the teenagers of all ages. It's all so very different to England! Goodnight.

Meanwhile
in Britain

We left Britain trembling on the brink of rock 'n' roll (see page 193). Just before the tumble, before home-grown rock stars appeared, there was the *skiffle group*. This meant acoustic guitarists (augmented with such illegitimate instruments as washboard, tea-chest bass, kazoo) playing and singing largely Afro-American folk songs, work songs, spirituals. A purely local phenomenon: clusters of guitarists began to be seen and heard on odd street corners, and especially underneath the arches, singing not 'Underneath the Arches' but songs like 'When the Saints Go Marching In'. As a pop movement, however, skiffle was directly inspired by Lonnie Donegan and his Skiffle Group who reached the top of the hit parade in May 1956 with a song about the 'Rock Island Line'. People said 'skiffle' was an American jazz word but I never found anybody in America who remembered American skiffle. And this railway line was in the deep South. The song story concerned engine drivers. A black American entertainer/murderer called Leadbelly had written it. All of this is interesting but not the point. *The point is* that almost anybody could have a go at skiffle and an awful lot of us bought guitars. I had been playing an accordion but now I exchanged it at Selmer's of Charing Cross Road for a Spanish guitar with a golden sun-burnt finish. Then quickly I formed a skiffle group. It was an instant success in Dorset, where I was attending a semi-progressive public school. Here is some of the flavour of that skiffle period taken from my diary for 10 July 1956:

Sticky weather for the first public performance of the school skiffle group. Shorts riding up thighs again. The Rev. said to be at the Fete by 5 but I decided to get the chaps there earlier so's we could rehearse the new record by the Vipers ('Don't You Rock Me Daddy O'). We never get a moment to rehearse as a rule but nobody seems to mind. The Rev. said he'd probably lend a voice to a couple of spirituals or 'Green Grow the Rushes O'. Waring got his tea-chest bass bashed in during some tuck-box room brawl so we had to go begging to Ladey, that acneyed ass-hole who was in his study, curtains drawn, burning joss-sticks. Sitting as per usual in a wicker chair gripping a cup of Nescafe with an ear an inch from his gramophone. Listening to some aged New Orleans jazz record. In the end he let us buy his waste paper box to make into a bass (you drill a hole in bottom, pull string through, knot at one end and at the other attach a broom handle). He shouted out as we left that skiffling was ruining the true jazz cause and anyway we only knew 3 chords. He also says we don't *swing*. He said the same about my Bill Haley LP and my LP of the Original Dixieland Jazz Band. But I think he just prefers 78s. At least we're popular and lots of juniors, including pretty ones, would like to be like us. Even the hearties are open-mouthed. That cretin McLain has started a group too. Knows nothing about music but I'm sure he's trying to woo beauty boy Gabriel. Christ-on-a-bicycle, there'll soon be loads of groups but at least we have the advantage of genuine Jaytex check shirts. I'm going to see if I can't get my guitar electrified.

I rounded up the other 7 guitarists and we all got down to the fete at just on Tombola time. So we had lots of time to rehearse. We all tune to an open E chord, then just slide a stiff finger up or down to change. Presto! We decided to do 'The Wreck of the Old 97', 'This Land is My Land' and 'Where Could I Go but to the Lord' but in the end we couldn't do them all because the Rev. gave a long speech about the place of skiffle in society and then there was only a few minutes till prep. Speech was quite interesting I suppose. He said skiffle was healthy everyday people music and that one could express oneself as the spirit moved one. Not everybody was Yehudi Menuhin but these young men were playing for nothing and had realized the school credo 'I Too Will Something Make and Joy in the Making' by building their own instruments (cheek! I paid £12 for my Hofner). He finished by saying that he hoped to hold a Skiffle Mass in the near future when hundreds would be able to *make cheerful noise unto God*. Then he sang and clapped with us on our one number. Afterwards some flower-hatted lady came up and said she hadn't an earthly what we were playing but it sounded *likely* and much better than the Hakkabod arts class singing wild selections from the Firebird Suite. A gang of local yokels sneered at us and one said that I wasn't a bit like Lonnie Donegan and he had an electric guitar. I must get one.

What we didn't know then was that skiffle was a side-product of the British traditional jazz movement, which had split from revivalist jazz movement, which had begun in World War Two – just about the time when Spike Hughes (see page 167) was renouncing jazz. All hated bebop or modern jazz, but beyond that they disagreed as to what was the true jazz. The traditionalists said that the seed was the truth and all its flowers were decadent. It lay in New Orleans and had never moved or sprouted. The leader of these jazz fundamentalists was trumpeter Ken Colyer who made a pilgrimage to New Orleans, sailing away in a rusty tramp steamer with a drunken skipper, witnessing many punch-ups and one mutiny but returning with the truth, which he spread around. His band sounded just like the old black men then living and playing in New Orleans. Traditional jazzmen in Britain spurned smart uniforms, preferring to play in braces, sometimes with shirt tails sticking out. Many held left-wing views and one of them – old Etonian Humphrey Lyttelton – was alleged to have said 'Boo!' to Harold Macmillan.

But traditional jazz wasn't all dour. During club sessions Ken Colyer used to allow his banjoist Lonnie Donegan to take up a guitar and do some folk songs whilst the band boys had a drink. These skiffle sessions became very popular indeed and when trombonist Chris Barber left to form his own looser jazz band he lured Donegan with his skiffle act too. Traditional jazz purists sniffed and went on listening to the real thing with head in hands but Donegan went on to stardom as the King of Skiffle. 'Rock Island Line', one of his skiffle session songs, first appeared on a Chris Barber L P. It got so many radio requests that it was eventually reissued as a single and soon became a top tenner, not only in Britain but also in America. Stan Freberg honoured it with a parody record. Success enabled Donegan to play venues like the London Palladium. He was a likeable, if waspish, entertainer and in time he found his place in another traditional field: British music hall. He had a hit with 'My Old Man's a Dustman' and he recorded a duet with his idol Max Miller, the great comedian.

I played skiffle at fêtes but it was also found in coffee bars (a fifties innovation). The top ones were in Soho, at that time the New Orleans of skiffle. Bars like the Breadbasket, the Heaven And Hell, The Nucleus and the Two 'I's. The latter was steamy, sweaty and tiny, and the music took place in a cellar, not much bigger than an average-sized drawing room. Nobody clapped or screamed because it was too sophisticated a place and also too hot. When customers fainted they were silently passed up through a grille in the pavement and on to the street. Skifflers who were to become rock 'n' roll stars through television could be found milling about in and around the Two 'I's. For example, Marty Wilde was Reg Smith of the Hound Dogs; Adam Faith was Terry Nelhams of the Worried Men; Cliff Richard was Harry Webb, part-time skiffle vocalist.

They were waiting for rock 'n' roll. Bill Haley's music caused bashing and cinema-seat ripping, but Elvis Presley caused imitation. Thousands of skifflers exchanged their home-made, unchanging, rather academic music for the more glamorous Big Beat. There was much more money in it. A lucky few got discovered by managers and exposed on television. Though they were more skilfully presented than their American rocker-uncles they never sold as many records, even in Britain. What's more, Lonnie Donegan's skiffle outsold them till the end of the fifties.

As a mass movement skiffle faded as Elvis boomed. Purist skifflers retired hurt and returned to folk music. But less rigid skifflers developed a taste for the blues and not only the old pastoral songs of Big Bill Broonzy and Leadbelly. They started listening to records of modern city blues – electric blues. Not really rhythm and blues but the country blues taken to the big city and pumped up through amplifiers. Chris Barber, who had helped start skiffle, arranged for US bluesmen to appear in British jazz clubs. Electric Muddy Waters, electric John Lee Hooker. Out of skiffle was born the British blues movement. I learned that afterwards, but at the time I used to drift into jazz clubs and sometimes catch a visiting bluesman. I was amazed, thrilled and stimulated by Champion Jack Dupree, pianist from New Orleans with rings on his fingers and in his ears, with songs about black

245

jack-bones making things disappear. Mick Jagger and his friends were on to the blues as well. So were others. But scattered in cells.

Meanwhile, pop proper . . .

The first British boy to be transformed into a rock 'n' roll idol was Tommy Hicks, an ex-merchant seaman from London's East End. He was just a member of a skiffle group playing the Soho coffee-bar scene until discovery. Definitely Britain needed an answer to Elvis, that's obvious. His story seems old-hat today yet in 1956 the operation that turned Tommy Hicks into Tommy Steele was ultra-new. Native show-biz was amazed at the nerve!

Briefly: a New Zealander called John Kennedy had been knocking around the world from odd job to odd job. By mistake he caught a cargo boat to England. Here he picked up work with the *Daily Sketch*, interviewing and snapping V.I.P.s as they arrived at London Airport. He knew nothing about famous people and once he asked Peter Ustinov what he did for a living. One night, after a spaghetti dinner in Soho, he dropped into the Two 'I's. The skiffle he found O K but Tommy Hicks was riveting. Somehow Hicks had got left out of the skiffle group, but, undaunted, he'd pushed his way through the crowd and done a one-man show – whipping gustily through Haley, Presley and plantation songs and all to the mere backing of his guitar. Girls squealed. Kennedy told me in a 1970 interview:

I followed him into the street afterwards and asked him to come and have a chat in the Heaven and Hell next door. He was scared – thought I was a 'tec. But he came after a bit. I told him that if he'd give me one chance, just one, I might help him become a star. He said it might be a lark and he'd give it a try, but he had to get his parents' approval. So I went to his home in Frean St, Bermondsey. Very poor: an out-door toilet and trains shaking the house as they go by. But nice people and proud; they told me I could go ahead so long as I promised not to make a fool of Tommy . . . I changed his name to Steele because there was a steel strike on at the time, and it had a nice ring of the untouchables about it . . . I had to get him talked about. Rounded up a lot of debutante types with three-barrelled names and some of their squires, then staged a posh party.

Meanwhile in Britain

The story of the working-class lad who jigged rock 'n' roll to nobs appeared next Sunday in the *People*.

This helped get us a date at the Stork Club. I tried all the other clubs but they didn't want to know. The Stork specialized in acts like Noel Coward and Marlene and I was pleased because I wanted to clean up the rock 'n' roll image after all those riots and delinquency taunts. I was out of cash by this time, but I bumped into Larry Parnes, a friend of mine in the rag trade, and borrowed a hundred pounds. He got interested in the business and later joined me in managing Tommy. I got Tommy a wardrobe of special shirts designed by Teddy Tinling, the tennis fellow, and a pair of real blue suede shoes. Lots of heavy aristocratic names came and saw us at the club – the Duke of Kent, for instance. Next we managed to get a recording contract with Decca – pretty good in those days. Only already established stars had record contracts.

The session band consisted of jazzmen. No rock experts at this stage. The two songs – 'Rock with the Caveman' and 'Rock around the Town' – were written by Britishers, Mike Pratt and Lionel Bart. The latter was a regular at the Two 'I's, sitting in with the groups on his solid silver washboard.

After the recording came music hall touring. Moss Empires, who had a big Northern circuit, weren't doing very well. They let Tommy Steele and the Steelmen top a bill and hoped. They were rewarded with full houses, for Steele was in the Formby–Fields line – a real live trouper. He darted about the stage grinning and removing all the sinister sex from rock 'n' roll. He had elfin charm. He did his movements at Mack Sennett speed, and sex is best in slow-motion. He was no *60 minute Man*. He was traditionally decent.

Kennedy accompanied him on the tours.

Up North it was grim. The local Empires were the only place alive, and they were full of jugglers and comics who always ended with a cheer-up song. They were war reminders. I spent my time rehearsing the lighting cues and sweeping cobwebs from the loudspeakers. Everything closed at 10.30 so there was nowhere to go after the show. Tommy took hours to unwind. What we did was to spend hours playing Monopoly and keeping the girls away.'

Off-stage Steele was the opposite of glamour or la-di-da. Like

Gracie Fields in the thirties, he had no time for gracious living. His favourite meal was egg and chips, and his art was a 'lark'. Colin MacInnes, a lone writer on pop, hoped that 'perhaps one day Tommy will sing songs as English as his speaking accent, or his grin. If this should happen, we will hear once again, for the first time since the decline of the music halls, songs that tell us of our own world.' (*Encounter*, December 1957.)

Eventually Steele did become all English and dropped the rock. He did panto. and then landed the part of Tony Lumpkin in *She Stoops to Conquer*, the eighteenth-century play. 'When he played Lumpkin his record sales fell off and kept on falling. The kids felt he'd gone toffee-nosed,' said Kennedy. He never became toffee-nosed but he did become serious about his profession; he studied other acts – comedians, dancers, singers – carefully from the wings. He started educating himself by reading a lot of world history and having his *Classics Illustrated* specially leather-bound by Asprey's of Bond Street so that they would be protected from the wear and tear of show business.

Thus Steele found roots at last. But many of the home-grown stars who followed him failed to get back home again, remaining Little Americans for ever. His success as a wriggler had brought about a host of rockers, complete with managers and comic-book names (e.g. Marty Wilde, Johnny Gentle, Billy Fury, Vince Eager). Off they went on theatre tours, supported by a comic and maybe a conjurer or tumblers. Said an aged stage-door keeper, 'For the children it was panto in the winter and rock 'n' roll shows in the summer. This was toy-town variety and the only non-kiddies were the old men who collected the lolly.' Any visiting US star eclipsed all the locals. Marty Wilde was uneasy in his role as rocker: 'We were terribly British, which we all are really under the whole thing. It was hard for us to latch on to this new thing of dressing up like they did, and lying on your back playing a bass upside down.'*

Actually, many of the Americans were hot on record but tame in real life – ordinary Joes singing, with a view to becoming family

*From an interview by David Epps for the BBC Radio 3 series *The Pop Scene*.

men. Alan Freed had done a certain amount of work in spicing rock 'n' roll, but he was never really more than a super disc jockey. Anyway, he soon got gobbled up by his own monster. US show business in general tried to forget rock 'n' roll by remembering the well-made musical. Filming was left to cheapie-quickie companies. Television was *American Bandstand* and the occasional variety show.

But in Britain there was a man, detached from all this grubby hurly-burly, who saw a tremendous theatrical potential in the music and eventually came to realize his vision on television. Jack Good, Oxford graduate and theatre buff, became the Svengali of rock.

I first came across him back in the summer of '55 when he led his Balliol Players into our school for a modern dress production of some Greek tragedy. I remember a male chorus line, in sports shirts and flannels, high-kicking its way uncertainly across our theatre. *Afterwards there were questions.*

In those days BBC TV was wide open to people with ideas. Good was taken on as a trainee producer and soon found himself co-producing *Six Five Special*, a new Saturday evening light entertainment show – sandwiched between the end of children's hour (6 p.m.) and the beginning of grown-up's viewing (7 p.m.). In fact teen-time itself, neither fish nor fowl.

Six Five started off as an avuncular romp, with camp-fire whiffs. By no means was it limited to rock 'n' roll. Some of it was quite good for you. For example the first show (February 1957), included not only the Bob Cort Skiffle Group but also Pouishnoff the classical pianist and Kenny Baker, the modern jazz trumpeter. Overseeing the fun were personable Pete Murray, the disc jockey, and vivacious Josephine Douglas, also co-producer. Sergeant-Major Brittain and boxer Freddie Mills popped up for laughs.

After a while Good was given his head and he proceeded to mould the little programme into organized shambolics at a gallop. He injected a spontaneous excitement by placing performers on rostrums from which they sang to a sea of boisterous youngsters. Often he himself acted as cheer-leader, 'hooraying' and dashing to and fro, exhorting one and all. It was a thrilling show to view from home and seemed the very end in modernity.

What fired him was a tireless enthusiasm for rock 'n' roll, as he received it. Pop was no longer wet crooning to twinkly violins. Here were songs that were absolutely positive as in the line 'She's my baby and I don't mean maybe'. (On analysis the finest of these invariably began with the word 'well', a tradition harking back to the opening 'Hwæt'* of Anglo-Saxon narrative poetry (see *Beowulf*).) And here was hypnotic music which bored the senses into a state of hypnotic attention. One plunged into such voodoo as one might a hot bath, with a response of 'Owwwww!!' rather than 'This bath is so many degrees'.

But, most of all, here were *free personalities*. Extraordinary figures appearing to live at a more intense level than ordinary people; so without inhibitions that they were able to do the first thing that came into their heads and to carry it off with uncommon aplomb. Good loved Jerry Lee Lewis's steel comb because it was Jerry Lee's and the latter brandished it. He loved Elvis's gold suit and his pink Cadillac because Elvis was in them. Pop objects held no intrinsic interest for him. He liked the way Tommy Steele would suddenly interrupt his stage act with something like: 'Anybody wanna hear "Giddy Ap A Ding Dong"?' In this current world, society couldn't afford mad characters but in the rock 'n' roll heaven all things were possible. What a gorgeous outlet!

His flaming vision was too ambitious for the folksy old *Six Five*. He moved to the Commercial channel to create *Oh Boy!*, the 'fastest show on television', and followed that with *Boy Meets Girl* and *Wham!* They were a tonic. Zap, zap, zap! – song followed song in musical montage. Costumes were carefully picked (a black shirt with a pink tie with a mauve jacket), sets were craftily lit (often the singer was circled in a spotlight whilst all around was inky black) and cameras whooshed in and out and around, under ace direction. Good was particularly keen on the big close-up of the rock face – 'then you flick your eyes right and we'll catch 'em'. Inspired by America maybe, but there was nothing like it over

*Pronounced 'waaaatt'.

there! Visually, I mean. Musically, it was tough work. Lord Rockingham's XI, the house band based on the Fats Domino and Little Richard sound, contained a high proportion of modern jazz men earning a living. In order to obtain a suitably raunchy noise it was necessary to evolve a ritual in which the jazzers detuned their instruments until each man pulled a vinegary expression. Then they knew they'd got it.

Good turned British boys into sensations, by painstaking rehearsal. Marty Wilde was quite scruffy and nervous before he worked with Good: 'He can be very john blunt, you know – but he can also make you feel like the king of the world,' Wilde says. Together they worked on the song 'Mack the Knife' for four days, discussing the story and getting the right motivation. Good combed the coffee bars and came up with Adam Faith and Joe Brown. Cliff Richard was just a shy boy with a group until Good metamorphosed him into lonely dark sexiness. After a bit of argument he agreed to remove his sideburns. Good wanted them off not because they diminished Richard's family appeal but because every coffee bar rocker had sideburns. Richard was to be something special: clean-cut but wild.

From films and photos Good had distilled in his mind the quintessential Elvis. He'd noticed, for instance, the way the Memphis rocker liked to grip his left upper arm with his right hand as if he'd been stabbed by a hypodermic needle. Good gave this image to Cliff Richard: 'You're waking up in hospital and somebody's giving you a terrible injection and oh! your face registers agony. Right – register now!'

Visiting American stars were rather intractable, on the whole. They'd whipped up acts some time ago and didn't need handling. An exception was Gene Vincent who arrived in Britain hot on the heels of his smash 'Be Bop a Lula'.

'His record conjured up in my mind a visual image of the artist,' Good told me in a recent interview.

He seemed the ultimate in the dangerous dagger boy, a frightening motor bike character, zooming down the street without fear of knocking down small children. His face seemed hard and drawn – El Greco-ish – so that I was terrified to meet him in case I said a wrong word to him and was cut from head to toe. But when I met him at the airport he turned out to be a Southern gentleman, very quiet spoken and very polite. So polite that he addressed me as 'Sir' and melted away from reporters and cameramen. He was wearing a red felt ice hockey jacket which didn't go well with my image of him, either. So I thought 'This won't do at all! This is not what my people want.' What was I going to do with him? Then I noticed that he walked with something of a limp and studying his footwear saw that one of his shoes was reinforced by some sort of iron bar.

The limp fascinated me and I thought, 'This surely is something we can build up on'. It struck me that what we wanted to achieve here was the evil Richard III malformed image. My mind raced ahead with the idea of Shakespearean types of costume. Richard III – YES! The limp, that's right! But also a touch of Hamlet – the misunderstood young man alone in the world. But also he *is* a motor cyclist, or should be, so he *must* have black leather. In the end we dressed him totally in black leather: black leather jerkin, black leather gloves. The gloves idea came to me because I'd once played the part of the murderer Lightborne in *Edward II* and had worn pink gloves. Well, pink gloves didn't seem right for Vincent but black was fine. Then black leather pantaloons, and to complete the picture a large barbaric pendant.

For his first television appearance I built a series of steps in order to emphasize his limp. But he was rather good at concealing it and negotiated the steps so well that I was reduced to standing at the side of the set shouting 'Limp you bugger, limp!'

The whole exercise achieved an evil effect which went over very well with the public. Three weeks later I visited the Trocadero cinema in the Elephant and Castle district of South London and was surprised to see that 75 per cent of the male audience was dressed in black leather, even including gloves and pendant. They looked at me askance and made derogatory remarks about the way I was dressed, which was quite normal – a grey chalk-striped suit and Brackenbury tie. I should have taken out shares in black leather.

How I Became
a Rock 'n' Roll
Star

In 1962 Jack Good, fed up, left the country and moved to America. Pop in Britain had gone wet with twinkly violins again. Many of his discoveries had turned into all-round entertainers and those that hadn't made the grade were finding the gigging hard. Pop was sung by well-groomed boys with suits and managers and aimed especially at girls – frequently twittering like birds.

The writer remembers being at a fairground, stuck miles up in the air in a broken-down Big Wheel with a girl he only slightly cared for, and Cliff Richard's 'Living Doll' being played over and over and over on the Tannoy, and she growing dreamier and snuggling closer as a drizzle fell that summer night. He remembers Roy Orbison's operas coming out of Alison's transistor all mini tin-foil sounding, on the beach. He remembers sneering at a group of males crouched round a portable gramophone in a sandy summer house enjoying Fats Domino. Domino grinding out the same old round of chord changes! Too simple to be clever.

That last year at school ('his absorbing interests, especially in creative music of a contemporary kind, suggest a playboy attitude to his "A" levels. A bad habit to cultivate a feeling that these passes are not vital to his career,' said the report) I'd got well in with the books 'n' art set, renouncing rock 'n' roll together with all childish things. They were an action-shunning, limp-wristed set – burners of incense, writers of verse dedicated to each other. Stormy 'affairs' and wriggling in the long grass. Night and day they burned with a hard gem-like flame and read German philosophy and listened gravely to Dave Brubeck's mental music, working out the complicated time signatures with slide rules. Giggling at odd bars. I was confused but anxious to get into it all and out of childhood that summer of '59.

I left school and spent a lot of time on my own, brooding in a funk. Soon I'd be twenty and I hadn't led a teenage life according to the articles. One day I bought a record by pianist Jimmy Yancey. A flash conversion to his amazing quiet blues-boogie with its graceful jog and Spanish tinges! In his piano was the whole of beat! I wanted nothing else ever. Endless, satisfying music. I was determined to make some too. On sunny afternoons – Saturdays even – whilst others were out playing I sat at the piano trying to work myself into a blues frame of mind; learning to crush notes two or three at a time, flicking the wrist around for certain effects, wiping notes, and keeping a steady roll going. No teachers around – just Yancey on the gram. Yancey at half speed, at quarter speed. Yancey taken to bits. Who was Yancey?

A photo in a jazz book showed him standing melancholy and black on the front porch of his wooden shack. At one time he'd been a vaudevillian, was reputed to have tap-danced in front of the King and Queen at a Royal Command Variety Show in Edwardian times. 'For 30 years he was employed as a groundskeeper at a Chicago baseball park and only played piano at rent parties and private functions,' said the back of my record cover.

About the same time I discovered Scott Joplin and the real ragtime. Stately and exact, chaos elegantly caged, it went well with the more down-homey Yancey. Difficult music to read (I fumbled it but eventually approximated it) but reading *about* ragtime helped. I read Rudi Blesh's *They All Played Ragtime* several times. And I read all about early jazz: shining trumpets that could be heard for miles on a clear New Orleans night, blown by legendary bronzemen in gay bordellos with fancy iron-work railings. Good-time high-yaller girls, diamond teeth, grinding all night, sweet lotus blossom and keep a knockin' but you can't come in. Then they all sailed up the river to Chicago! Did I want to get to the USA! Sickening to close the book and face Putney Heath!

Next I went to Trinity College, Dublin, Eire. I had some friends there and also the Trinity Handbook was luring:

How I Became a Rock 'n' Roll Star

Living in rooms in college is a unique and complex experience. The walls, once adorned, become the mirror of the student resident's personality. How depressing they can appear on a murky, joyless morning, but how splendid and intimate at night. For only when evening falls can rooms really come into their own. Round college fires, over supper, world problems, politics, religion and sex in that order are discussed far into the night, while Beethoven or Brubeck tries to make himself heard. Perhaps the only feature common to every resident's day is Commons, where between well-rounded sentences there is an ordered camaraderie which will remain in the memory when the rest of College life is forgotten.

But for the first few years I had to live in digs. I took a course in modern history and political science. I'm not sure why. The head of our department gave us an introductory lecture which went: 'Freshmen! I ask you: what is history? History is the past,' and left it at that. Julian, the college postman, told me: 'History? Why study history? It's all happened and there's nothing you can do about it.' I was confused. We all scattered and I got going on other things. By now I was absolutely dying to be black. I was utterly hooked on black men, through reading and records. Luckily, there were a number of actual black men from Africa herself at Trinity. Quite a few sat together in our history class.

Mr Balloodadan, very friendly, wore a blazer with 'Mauritius' sewn on the breast pocket. I figured that it must be the name of the ocean liner he sailed over in, that he'd won the badged blazer in a deck quoits competition. My pal J said no – Balloodadan was from a country called Mauritius where he owned a chain of brothels and he was over here on business, buying white slave girls. Also in our class was Mr Anangoola who had tribal scars on his face and applauded everything, especially lectures. I persuaded him to come out to my digs one evening to hear jazz records. He turned out to be a disappointment, enjoying the tea and iced cake but not really responding to the jazz. I thought it might trigger him off so that I could then quiz and study him but it didn't and that night I learned a truth: not all black men have innate beat. He returned to his degree course (eventually winning a first) and I dived headlong into college jazz life. That was the next best thing to being black.

Our Time

JOURNAL (November 1961): I wore my US army combat jacket under my gown for a ghastly lecture on Descartes and his candle. 'That the mind is more easily known than the body.' After filling my pipe with the Provost's Mixture I set off in freezing cold for a rendezvous with the Trinity College Jazz Band, at home. They live together as one man in a seedy part of town, sharing a room. I've been asked to join on piano and mouth-harp. I'm reading *Mr Jelly Roll* and *The Country Blues* to get the feel. The band was all in bed together, plus 'free' girl scrubbers including one-eyed Edwina, Dublin's Queen of the Blues. She sports mauve legs and buttered hair. Her dad's an IRA sergeant and she's really been through the blues, green-style. A blanket, hanging out the window to air, was so stiff with the stuff of life that it banged noisily against the wall. A jam session was in progress together with a breakfast of toast 'n' marge. That's all they ever eat, 3 times a day. Sean Banjo lost his strumming hand years ago in industry but he plays acceptably by sticking a pick in the stump. He manages to keep a rigid rhythm, bleeding a bit on up-tempo stuff. That afternoon we formed up as The Paragon Marching Band under the direction of history student Barold Pilchardson – strapped into bass drum, tishing a tiny cymbal with a kitchen spatula. We weren't playing a funeral but advertising a hurling match. We marched proudly through the rain but nobody much could hear us because chinless wonder types were out in force too, blowing hunting horns and yelling slogans like 'T-R-I-N-I-T-Y', 'No Popery', 'Pull the Chain' and so forth. We had our revenge, though, that very evening when we turned up to play an Anglo-Irish aristocratic gig. 'I don't think I know your face,' drawled the velvet-jacketed host after creaking open the castle door to Harry Trombone, our tough leader. 'You won't know yours, matey, by the time I've finished with you si vous don't open up sharpish!' slashing mine host with a handy trombone. Next morn Harry woke up in an upstairs chamber and, full of overnight beer, pissed into a nearby Celtic vase which he then politely emptied out the window hoping it might disappear into the moat – only it didn't. It crashed through the plate-glass conservatory roof arriving smartly on the breakfast table to join the scrambled eggs and kedgeree being served to the weekend guests. I'm also reading *Really The Blues* by Mezz Mezzrow.

Whilst I was studying and living jazz in Eire a new movement was bubbling underground in London and a few Northern pockets: rhythm and blues, GB fashion. Like yours truly, it was inclined to be academic. Like skiffle and traditional jazz, too (after all, we were a long way from the scene of the action). R&B was

256

slightly different, though, because it was a more up-to-date move-ment than jazz and that. Its electric blues bands played in trad-jazz clubs mostly. Rather grotty spots with hot coke and floppy crisps. The big ballrooms were using neat 'n' dainty pop groups with their light rock à la Shadows (Cliff Richard's extremely popu-lar backing group). The fighting little jazz underworld was split over the electric blues question. Of course, all jazzers must love the blues but the blues is a trillion things to its lovers. Tradjazzers preferred good old comfortable bluesmen like Big Bill Broonzy and nicely experienced vaudeville blues ladies of the twenties like Bessie Smith (if tradjazzers dug jazz singing at all – mostly they dug instrumentalists) to the post-war angry electric blues. R & B, they felt, was decadent and commercial, and far too new.

The Grand Old Man of British R & B was Alexis Korner, singer/guitarist/historian. I used to read him on the back of record sleeves. Anybody keen on R & B had to hear his band (because there was nothing else here) and perhaps have a blow as well. Jack Bruce, Ginger Baker, Eric Burdon, Charlie Watts, Mick Jagger – all of them played gigs with the Korner band one time or another.

Not surprisingly, Korner was the son of an Austrian cavalry officer. He soon found a way out through Afro-American music. During the fifties he served in trad bands but his trouble was he just couldn't contain himself; he liked bebop, R & B and Chuck Berry too. (My trouble was even worse because I liked Al Jolson, Billy Cotton, Bessie Smith, Albert Ammons, Vera Lynn, Hank Snow, Woody Guthrie, Joe Hill, George Formby, Scott Joplin, the Big Bopper, Connie Francis, the Original Dixieland Jazz Band, the Honeydripper, Fats Waller, Whispering Jack Smith, Glenn Miller, Speckled Red, and Ragtime Bob Darch.)

Anyway. Around 1960 Korner formed 'Blues Incorporated', a ravishing all-electric blues band. Jack Good went wild for them, cut them live at the Marquee. I caught them at a club in Ealing. Changed my life: the loudest, beefiest, raunchiest, most thrilling sound I'd ever heard. Better than my records! And all locals. I was struck by a boy singer in plimsolls (unusual) who had full red lips and was shouting hurtful, hateful blues, not about cottonfields at all. How great! Very reassuring. So you didn't have to be a grizzled old black varmint of sixty to sing the blues. Nor did you have to have been bred in an urban ghetto. You didn't even have to be American. Much later I realized I'd witnessed Mick Jagger.

At that time he was barely existing off mashed potato and an occasional egg in a rough Chelsea flat together with other embryonic Stones. He was still quite serious about his course at the London School of Economics, but Brian Jones just blew mouth harp all day long. An outpost of R & B, one of many.

I returned to Trinity and came out into the open about R & B. It was a real pleasure to – after all, lots of it had honking sax, chinking piano, telstar guitar. If this was blues it was also rock 'n' roll! Chuck Berry, I learned, was an R & B artist as well as a childhood memory. So I formed a band called 'Warren Whitcomb's Bluesmen' which did well at the Jazz Band Ball. Undergrads came up afterwards to say they dug the 'sound'. It got around college that I was resident R & B expert, therefore left-wing, iconoclastic and in favour of change. I became associated with movements when all I liked was music. Still, a gig's a gig and I put away my pipe. Roger Question and his New Theatre Group approached me in Front Square to ask me into their rooms for a discussion about a revue they were about to write. Only they didn't call it a revue, they called it a 'thing'.

'This thing will be an anti-revue revue. We cast a spell on the audience by giving them melancholy with a bang, but leave them with a bitter after-taste,' explained Question, whirling round and just missing a wicked-looking chianti table lamp. 'Good,' I said, 'I'll take care of the chores.' 'What chores?' 'A pint of stout!' said I. Ignoring this he carried on with: 'You hated school, right?' (No, on reflection, I quite enjoyed it.) 'Well, we're gonna destroy such institutions and also send up Shakespeare – you know. "Hola! What manner of man is this that holds his privates in parenthesis?" and so forth. Your job is to write some high-speed nasty boogie-woogie to support this.' I got a lot of requests to accompany demonstrations – 'The Right to Protest' march, the 'South African Fruit' march. Students in battle-dress used to say 'Sit down and play me some R & B.'

How I Became a Rock 'n' Roll Star

Summer of '63. The Union of Students of Ireland advertised a charter flight to the USA and I signed up in a hurry. OK to fiddle about locally but America was still boss. For decades I'd dreamed of landing there and kissing the soil. Americans had better bodies, sculptured skulls. They *were* sex, I thought – next only to the French, of course. Most of all, though, America was the home of all my technicolor music. Oh boy, oh boy! I got a crew-cut in readiness. The night before we flew off I was just walking out of Front Gate when who should purr past in an open Cadillac but President Kennedy himself! Plus his wife. They waved at me and, quite spontaneously, I dropped my music books and clapped. In a daze I rolled off to my hotel where, wrapped from the cold in a Papal flag, I slept like a child.

Letter from Seattle, Washington (August 1963)

Dear All,

Sorry not to have sent an epistle earlier but it has been such a whirl! The burgers are great. Had my first at the Greyhound bus station, after I'd bought a 99 day 99 dollar ticket to See America Now. Then we looked at Greenwich Village (which is like Chelsea except more so). Full of frowning folksingers with guitars slung on their backs and policemen who won't tell you the way. I'm always being asked for I.D., (identification papers). Hard-backed British passport foxes them. Did you know that the Village has more coffee houses per square foot than any other community in the USA? 'And that's one helluva lotta punks,' said a policeman I met – with a college degree. Everybody has a degree here.

I went in search of American music. Spent a day in the Library of Congress asking. They said look in the hills around Nashville. I bussed to Nashville. Walked into radio station WLAC to enquire but instead they put me straight on the air as a newsflash, quizzing me about Christine Keeler and Profumo. They said it tickled them pink, that story from the land of bowler hats. One man asked me if I drove across to France often. I was terrified of playing a blue note here in the South, home of it all. But eventually I did and was asked to do a TV show on the strength of it so I sang 'Maggie May'.

Very embarrassed by my accent at first but now I'm feeling re-assured because people are fascinated by it. A girl in a drive-in burger rendezvous left work early and drove me all the way to her parents' place (50 miles away) so's they could hear the 'cute' way I talked and then the parents called up their parents to tell them. Later, alone with the girl on her 'Davenport' couch, I was only chatting away amiably when she said breathily: 'Quit it, Iron, you're *turning me on*!'

Bussed off to New Orleans. Visited Preservation Hall, the jazz exhibit, to hear some veterans play. In the interval I dared to play some boogie. One by one the band returned to join in, just like a film musical. Dreams come true!

My courage is growing: I arrived in Seattle (the Northwest tip on the map) via Los Angeles to visit cousin Anna and, believe it or not, landed a job in a student coffee house in the downtown Skid Row area. I get room and board in return for singing, every night, blues/ragtime/rock 'n' roll at an upright piano. Talk about carrying coals to Newcastle! A columnist, well-known in Seattle, described me in his column as a 'hip, fresh-faced lad who mimics Ray Charles and generally laughs it up in a manner calculated to shatter completely the traditional image of the reserved sedate Briton'.

I've been having trouble with my fellow artistes, the Hootenanny folk people. Every other act seems to be a group of crew-cutted college types in short longs and long shorts strumming guitars and singing about Tom Dooley (a chap who was hanged) with a smile, or 'Three Jolly Coachmen'. Mothers, fathers, wives, husbands, children all love these folk songs and join in by clapping their hands. But there are other folk acts who aren't so smiley and have no fixed address. Billy drifted in from Canada, lives off raw beef, did a week at our coffee house singing his own tough songs and hopped a boat to Madagascar. He sang eyes closed, head down, motionless (except for a bobbing Adam's apple). A few nights ago a po-faced but beautiful virginal girl with straight flowing flaxen hair who was singing plaintively about being '10,000 miles from home' walked off stage in a huff because a customer was munching his pizza too noisily, so yours truly had to dash on and sing a breezy version of 'Brother Can You Spare a Dime?' to keep the show rolling. I don't know – is this entertainment, I ask you? Still, most of the time, this music is (in the words of the leader of the Wanderers) 'not just folk music but also *fun music*'. Sometimes local disc jockeys drop into the place. Maybe I'll be discovered. See you soon, IAN. xxx

I had landed slap bang in the thick of the Urban Folk Music Movement – Hootenanny period – but it looked like skiffle to me. Fortunately I ran across L. M. S. Farquhar's Dwayne Hickenhacker (now calling himself 'Rovin' Stearns Eliot' and crisscrossin' the country with his guitar, stoppin' off at campus and coffee house to perform ramblin' songs). He got me an appointment with local university professor Jack Feeny who, sitting in his department office, put me wise about the Hootenanny craze: 'It's not a craze, Iron, it's a *movement* – right outside of the pabulum stream of popular music – in fact a reaction against such rampant commercialism. It's a fairly old movement too, at least from the political angle. Now you're interested in ragtime and goodtime stuff and that's an OK field but there's another history of song – protest, meaningful song – that runs parallel with your money music. I guess the torch was first lit by Joe Hill back in the rag days. He put new words to current hits and made them gut songs, union propaganda. For example he changed Irving Berlin's "Everybody's Doing It Now" to "Everybody's Joining It Now" and he meant *one big union*. He contributed these "songs to fan the flames of discontent" to the famous *Little Red Songbook*, issued by the Industrial Workers of the World. The bosses didn't like the I.W.W. or Joe Hill. He was executed on a trumped-up murder charge in 1915. But he never died; his torch burned right on and in the thirties it was taken up by Woody Guthrie, a genuine working Oklahoman with a zest for learning, a strong sense of right and wrong, a feeling for the little man and a store of great songs. Woody fled the dust bowl storms of Oklahoma and went hard travellin'. He picked fruit in California and eventually turned up in New York around 1938. Now there was growing up quite a bit of interest in our folk songs at this time, largely stimulated by work on folklore projects set up by the Roosevelt Administration. A lot of getting back to fundamentals, discovering our great heritage. Pure untrammelled folk songs, warts and all. Hillbilly music was considered hopelessly commercial – Gene Autry and Jimmy Rodgers, etc. – but when Woody came along like a research project come to life, with his songs of point and truth, folk song enthusiasts were ecstatic. He radicalized the intellectual antiquarians. He was about the present and future, not just the rosy far past. He said America was basically a good place but a few things had gone wrong. For the whole world he wanted One Big Union. During the forties he became a part of the New York folk scene, a tight little one, and lived in the co-operative settlement called Almanac House. This house spawned the Almanac

Singers, the very first folk group. It was a quartet and it included Woody and Pete Seeger, a Harvard drop-out and the son of a distinguished musicologist. The Almanacs did the subway circuit in New York and a lot of Labor Rallies and Anti-Fascist Rallies. All this was OK whilst the war was on and we were all fighting together but afterwards the Iron Curtain crashed down, and not just in Europe. Crashed down here as well and the folk radicals found themselves branded 'unfriendly'. Senator McCarthy and his witch-hunters blacklisted Pete, making it impossible for him to get regular dates – but not before he and his new and more professional group the Weavers had gotten hit parade success with such old songs as 'Goodnight Irene', a black piece, and 'Kisses Sweeter Than Wine', from Ireland. The fifties was a bleak period – a silent generation – and Pete found his only welcome audiences at colleges, though some Deans weren't at all gung ho, but he kept the flame a-burning and inspired a lot of kids during those Eisenhower years. Rock 'n' roll was temporary bread and circuses for the dumb ones but by the end of the fifties things were brighter. The Kingston Trio continued in the same line as the Weavers – a bit slicker and with touches of Caribbean. They were a part of the coffee house and campus folk group movement. Today you'll find that the same kids who are singing 'This Land is Your Land' are also anti-John Birch, anti-segregation and pro-Peace Corps, pro-Civil Rights. They sing songs of the soil – they have strong roots and no identification problems – but simultaneously they're full of hope for the future. They feel, like the President, that things can and will *get better*, Iron.'

Full of folk, and dressed in a letter-man jacket breasted with a huge purple 'I' and a Seattle University sweat shirt, I turned up at Idlewild Airport for the return home (except that my home was America). Very depressing to see again my companions, that grey mass of porridge-eaters. They'd seen National Parks. The worst of the boozers were evicted at Shannon after they'd tried to hijack a hostess.

London. I mounted a bus and the cheeky conductor pointing to my sweat shirt said 'Wot's that then – Beatle University?' No,

Seatle. Everybody was talking and reading and seeing Beatles. What a dreadful pun! A group neither folk, R & B nor ragtime, but all-British pop. Thundering down from the grim North, which I'd only heard about in jokes like the North countryman in Harrods who was asked by the posh sales lady, 'And what is monsieur's fancy?' 'Pigeons and fucking but ah coom 'ere for a flat 'at.' That reply was foolish or nitty-gritty depending on your outlook.

What a winter it was going to be! I retired to bed confused as usual. The Liverpool sound swam around me. Apart from these Beatles there were the Swinging Blue Jeans, Billy J. Kramer and the Dakotas, Freddie and the Dreamers, Gerry and the Pace-makers, etc. I read about Liverpool in bed and learned that it had been the centre of the African Slave Trade and was known as a 'knuckle-dusting city'. The Beatle-type groups had forged their music in grubby little clubs that sweated like hot salamis where sailors were liable to follow you home. A pal of mine popped up to have a look at the North. He ordered a cup of tea in a cafe and the proprietor called out his cook and all his dishwashers to tell them, 'Just hear how this bugger from London talks.' Well really! First Gracie Fields, then George Formby and now this!

I looked at pictures of the groups. Gangs with guitars – they didn't look a bit like Cliff Richard. 'No,' said my friend who'd been North, 'I have it on high authority that they're raised on tripe and jam butties and never have tits in their mouths until they're engaged.' I thought that was a bit strong but life in general was getting tangier. I read some more mags: John Lennon's ambition was 'money and everything', Paul McCartney's was 'money and to do well', George Harrison's was 'to retire rich' and Ringo Starr's was 'to get to the top'. I always thought glossy statements got you to the top. They also said that Sophie Tucker was their fave group, which I might have said at a college smoking concert but not on stage at a Royal Command Performance. However, the Queen Mother said she 'found them most intriguing'. What on earth had all this to do with folk music?

R & B was in the public air though, thanks to the Rolling Stones. They had emerged from the minority blues scene in the light of

263

pop and now Mick Jagger was everybody's property. I watched him pout on TV and he even nearly annoyed me! Surly was all right for blues but for life maybe too close to the wind? 'We just act ourselves,' he told a reporter.

All these groups appeared to do what they liked yet they had precious record contracts. Hitherto hard things to get hold of. Toytown in adultsville? I got much better but had to get back to college for the winter of '63.

At last I'd got rooms and would now be able to enjoy calling at the co-op, Julian the postman on his rounds, cacophony in the bath-house, Front Square quiet and mellow on a Sunday afternoon as yellow leaves blew off saying 'pardon'. I pushed open the old oak door and was surprised to see history student and arch jazz-man Barold Pilchardson sitting on a bank of black amplifiers with chrome knobs on, flanked by crossed guitars with sun-burnt finishes. With a flourish he snapped his clarinet in two as he announced 'Let's go. I've formed an R & B group and you're in it on piano.' He'd rustled up electric guitarists, electric bass players, electric drummers but no name so I called it Bluesville Mfg, after Alexis Korner. Off we dashed to our first date – for the 'Save The Children Fund' at St Anthony's Hall. There was much wiring up to be done, testing mikes with 'one, two, three, testing!', shoving plugs up junction boxes and pretending to inspect my grand piano. Barold heaved a few mikes in it so that it gave off like slivers of hot steel. Electrification! It was as exciting to us as it had been to Lenin after the Revolution. A small chap could strum up a thunderclap. Blow-up notes like giant flies devised by mad scientists. Soon the scrubbers and guerriers assembled out in the gloom. When I sang about the 'Hoochie Coochie Man' I truly felt angry and I kicked the black coffin amps. This got a howl. My tongue hit the round metal grille top of the mike and it tasted tingly, refreshing. Electrification! Another howl. So I lifted my leg and the scrubbers screamed, I shifted a bottom cheek and they screamed. Raised an eyebrow. Scream. Then I stamped on a live wire in the junction box, shot eight feet in the air hitting a dangling crucifix and fractured my thigh on landing and they screamed and my God so did I! Still, it was a revelation, all this idolatry. I went to bed but someone told me afterwards, at a gang-bang in Goatstown,* Maisie opened her eyes after her tenth man and asked 'Have I had the one that looks like Mick Yaggers yet?' She meant yours truly.

Lord love old Ireland! Everywhere I was mistaken for him – even gold-braided commissionaires outside ice-cream parlours in O'Connell Street saluted me smartly and whispered 'Have you got a few shillings for me then, Mr Jaggers?' Girls tittered. I'd never thought of myself as God's gift before. My mirror showed me that my crew-cut had gone to seed. Quickly I took the trend in my hands – (1) I determined to let my hair grow till it was as long as the new groups'. Hitherto long hair had been confined to art students and anarchists but now the world was worried over the general spread of hair. Wallace Scowcroft, President of the National Federation of Hairdressers, said about the Rolling Stones, 'One of them looks as if he has got a feather duster on his head.' I had hair trouble: after it reached a certain length it about-turned and grew back up, ending up looking like the Dutch cap which Ginger Rogers wore in *The Story of Vernon and Irene Castle*. (2) I determined to slim down to a hungry size by eating yoghurt. (3) I bought a chest expander.

Bluesville was rapidly becoming the toast of Dublin youth. Fans referred to us as the Bluesvilles and in return we glided swiftly from academic blues into current pop. We learnt up the current Top Ten and in so doing I came to appreciate Beatle songs. I took them apart on the piano. They had odd codas and stretched notes and shuffled chord sequences and yet they weren't avant-garde – more like the son of a friend. Driving a Land Rover, though, not a Cadillac. There was no middle in their sound, no belly of fiddles or horns. But an obese bass in seven-league boots and a shrill spartan harmony from the head. Their melodies took steps avoided by most pop songs. 'They're medieval,' said a college music professor, 'and the words are nursery rhyme.' We didn't pay too much attention to the words because you weren't supposed to in those days. Mostly the Beatles sang simple messages

*A Dublin suburb.

of love from him to her. Reminiscent of Buddy Holly. His songs, together with the Everly Brothers' souped-up country harmony singing had had an enormous influence on British pop musicians. Whilst the girls had been mooning over Holly and the Everlys some of the boys had been analysing the music. I'd been in a blues haze, never dreaming of attempting to write blues about Britain. *Muddy has the blues* – Yes! Even, *President Johnson has the Blues*. But *Harold Wilson has the blues* – NO!!!

But the Beatles wrote straight pop so I had a go at that. I locked myself in the College Library, surrounded by swots swinking over such set texts as *The Dark Passage: some medieval problems* by E. Musco Biggs. I wrote a whole bunch:

> Now listen here sweet miss
> I ain't asked you for a kiss
> I ain't asked you for a date
> I only wanna see ya work out
> 'Cause I like it – dance again one more time.

and

> But in the evening no-one comes and outside
>   the rain it just drums and drums
> I see the sign and it says THE END.
> When you go I'll be left with Satan
> And he just sits there waitin' and waitin'
> I see the sign and it says THE END.

and

> Sittin' with my baby in back of car
> we're going strong but not too far
> when all at once we hear a knock
> 'You better move on Mac' says a great big cop.
> (*chorus*) There's too many secret police
> Ya can't do a thing today
> Too many Big Brothers too
> Always gettin' in the way.

And then, running out of themes, I fell back on an old folk song I'd remembered from skiffle days:

> I'm getting tired of just hanging aroun'
> I'm gonna get married and settle down
> And this sporting life is gonna be the death of me.

266

How I Became a Rock 'n' Roll Star

I changed the time from 4/4 to 6/8 and put an E♭7 here and a D♭ there, although the tune was in F. I heard swishing drums, swirling organ, clanking arpeggio guitar, and anguished vocal. I'd also heard a current hit which had most of these ingredients, 'House of the Rising Sun' by Eric Burdon and the Animals, from Newcastle.

There was a recording studio underneath Merrion Square, near where Oscar Wilde had been brought up. I took the lads there with all the clobber because I was sure we could have a hit. A Bush Baptist brass band was still recording when we arrived. Would they be long? 'Friend, we'll just play the last few bars of "Holy Holy Holy" and then fuck off!' said the leader. Soon we were blasting away on our hit. Trouble! The studio owner, an ex-British army wallah who'd been first man out of Dunkirk (six months before anyone else) owed a bit of rent. Enter bailiff's man by way of one foot in the door, threatening to whip all the movables. I flashed a card which read 'Know Ye That *Ian Whitcomb* Holds Ye Commission of Honorary State Trooper' (I'd been given it whilst touring Alabama). The bailiff's man tugged at his bowler and asked if I could spare a few shillings. We let him conduct us on the final take of 'Sporting Life'. I was carried away and sang one verse very high-pitched.

The Seattle coffee house was calling to me. I returned in the summer vac. of 64, with a suitcase full of leather gear and our Bluesville tape. When I arrived I found a huge banner over the coffee house: 'IAN WHITCOMB – DIRECT FROM LONDON VIA LIVERPOOL'. Beatlemania had hit America, wham! Janet Leigh had appeared at a Hollywood party in a Beatle mop-top hair-do. But kids complained that I didn't sound as British as the Beatles. All that money spent on a progressive public school in the heart of Dorset! Still, when they asked me whether I knew the Beatles I was able to say truthfully that our sax player was a friend of Peter Asher of Peter and Gordon fame and that Peter's sister was currently engaged to Paul McCartney. 'I'm none the wiser,' said a disc jockey. 'No, but you're better informed,' I replied, like a college student.

Things had changed since the first time I'd been in the States.

267

Britain called the tune and I was out to exploit. First I looked up 'recording companies' in the Yellow Pages. Second I was told that Jerry Dennon was the man to see because he'd produced 'Louie Louie', a top five smash by the Kingsmen. He was a busy man but finally I was able to burst into his office to tell him that I could be hotter than the Rolling Stones. He nodded. He pondered a few weeks and then drew up papers for me to sign in order that he might release 'This Sporting Life' on his little local label. During my cross-continent Greyhound trip to Seattle the tape had got crinkled and torn. Clever engineers smoothed and sealed it. Then we dubbed on an extra organ plus some maraccas to give it 'balls', before sending our 'product' off to an ace mastering company in Hollywood for final echo treatment. The result was a whirlwind of a sound and all housed in a tiny 45 with a blue label. Last thing at night I gazed at this label: IAN WHITCOMB AND BLUESVILLE. Dreams come true! Years before, I had stood on a windy hill on a Surrey golf-course shouting 'I will be Laurie London.* I will be a star,' across the greens, frightening golfers. The night before I left Seattle for Dublin and the spring term I was guest of honour at an all-girl shower party. During the proceedings I found myself french-kissing a schoolgirl while she murmured 'You're TURNING ME ON'. Again that phrase! A song formed in my mind but I had to dash off, as there was an exam in two weeks – the first part of my Honours History Finals.

'Discuss Owen as a fore-runner of socialism in your period.' 'How far is Marx an original thinker?' 'Outline the place of the King's Wardrobe in the development of Parliament.' These were some of the questions I had answered. The dreaded exam over, once again students and faculty could relapse into college life: setting fire to our furniture, organizing marches, listening to Julian the postman on his rounds, watching Front Square as the leaves fell. It was cold that February of 65 and I had a feeling that something odd was going to happen. I returned from a walk consisting of following in Bloom's footsteps, to find a telegram waiting: 'RECORD OUT NATIONALLY VIA ZOOM LABEL SUBSIDIARY

*A child star of the fifties known for 'He's Got the Whole World in His Hands'.

How I Became a Rock 'n' Roll Star

OF CAPITOL RECORDS FANTASTIC REACTION HERE IAN
I FEEL THIS CAN BE A LEFT-FIELD SMASHEROO REGARDS
JERRY'. The comparative strangers in my rooms and on my easy
chairs moved in their hacking jackets and laughed. The kettle was
forever on the hob singing a Celtish lament. The fire spluttered.
'It's going out,' said someone. 'Well, I hope it's got a woolly on
for it's chilly tonight,' said another. This was the kind of banter
that was roaring round our block (where once Oscar Wilde had
roomed quite near Edward Carson). The only signs of pop life
were the banks of amplifiers draped in gowns and a framed fan
letter which read 'Ian, I would like to have sexual intercoarse
with you at your own convenience. Yours, Moira.'

I watched the minutes, hours, days, weeks go by. The fire
crackled. Julian the postman trundled up over the ancient cobbles
in a van, not his customary bicycle. He tipped a heap of mail into
our rooms, saying, 'And I trust that's the feckin' lot, friend,' and
left spitting.

Cuttings from US trade papers: 'This Sporting Life' was No. 90
with a bullet in *Record World* ('newcomer stretches the blues out
into a taut performance. Slice is a worker'). The *Fenway Reporter*
said 'like it's weird. Definitely a record. Requests should be
coming in after a few days' play.' Bill Gavin's Tip Sheet had it as
a 'significant regional'. *Cash Box* placed it at 22 per cent airplay
in their 'Radio Active' chart. Radio stations throughout America
had put it on their playlists – KJR, Seattle; KYA, San Francisco;
KFWB, Los Angeles; KRUX, Phoenix; WAPX, Montgomery;
WKDA, Nashville; KAKC, Tulsa; WWDC, Washington;
WIBG, Philadelphia; WBZ, Boston; WDRC, Hartford;
WMAQ, Chicago ... PLEASE GET BLUESVILLE IN ACCORD
AS I WILL BE OVER BEFORE YOU CAN SAY PHIL SPECTOR
TO RECORD ALBUM REGARDS JERRY.

Jerry Dennon arrived safely and I put him into a lovely hotel
with iced water. We were on the fish course when a phone was
brought to our table. Long distance from Hollywood. An agent.
He had just caught this fantastic record of mine on his car radio
and was I signed? Later that evening, over coffee, I signed Jerry's
papers. Even later a deputation from Bluesville arrived and they

269

signed some other papers, I think. It was an awful long time ago. Next evening we cut our LP in a tiny studio very near the famous Post Office where in 1916 the Irish Republic had been declared. Amongst the numbers we laid down was one that utilized that phrase I kept coming across in America, 'You turn me on.'

The tape rolled, driven by another Trinity College student. Jerry paced the room, nodding. Bluesville* set off at a comfortable boogie pace. They were using a lick popular with Albert Ammons, Jimmy Reed, Chuck Berry, Jerry Lee Lewis, Marvin Gaye and countless others. It's still fairly sure-fire:

```
            ↗ DING-DING↘
        ↗ DING-DING  F7  F7  DING-DING
     DING-DING  F6  F6          F6  F6
  (chord):  F      F
```

Our drummer did a wonderful back-beat laced with solos on his bass drum – a novelty at that time. One of his many cymbals dug into my back. During the instrumental opening chorus a weighty ash-tray, powered by the music, slid off my baby grand piano and thudded on to the only bit of free floor space. A studio no bigger than a potting shed! The twin guitars chugged on and pretty soon I decided to contribute a vocal. Actually, I could hardly hear myself above the rock but I sang ad-lib into a near by massive ex-BBC talk show microphone. Here is a transcript:

COME ON NOW HONEY – YOU KNOW YOU REALLY TURN ME ON!
COME ON NOW HONEY – YOU KNOW YOU REALLY TURN ME ON!
AND WHEN, WHEN YOU DO – HUH! HUH! HUH! HUH! HUH! HUH!
            – THAT'S MY SONG!

COME ON NOW BABY – COME ON AND DO THE JERK WITH ME!
COME ON NOW HONEY – COME ON AND DO THE JERK WITH ME!
AND IF, IF YOU DO – HUH! HUH! HUH! HUH! HUH! HUH!
            – THAT'S MY SONG!

COME ON NOW BABY – YOU KNOW YOU REALLY TURN ME ON!
  (Ohhh!)

*That February night Bluesville consisted of Mick Molloy (lead guitar) Deke O'Brien (rhythm guitar), Gerry Ryan (bass guitar), Ian McGarry (drums) and me.

How I Became a Rock 'n' Roll Star

COME ON NOW HONEY – YOU KNOW YOU REALLY TURN ME ON!
  (Ah yeah)
AND WHEN, WHEN YOU DO – HUH! HUH! HUH! HUH! HUH! HUH!
                    – THAT'S MY SONG
(Let's GO!!) . . . (Oh YEAH!) . . .
HUH! HUH! HUH! HUH! HUH! HUH! – THAT'S MY SONG!
Copyright for USA and Canada, Burdette Music, Seattle, Washington.
1965. (US selling agent: Edward B. Marks Music Corp., New York,
USA.)
Copyright Sparta Music, London, 1965, for the rest of the world,
Assigned to:
  Editions Musicales Catalogue, Paris, France, 1965
  Fermata do Brasil, Sao Paulo, Brazil, 1966
  Carl Gehrmans Musikforlag, Stockholm, 1965
  Edizioni Musicali R.I.A.S. s.r.l., Milan, Italy, 1966.

Afterwards experts told me I'd sung in a *falsetto* voice. Why had
I sung high? It's such a long time ago but I think I was doing an
impression of the Supremes. Why did I HUH! HUH! HUH! HUH!
like a baby whimpering for milk? You may ask but I really don't
know. I never suspected that POP HISTORY WAS IN THE
MAKING!

The next thing I knew I was at a lecture in Medieval History
and roll-call had just been finished. Suddenly a voice from the back
shouted smoothly: 'Hi, dear! You've forgotten S for Shaper.' We
all turned to catch a sun-tanned figure in polo-neck sweater and
blue blazer, finger snapping. As he was ejected, humming 'Just One
of Those Things', he beckoned to me with a jerk of the head. I
followed and discovered that this was Hal Shaper, my song publisher for Britain and the World (excluding USA and Canada).
Quickly we linked up with Jerry and, as I led them round Dublin
in Bloom's footsteps, they discussed contracts. Hal had a great
love of life which he demonstrated by swimming across the river
Liffey and by defending us with karate chops when, returning to
my rooms that evening, we were attacked by a mounted college
fraternity group. Chop! Ha! Chop! Ho! Toppers went flying and
dickies too. The students clattered off in a hurry.
Safe in my rooms that night Hal, Jerry and I discussed my future

271

over cocoa, whilst my friends dreamed of future exams or worked out a thesis.

A few days later Jerry flew off to Hollywood with the tapes, anxious to play them to the Zoom Records executives. And I flew to London with Hal in order to 'come out' and meet the British pop people. I met the press and I visited the clubs. An extraordinary number of public schoolboys had entered rock-pop who might otherwise have gone into the city or become mercenaries. One, a record producer/baronet, was deep into West Indian banana blues – so much so that he attached himself to the girl of one of his artists when the latter was away at sea, only to be interrupted just when he was *on the job* by the sailor's return. In the ensuing fight the baronet had an ear sliced off but fortunately he managed to pick it up as he beat a retreat back to Chelsea. I met the pop baronet through Denny Lavarack (afterwards Denny Cordell), another ex-public schoolboy on the pop scene. I knew Denny from my jazz days when he was a keen officer's training corps drummer and tea-chest bass player. Now he was involved with the Moody Blues and Georgie Fame, and in future years he was to produce hits with the Move, Procol Harum and Joe Cocker. Well done, Denny!

At certain parties I went to during my 'coming out' fat cigarettes were passed around and I passed them on until I was told that this was Indian hemp. I'd read in the evening papers about hemp being smoked in Britain but I'd shrugged it off as eccentric because who'd normally want to smoke old rope? But I had to decline great puffs of the pleasure on account of a recent illness. 'My doctor says no,' I explained.

For weeks and weeks I dillied and dallied until I suddenly realized that the summer term was almost over and I must return to Trinity if only to lead Bluesville at the Summer Ball.

College had never looked lovelier that night of the June Ball. A fairyland of twinkling electric lights aided by a ceiling of real Irish stars; you could hear the angels sing. A dream of fresh strawberries and stout. Bluesville, playing from the summer-house in the Provost's garden, were a centre of attraction – for word had spread around campus that we were riding into the US hit charts and that I would be jetting off to Hollywood and stardom. Julian, the postman, was spreading a lot of four-letter words as well, weighed down by great sackfuls of US mail for me:

' "You Turn Me On", the ad-lib HUH HUH song, is a "pick" in *Billboard, Cashbox, Record World, Music Business* and a "national breakout" in Los Angeles . . .' 'We're shipping 50,000 of these mothers a day! Are you ready for this, Ian baby??' scribbled Zoom's West Coast Promotion Man Geo. Rainbow. IAN YOUR RECORD IS GOING TO MAKE IT BIG WE ARE WORKING HARD TO PUT IT IN THE TOP TEN WITHIN THE NEXT THIRTY DAYS IT WILL APPEAR ON OUR HIT CHARTS NEXT WEEK REGARDS JG KLOPMASTER PRESIDENT ZOOM RECORDS . . . IAN YOU ARE SCHEDULED TO DO THE NET-WORK TV SHOW "SHINDIG" NEXT WEEK REGARDS JERRY.

Oh, it's pure pixilation in pixieland as we crash into our numbers! Gleaming at the front of the bandstand is my political theory professor, enraptured with a glass in his hand, every now and then shouting out 'Yes, I helped teach him that!' Right out into the dark glow of night I peer and spot Mr Balloodadan arm in arm with Mr Anangoola. Both are dressed festively in pin-stripe suits, both are sparkling with smiles as they sway away in rhythm. 'Thanks, Ian, I've got it! I've really got it!'* screams Mr Anangoola to me in pure delight. Nearby I see the college jazz band sitting under a rug, waving at me. And there's my landlady, and there's Roger Question, and there's my history set! Will I come and say hello in a tent to a notable Dublin politician? 'You've done well, Whitcomb. Are you Irish? I'll wager you've made a few shillings and now you'll be away over the water! What can I do for you?' I reply that I'd love a lectureship after my star has fallen. 'Don't forget us,' he says, chucking me under the chin. Now dawn is breaking and we're all singing a linked-up arms version of 'We'll Meet Again' . . .

Hollywood. Stardom at last! It happened this way: I'd had a pleasant trip in the jet (en route for my appearance in the rock 'n' roll TV show *Shindig*), chatting sundries with executives, talking

*The big beat.

273

Marx with a University of California professor, listening through headphones to great songs of the past like 'California Here I Come', availing myself of heated face towels and personal gift perfumes, enjoying the captain's flight commentary ('I hope you folks are having a happy day. Down there is the Grand Canyon and look there's the Rose Bowl. Big game on and I'll keep you filled in on results.') Just as we were getting off at Los Angeles, swapping addresses, a hostess said 'Hold it! Get the kid off first.' After a friendly tug at my hair, she guided me down a fabric con- certina-ed corridor and out into the arrivals lounge. Oh boy! It was jam-packed with teenagers and directly they saw me the cry went up 'It's Mr Turn-On himself!' Girls snatched at my cotton blazer; boxes of chocolates, books of poems, furry animals, brownies, Bermuda shorts, were thrust into my hands. I attempted a wave, remembering how the late President Kennedy had done it that night long ago in Dublin. Coloured policemen assisted me through a getaway exit. 'You've shut down the entire section, boy,' one of them told me. I was helped into a police car and then transferred into a civilian car. We roared off, pursued by teenage cars. 'We'll give them a run but just keep in touch, know what I mean?' said my driver, smiling winningly from inside a glinting suit. Holding out his hand: 'Hi, I'm Jumping George Rainbow, the West Coast Promotion Man, and you're a star.' I asked what was happening. 'You're what's happening, baby! You're the hottest property around at this moment. Everybody wants to know who and what you are. Are you really truly British or are you a coloured Ohian Jew? That type question. Listen! I'll prove how sizzling you are.' He punched a station button on his radio: 'HUH HUH HUH HUH' came out. He punched another: 'Come on now baby – you know you really turn me on.' And another, and another. 'British chanter Ian Whitcomb, the high-screech Turn-On boy, was mobbed at Los Angeles Airport today when he arrived in the Southland for personal appearances. Stay tuned for upcoming details. You heard it first on KHJ Boss Radio – where the hits roll night and day!' I was flooding the air- waves. George punched back to catch some more bars of 'Turn On' and he pounded the steering wheel on the off-beat. He was a glamorously silver-and-crinkly-haired man in solid rhinestone glasses. I wiped my brow. It seemed I was breaking out all over America and even infiltrating Brazil and Canada. But controversy was collecting: authorities in Portland, Oregon had banned me; in certain quarters it was suggested that my record was orgasmic and drug-sodden. 'But cheer up,' said Geo., doing the Jerk with his left elbow. 'You're a *star*, one of the great brotherhood of *stars* and you must dress like one, smell like one and act like one. You need a plethora of *velour*, *personal deodorant* and *special actions*.'

We saw to these in Hollywood. *Hollywood*. Wood of Holly. The foundress, homesick, had named her dusty ranch after a cheerful wood near her English birth-place, so I understood. Star name-mosaics set into the sidewalks. Some blank stars – would I be there some day? 'If we work at it. Let's get the velour.' Low-slung plaster box shacks in a wide street, a western street with stretched purring cars, everything trapped forever in the glaze of High Noon. I saw cowboy types hanging around and the most perfect bodies in the world, fed on ice-cold milk and constant flash-bulb sun. This, surely, was the MILLENIUM and to hell with Marx! I need read no further.

The velour turned out to be a plush carpet-like material fashioned into trousers, sweaters and very current. Soon I was dressed up. Geo. got me some pressure-can deodorant at the drug store. Then we retired to the Tel-El-Pal apartments, Geo.'s home and just round the corner from my swell hotel, where we lunched off pulped bananas and carrot juice. After spraying my hair with a lacquer, Geo. showed me a movement routine for performing 'Turn On' on TV: 'Your back to camera for six bars, spin round slow and British, sidle about and cup hands sexily for the panting on the "HUH HUH" break.'

In the afternoon we dropped into a coffee shop just in time to catch some key disc jockeys as they came off the air and in for a snatched burger. Geo. said: 'Hey King Daddy-O, say hello to Ian Whitcomb, currently number 6 and climbing on your top 40. My but those eggs over easy look good, Daddy, and the ham looks expectant. How's your wife? . . . Let me ask you this, Daddy-O:

can I take it as affirmative that the new Suntans record is on your playlist? No? It has a real gut sound that makes you want to go go go for some exercise, indoor and of the horizontal kind.' Daddy-O was very cool, just went on eating his patty melt (a slab of ground meat topped with toasted cheese, and really delicious). Geo. was now acting out the new Suntans, chanting and swaying and glistening all over, highlighted by the single razor-thin white light in that otherwise dim coffee shop.

We went visiting jockeys on the air (afternoon shift) and I said 'Hi, this is Ian Whitcomb' to them, from the other side of their glass booth. Solemn men kept slipping plastic tape cartridges into slots and out came beeps, jazzy fanfares, forties cool harmonies. Hard-solemn, but gorgeously built girls delivered news flashes on lavatory-like paper: Vietnam, the Dodgers game. 'That's the score and you know it!' shouted a sweating jock. I shook more hands and accepted coffee from paper cups. Geo. sang some more of his releases to passing jocks in a crooner voice. 'Look at your mother – right up with the stone foxes!' he whispered to me, pointing to a hit sheet pinned on a passing wall:

TUNEDEX

This week	Last week	Title	Artist
1	1	WOOLY BULLY	Sam the Sham & The Pharaohs
2	2	HELP ME RHONDA	The Beach Boys
3	4	BACK IN MY ARMS AGAIN	The Supremes
4	5	YOU TURN ME ON	Ian Whitcomb & Bluesville
5	9	MR TAMBOURINE MAN	The Byrds
6	13	JUST YOU	Sonny & Cher

'You're gonna meet these big, big, big cats on your shows. You do three TV shots in the next two days: *Hollywood A Go Go*, this afternoon; tomorrow, *Shindig* and *American Bandstand*. Next, meet the press. Then west-coast tour from San Diego to Seattle with the Beach Boys, Sam the Sham, the Righteous Brothers, the Kinks, Jan and Dean, Sonny and Cher, Sir Douglas Quintet. After that, join a rock 'n' roll trailer of biggies tour. And after that, Ed Sullivan, the moon.'

'But I have to get back in August to prepare for my finals at college.' It was sweltering in my velour.

The first TV shows were interesting because of *lip-synching*, popular at the time. You stood on a rostrum surrounded by the sea of teens and you pretended to sing and go through anguish. I felt odd doing this panto so I added pointing actions, shook my hair, slid my hand up and down the mike. 'Bitching record,' boomed the director over a monolith giant speaker swinging miles high in the studio. 'And did we get some boob shots of the dancers!!!' Indeed they *were* the most pneumatic girls I'd ever laid eyes on and one of them gave *me* the evil eye. She wore buckskin afterwards, her name was Gail and she was indifferent to my suite at the glamorous hotel (more a home than a hotel: palm trees and liver-shaped pool outside; inside your personal cooker and fridge). We talked long into the night. I remember she told me that Dylan and the planets were her life, but she also dug the Beach Boys. 'I'm doing a show with them,' I said. And so to bed. I can't even remember what book I was reading.

Next day on the great *American Bandstand* I jumped into the piano. Also, I met Dick Clark and Chubby Checker. At other times I met the Everly Brothers, the Crickets, Bill Haley, Brian Hyland and Bobby Vee. *I have photographs of all this.*

Shindig was the big thrill. Like a Christmas party with Jack Good as Father Christmas. Jack, also calling himself Art Gridestone, had been able to launch this whizz-bang of a rock 'n' roll show only after years of struggle. Big-time executives disliked the fact that there were black people in it. 'Too many of 'em' complained a veep exec. and Jack took a swing at him but missed and smashed through a plate glass window instead. Jack assembled the best rock 'n' roll band ever. Just look: Billy Preston, James Burton, Delaney Bramlett, Glen Campbell, Jim Horn, Chuck Blackwell, Leon Russell, Earl Palmer, Glen D. Hardin. (Today they're very heavy names, but then they were simply on the job.)

I met most of them the day I went in to a recording studio called Nashville West to lay down a backing track for 'Sporting Life', the song I was to do on *Shindig*. You see, 'Turn On' had been vetoed as too suggestive for family audiences.

277

These big session men were lazing around in the barn of a studio, sipping cokes and chewing candy. In the control booth were banks of levers, buttons and dials. Girls with clip-boards relaxed in arm-chairs. Piles of tape made a carpet. I'd read that Southern California was the electronics centre of the world. Electronics for defence mainly, but here in this studio it was electronics for pleasure.

In a trice (but with no sweat) grown men got up and produced shattering rock 'n' roll. As if they'd been born with it deep inside them. No one had to teach them my quite complex chord sequence. They added deft tricks of their own. They never seemed carried away, yet the most heart-wrenching cries came from their chromed saxes, their wooden lumpy guitars, even their polished organ. I had to suppress a cheer.

Then off Geo. bundled me to the TV studio for *Shindig* proper. I noticed that Geo.'s suit trousers ended above his ankles. Dressers put me into a leather motor-cycle outfit and floor directors placed me in the middle of an all-girl group called the Shangri-Las. I was their guy in the song 'Give Him a Great Big Kiss'. After that the stage was mine and I whipped off cycle gear and lay down on a ramp to sing 'Sporting Life'. Geo. rushed up and said 'Jeez, cover up, cover up! Camera's getting a massive shot of your joint!' Jack Good, in bowler and braces, put a stop to it saying 'Sorry. I wouldn't have put a dog through that!' On the night all was well; the audience kids screamed on cue, the ads for face creams ran smoothly, the Beach Boys sang 'Help Me Rhonda', and I got through my act without a hitch. Afterwards Geo. took me to a music-business restaurant where I shook hands with a lot more disc jockeys and programme directors. Geo. spotted Phil Spector and said 'Hi, Phil!'

About this time something was happening which I wasn't too sure about. Later it was called folk-rock.

Folk-rock, then rock, and finally the rock counter-culture, was to haunt me in future. I never haunted *it*! In 1963 Seattle I had been bothered by folk music of the crew-cut college kind, with its finger-pointing and its lecturing. Here in 1965 I was about to enter an evil world as a knight from Trinity College and the folk people were getting there first. A year of great change, of electric Dylan, of 'The Eve of Destruction', and I desperately wanted a part in it . . .

First of all, I was visiting a go-go club on my second evening, I think it was. As I entered, flanked by record executives, the band struck up 'Turn On' and luscious go-go girls offered me champagne 'n' coke. A delightful couple in furs, medieval wanderers, came up and shook my hand. They were Sonny and Cher and I thought no, not so much medieval but more 'Buffalo Bill and Hiawatha in Alaska'. Anyway it turned out that Sonny had been involved in pop quite a few years. He'd been apprenticed to Phil Spector, king of the cavernous sound. I'd caught Sonny and Cher's songs of pure love in a harsh world on Geo.'s car radio. Sonny was, at present, busy writing protests about those who disliked the length of his hair and the cut of his clothes. After I met him he got ejected from the famous music-business restaurant (where Geo. had said 'Hi' to Phil Spector) and all because of looks. He was to go on to write 'The Revolution Kind' and to show the futility of war.

But that evening in the Crescendo Club I was charmed by Sonny and Cher and they gave me a lift home in their Cadillac.

Secondly, amongst the acts lip-synching with me on a show called *Hollywood A Go-Go* was a group called the Byrds. Now, whilst everyone else and me was clapping along to the beat, smiling and showing teeth, these Byrds stood like ice-cold tombstones. They didn't wear band-suits; they wore buckskin with fringes, and soiled polo-necked sweaters and jeans. No velour in sight. They only half-heartedly lip-synched and I could have sworn they were having a chat whilst they were supposed to be singing on the air. But the main surprise was: *they didn't smile.*

They sang 'Hey Mr Tambourine Man' to the accompaniment of drums, and electric guitars (notably a twelve-string affair that sounded Elizabethan). Afterwards I went up to their rostrum and, flashing a smile, asked them who wrote the song (just for polite conversation). The twelve-string guitarist, wearing National Health type glasses and a wry look said softly so I could hardly hear: 'Dylan, man, like don't you know?' I said no but I do know the other song you sang, 'We'll Meet Again', originally made famous by Vera Lynn, the Forces Sweetheart. 'We think it's kinda funny and old,' said their spokesman. I said that the song meant an awful lot to those who had fought in the Second World War. 'I trust everything will turn out right,' replied the spokesman mysteriously.

But these were minor blemishes in my astral life. A star I was – and one of the great brotherhood of stars! Fortunately, so far, nobody had suggested that I be changed in any way (after all, remember how they'd glued back Bing Crosby's ears and mowed back Rita Hayworth's hair-line?). Occasionally Geo. would comb my hair forward Beatle-fashion but then, with a swish, I'd mess it up in a Jaggerish kind of way. On top of this hair would go my Sherlock Holmes deerstalker hat, which seemed to go down well with the younger girls – little did I know that it was to be the cause of my undoing!

In the privacy of my hotel rest-room I now began noticing hairs in the wash basin, hairs in the lavatory bowl, hairs clogging up the bath plug-hole. However, a digest magazine assured me that loss of sixty a day was quite usual and I gathered up only fifty-five. High summer would bring re-growth.

I am lounging in the celebrity hospitality room of a big network TV studio waiting to take part in a new teen quiz show called *Big Date*. My fellow contestants are folk-rock singers, rather solemn but with occasional bursts of frantic private laughter, and they too are lounging. Many are throwing lines together for future recording songs, encouraged by their agents and managers. A glamorous wiggly girl/woman production assistant has just briefed us on what we should do on the air: 'We want reaction, reaction, reaction! You singers will be placed on one side of a screen and your girl quizzer on the other. She will then ask each of you personal fun-type questions which you'll answer with *tingle*. Finally, she'll decide which voice turns her on most and that is the winner. It's a warm family show and we want you to animate, animate, animate!' The folk-rock singers stared into the far distance.

I must get a follow-up to 'Turn On' because it's climbed as high as it ever will on the national charts (number 8) and next week it'll start plummeting like a lead zeppelin. Earlier today I had a 'meeting' (as they say out here) with J. 'Gene' Klopmaster, our record company vice-president, at which I suggested that a good follow-up might perhaps be my humorous monologue 'Jottings from an Active Life' (the memoirs of an old soldier). With the best will in the world the vice-president told me in his ocean-deep voice: 'Ian, I have been twenty-five years in this business of ours. I have seen many a platter rise and fall. *I have walked with Sinatra.* It is my experience that the "spoken word" is the kiss of death, sales-wise.' So we decided to follow up with my recording of 'N-nervous', a stuttering blues with teen appeal.

From these thoughts (almost *worries*, and who would have believed that I might ever *care* about pop?) I turn to my fan mail and press clippings which I have spread around me on the glossy black plastic sofa of the TV hospitality room . . .

A letter:

Ian baby.

I'm crazy about you, Ian baby. I love you too. Your singing marvellous, your looks marvellous too. I like your cuteness, hair, singing, your looks. I like the way you snap your fingers. Ian is a pretty name and you are a pretty boy. What kind of girls do you like? What kind of girls do you dislike? Well, I have to go now but I always will love you.

Your lasting fan,
Beverly.

Another letter:

Dear Ian Whitcomb,

I have watched you several times now and I want to say that, sure you have talent and you're magnetic, but why, oh why, do you screw it all up by horsing around, by being coy, by camping – as if you're embarrassed by show business? You could be great if you faced your potential and saw it through but that takes guts. Instead you mince, or treat it all as a big joke. Come on now!

Yours, Arlene.

281

Our Time

An article:

THE THINGS THAT TURN ME OFF AND THE THINGS THAT TURN ME ON

By Ian Whitcomb.

I get turned off by bureaucracy and government thinking; by fat, middle-aged, right-wing people who like Lawrence Welk music. *I get turned off* when I hear of even more war and violence erupting all the time. *I get turned off* by Bermuda shorts, Madras blouses and rollers in the hair.

I get turned on by all American girls, especially those with long, flowing hair, wearing jeans with those knitted tops. *I get turned on* when I get letters so don't hesitate to write and you will be sure to get an answer.

A poem:

Sweet Ian, my Jeannot with the lovely hair.
I wonder why I love you.
Are you
      the one who speaks sweet words
      as we lie under the everlasting?
Place thy gentle head upon this pillow
      while I drape myself in willow tears
And sing thee twylight songs, my dear.
Jeannot
      (the-petals-of-my-dreams-are-ragged-and-torn-the-petal-of-my
      skin-is-withered)
         Where
           art thou
           ou
             ou . . . ?

Suddenly! 'OK everybody, rally round! Let's get in the groovie and make a movie!' It's the female production assistant and we all troop down to the studio for the quiz game.

'Mmmmm, but that was a funtabulous evening, Ian baby,' she said, lying back deep and low in the plush leather of our gliding Cadillac. I had won the quiz or, at least, she had won me because she liked the way I answered her questions in my British accent. Matter of fact, I was beginning to like it, too. The first part of our prize was a 5 p.m. hot dinner at the King Alfred & The Cake, a new restaurant. There we had eaten T-bone steaks as big as shoes, with baked potatoes filled with chives, sour cream and crispy bacon chips. Outside the sun glazed down but inside the Alfred all was low-lit. We had the place to ourselves save some coloured waiters in tails and a blazered man from the TV studio who'd been sent to take pictures of the winners enjoying themselves. As he clicked away and arranged us my partner told me about her life in the valley: about paddle tennis, art classes, and her DC5 collection.

After dinner we were driven to a Herman's Hermits concert where I was mobbed, much to her amusement. Finally we were guided into Sunset Strip's famous Whisky-A-Go-Go to hear a new group. The TV blazer man said for us to get up and dance for pictures. This was hard because the group was jamming on a single Eastern chord, building it up into a climax – and the buckskinned, beautifully built, sunkissed audience was intently listening, not dancing. Still, we had a go, all alone there on the floor with the TV man hovering about us telling us what movements to make. 'Many of the quiz winners end up as life partners,' he told us and I could have sworn he goosed me but maybe not.

'Mmmm, but it was so really action-full!' she continued from the plush as we creamed on to the freeway. The car radio said 'Here's Ian Whitcomb's new number called "N-nervous", a station exclusive, and we're wondering nervously: will it make it? Still, if it ain't right turn it over and do it again, hey?' Slowly she was pushing herself up from the depths and her eyes were closed and her lips were pursed but she managed to say dreamily: 'You're not nervous, are you, Ee-on?' It was then that I removed a chip of crispy bacon from her upper lip.

In no time at all we were descending from the freeway and into Panorama City, her home. Afterwards, I got our driver to drop me off at the apartment of Gail, the dancing girl, because I wanted to discuss some more Dylan with her.

Notes on Odd Scraps of Paper

We have just entered the state of Kansas. I am writing these notes on a bus, which is our home during this rock 'n' roll Galaxy Tour.

Our Time

My notoriety as the 'Turn On' boy/girl at first affected my relationship with the other rock stars, but now I'm accepted. Mostly, the 'soul' singers keep to themselves – playing poker and humming blues phrases. I have palled up with a member of a British group. He's a fast reader and has whipped through my college text books (it's the Finals in the autumn and I'm working on the bus). He thought that *The Anarchists* was cool, but added, 'directly you try to make anarchism work as a practical solution it collapses because by its very nature it's anti-form'. I'm very excited by Prof. Tucker's book *Myth and Philosophy in Karl Marx* – it paints the old ogre as quite human. Tucker says that Marx had a terrible good *v* evil struggle in his interior self as a young man and was rather religious too. Then he decided to *externalize* his *internal* struggle by setting the proletarians as the good men and the capitalists as the bad men in a revolutionary battle. Unfortunately his followers took him literally and tried to make real this private nightmare. Moral: dreamland is bestland. One of the singers has just done a 'B.A.', i.e. pulled his trousers down and stuck his bottom out to annoy a passing station wagon.

~~I have been very worried about the fights.~~ There have been some very unfortunate incidents during the last few months which I must write down so that I can understand them. They happened before I joined this particular tour:

1. In mid June I joined a rock package in San Clauso. Big names were on the bill. Just before I went on with my act an important-looking impresario told me: 'Sitting out in the audience is a friend of a friend of yours from England who's now a disc jockey out here. His name is Lord Jeremy and won't you just mention him on stage?' I did this to oblige, but as I mentioned the name a spotlight swung on to the jockey, as if on cue. He stood up and took a bow in his deerstalker hat and heavy tweeds. Then he kicked up his heels (revealing sensible brogues with high heels) and waved a Union Jack. At the same time a doom-laden voice in heavy echo boomed from the public address system: 'It's Lord Jeremy himself! Tally Ho for KLAP, the station of sockeroo!' After I exited the stage to loud applause I was approached by a long man with a Lincoln face and beard who

284

grabbed me by my velour pullover and screamed 'You stupid ass-hole! Lord Jeremy is a jock. from a rival station. We're presenting this package not them, and I oughtta slug you!' 'How dare you speak to me like that. I ought to tweak your beard.' I did just that. It looked like a scrap but various nearby rock acts came to the rescue and all was made peaceful. Unfortunately the Lincoln man turned out to be a powerful radio-station 'programme director' and the net result is, I'm told, that my records are black-listed on all his affiliated stations. This means I'm banned in most Cali-fornian urban areas so Geo. and I will have to plug the rural regions.

2. Geo. and I dropped in on a rural rocker station up a dusty track near San Francisco. We were armed with promo. copies of 'N-nervous' for what we call a 'hyping trip' (i.e. wholesale plug-ging). A red-tiled bungalow with parts done in thatch. Inside a gale of air-conditioning was blowing. The programme director, 'Swinging Swallow', kept us waiting for what seemed like hours while he organized a listener contest: to find out which kid had the fattest lips. Then, when at last we were allowed into his inner sanctum and Geo. had swiftly managed to get 'N-nervous' spin-ning on the audition turntable, all 'Swallow' did was to lie back in his expandable chair, sip a beer and talk about last night's baseball game on TV. Geo. played along skilfully with the occa-sional 'You're so right, Swallow,' but Swallow, as he talked, kept picking up the record-player arm in order to skip grooves on my record, the record that my pop life future depends on. 'When are you gonna make another record, son?' he asked vaguely in my direction. Before I could reply he said, 'Have you guys heard this "Eve of Destruction" mother by a kid called Barry McGuire? No? Well, it's gotta be a stone fox smash!' and he bust open another beer, soaking 'N-nervous'. He went on with: 'A lot of the lyrics I can't make out but what I can is goddam *treason*! Can you believe a guy who knocks our draft, our senators, our church, our H-bombs, and all on a pop record?' 'So I can take it,' said Geo. with a boogaloo gesture of the hips, 'that the disc, Swallow, is negative as far as your big boss playlist is concerned?' 'Not on your Hollywood scalp doily! It may knock

285

the USA but I don't knock success. Never knock success, Whitcomb. That "Eve" record is Dylan made commercial and it's a new kind of *loot music* under the title of *protest* – remember that!' (He said everything on one-note like a parson at prayer time.) 'Now, Whit*comb*. You got something I can play and I'll spin it like a fat lady farts, like a wild bear shits in the woods, but until then it's so long and remember: the clowns at the circus are real funny but on the road they're murder; see you soon and don't do anything I wouldn't photograph – get me? And get out!'

3. It was my birthday and I was back at the hotel after doing a very important show somewhere in the North-west. I was on my own, unprotected by Geo. I was signing autographs for a couple of girls in a bedroom. Their mothers were there, as well as other rock stars. All at once a policeman and a security guard came in and shouted 'OK, everybody out! No adults in a juvenile's room.' The others scrambled but I went on signing, calmly. A stomach appeared in front of me. 'Punk, you better GIT!' I looked up slowly through hooded eyes and made out a fat blue officer. I said, 'Don't you ever speak to me like that. Ever.' 'Wise guy, huh?' and he and the guard laid into me with punches, so I defended myself with my hard-backed passport. Within moments they had me up against the wall in handcuffs. Mothers were shrieking. Only kind words from the rock package promoter saved me from jail. All I wanted was to be back with my books.

Just a few moments ago one of the people on the bus, a lead guitarist, placed his wedding tackle right in the middle of my Marx book, right on the page I was reading. I can't understand it! What has this got to do with pop music? And speaking of genitals I have had a sexual baptism of fire on this tour. The other night an orgy was arranged at our motel. Come and see it, they all said. In a huge suite, decorated with French Impressionist reproductions, lay a fan-girl naked, homely-looking and spread-eagled on a double bed still with the counterpane on. Waiting in line were members of our tour all with their engines out, some primed, others priming. One after the other they ran the fan-girl through with shouts of

'Eureka!' and so forth, whilst a guitarist accompanied the action with synchronized ragas. A rich blood-red dawn was bursting through the windows behind the queue making the whole thing almost painterly, but as the last member, a grotesquely fat road manager, lumbered up and in I thought 'this is a violent scene on the lines of the French Commune or Berlin, 1918'. Staggered, I retreated to a private room to chat to one of the girl friends of the spread-eagled fan-girl and we had been getting along well for an hour or so when in reeled one of the chief orgy-makers, a teen idol sporting an enormous thick and stretched dong – like a great red yule-log entwined with blue ivy. 'Hi, gang! Say hello to Roger!' he screamed, pointing to this thing. 'Come along, Roger, don't be shy. Up, up and fight fiercely! Who d'you wanna do next?' I bundled him out and when, shortly afterwards, there was a knock I ignored it until the door was actually broken down by two squat officers. I asked them what they wanted and they said, 'You, kid – for cohabitation with a minor,' and banged a notice which was attached to the back of our door. 'We've been listening for an hour in the connecting room next door to all that junk you were giving out about your lumbago.' I wished that Geo. could have been there. I said, 'What can I do to help?' They said, 'Got any albums?' so I gave them several of my 'Turn On' albums, all signed to their children. 'N-nervous' is hovering at number 80 in the national charts.

In Nebraska: I just picked up a pile of mail which Geo. had kindly forwarded to our motel. One of the letters is very interesting. It's from a new liberation group called the 'Jolly Boys of America' and they inform me that they have adopted me as their mascot. 'Turn On' is their rally song, a 'We Shall Overcome'. They enclosed a song which they feel I might have a hit with:

> I want to ask you a personal question, Aubrey dear.
> It's really an awfully personal question, Aubrey dear.
> Won't you come along and have lunch with me at your
>   own convenience?
> But when I appear in my Burberry, please don't scream:
>   'Where *have* you been, Lance?'

287

Our Time

We'll talk about Klee during gratinée, won't we, Aubrey
    dear?
And how good Mae was at matinée, won't we, Aubrey
    dear?
And during our crème caramel I'll say 'It's all very well
But here is my personal question,
A terribly risqué suggestion,
But can I borrow Bobby tonight?'

I've sent this off to Zoom Records for their comment. Maybe I
should record it?

Today I got this cable from 'Gene' Klopmaster, vice-president:

IAN TWENTY-FIVE YEARS IN THIS BUSINESS WALKED WITH
SINATRA KISS OF DEATH APPLIES NOT ONLY TO SPOKEN WORD
RECORDS BUT ALSO TO SONGS OF A HOMOSEXUAL NATURE AT
THIS POINT IN TIME TRY AGAIN GOOD LUCK AND KEEP
KOMMERCIAL EXCLAMATION POINT YOURS J G KLOPMASTER
VICE PRESIDENT ZOOM RECORDS

> Trinity College,
> Dublin,
> EIRE.

My dear Whitcomb,
    You'll be glad to learn that we've awarded you a second class degree
in History Honours. Under the circumstances – I mean your musical
career and success in America – we all feel that you performed remark-
ably well in the exams. I speak for all of us on the faculty, including
even Julian the postman, when I say 'well done' and 'good luck' in
your future life as a degreed star.

> J. D. O'Hill.

*(The following pages are the work of Jon Steverstein, a post-
graduate student in rock at the Jim Jones University, Ohio. His research material consisted of Whitcomb's occasional diaries, his
letters, records, tapes and photograph albums.)*

Whitcomb's ultimate problem seems to have been that, despite his
adoption of, on the one hand, highly seasoned furs and cowboy
boots and, on the other hand, a belief that the next pop movement

would be a return to the roots of authentic classic ragtime, he himself was unable to get a hit. He was also entirely *irrelevant*, representing nobody but himself and maybe a few, a chosen few: his relatives, friends and those who were polite to him. He was unaware that he was remaindered in the middle of the revolutionary ferment of 1966–8. That was the key period in rock history: the ultimate negation of the sweet-corn, coke-soaked, cream-style suburban pop by the new consciously purposeful and relevant 'adult rock' of Dylan and the San Francisco groups, in which rock became the cosmic mirror of change – whether that change be in Chicago, Paris, Cuba, Columbia or Hollywood. As Lennon said of his penis exposure: 'I mean, you're not used to it, being naked, but it's got to come out.'

Thus a totally *aware* and *meaningful* new moon replaced the old *silv'ry* one. A moon at once both personal *and* symbolic of the new universality celebrated by electric youth subculture. Incoherent to the Establishment, its message thus emerges uncensored (as with nineteenth-century Russian poets and novelists, anxious to bypass a deaf and irrelevant Establishment in order to communicate a message to their people).

So the molten rock of the subculture melted the plastic walls of a dying wash 'n' war civilization. Not for nothing did our tin buttons read 'If you're not part of the solution you're part of the problem baby'. A rock writer put it even more succinctly when, at a demonstration, he ordered a University of California faculty chief to 'get off the truck you fucking Fascist!' All this and more was contained in the key work of these important and disturbing rock years: 'Sergeant Pepper' by the Beatles. Whitcomb's part in the Revolution is shadowy and difficult to determine – a Konchik* rather than a Lenin.

From the Spring of 66 to the Fall of 68 we see him moving slowly in the orbit of Hollywood, trying to 'get arrested' (in the words of his PR consultant) and finding that shows and records become fewer and farther between. 'It's hell when you're balding,' he wrote in a diary. Much time was spent floating in the dinky

---

*Famous society orchestra leader of Tsarist Russia who was ruined by the Bolshevik revolution.

swimming pool of the Tel-El-Pal apartment block on North Cherokee, just off Hollywood Boulevard. This block was his permanent home (it is now a supermarket). 'Is the Holmes hat outmoded?' he wrote. There were, at this stage, advisers around to answer: some said he should go with the fur and nix the velour; others said he should wear herring-bone tweed and get like a 'young Peter Sellers'. The movies was an exit and eventually Whitcomb was persuaded to enrol at the Jack McTodd Acting School, a battleship grey block decorated with plywood pillars and within a quarter mile of Monogram Pictures. Many other one-hit rock stars were studying there.

'McTodd, a leathery puff-pastry face of between 30 and 50 on a body dressed in baggy beach wear, greeted me with his famous Roman shake, which means a mutual clutching of the wrist rather than the hand,' wrote Whitcomb in his diary. 'Straight after the shake and a swift up-and-down look of appraisal he suggested private tuition for me. Here, apparently, they study a form of method acting ("But never ever voice that word in my presence," said McTodd, grinning for a fraction of a second). We fixed coffee from a machine and then sat down with our foam paper cups in canvas chairs – facing each other in close-up. "G-good morning," I said to break the silence and his stare. "Look, I never sleep," he replied, and at once we got down to work.'

Whitcomb studied with McTodd for several months. The singer just *had* to find a way out of pop. McTodd used to teach like this: 'What we need to ascertain is what the body feels like doing, *not* what the rational brain thinks we *should* feel. We must forget that area – I have a rhyme for the problem: "Neglect, neglect the int-ellect." See? For this feel-music we use tools such as the psychological, creative, super- and life-objectives. So, we involve the whole being from head through cock to toes by thinking up a phrase, no matter how crazy, which expresses our physical involvement. Like, for instance: "I desire the cuddly bear now!!"' As he spoke this he grabbed Whitcomb round the waist ('breathing hard instant coffee fumes that watered my eyes') and added: 'Quick, quick! Use your super-objective phrase to answer my life-object! Pronto!' Whitcomb said, 'Wash away the smelly cheese!'

with a push that toppled McTodd. Luckily the teacher was wearing springy tennis shoes which enabled him to bounce back on to his feet again so that the whole incident looked like one continuous action. On landing McTodd said, 'Great goo-goo moon, but we're making progress!'

The end of the acting experiment came suddenly one afternoon in May. Teacher and pupil were reading together an old script from a TV hospital drama series. They'd reached the point where Whitcomb, as a young intern, has to watch a patient – his girl friend – die in a hospital bed. The script said: 'He breaks down and sobs . . .' Whitcomb said, 'Sob, sob,' in a galloping mono-tone. McTodd chided him with: 'Come on now, baby – use your tools and try again.' 'Sob, sob.' 'Look. I want emotion. I want tears.' 'I can't just turn on the tears. Can you?' 'You bet. Watch and listen,' and McTodd broke down and cried great tears, which splashed everywhere. 'Now d'you see,' he asked through his agony, 'how the right tools can achieve reality. I think . . .' But Whitcomb had got up to leave, and as he did so McTodd fell to the floor for he had been leaning on the singer. At the door Whitcomb said, 'I think it's *disgusting*!'

The end was near. 'I keep my tears for the Tel-El-Pal,' he said into his tape recorder when he got home. From now on he spent more and more time mooning in his Tel-El-Pal apartment, mostly sprawled on the grim bed. 'Could there be a more depressing and futuristic object than this bed? – except another one like it. There are millions of them, I'm told, that pull down from the wall. Like a coffin calling me home. Has the habit of suddenly springing back up the wall' (tape). In other words, the bed had Whitcomb 'up against the wall'.

He read voraciously, particularly biographies of successful generals and a book about hair. 'It says 2·5 million US males wear rugs. Some allow the scalp to breathe. Some made of stretch material, pull on like a bathing cap. In a transplant, plugs of hair are taken from different parts of the body. Even from under the arms. Surely a Semitic effect?' – (notebook.)

Best of all he liked to read *Billboard*. On the 'Hot Hundred Chart' he circled singers whom he'd encountered on the road.

291

Our Time

'They may be going up with a printed bullet at present but soon I may present them with a real bullet, peut-être?' he scrawled against one chart.

On certain days of the week he would clamber into his automobile and tour around Los Angeles. He rented many different kinds of autos but the most impressive was yellow, had front and rear suspension boosters and reinforced fenders – 'the widest car that General Motors makes' (notebook). Inside was furnished with ice-box, grill and camp bed. He liked to race down Sunset Boulevard with windows up, air-conditioner raging, tape pounding, radio chattering, as he winged parked autos and knocked bits off trees. One time he ripped away the entire side of a restaurant – at only 5 miles per hour (the one next to The Troubadour on Santa Monica Boulevard).

A similar murderous mood is to be found in his songs of this period. We might note, in passing, such lines as: 'Hear the roar and rattle as the rockers ride and hear the hippies moan.' These rockers will 'trample your hydrangeas with their boots, use their daggers on your Nehru suits, pass some water on your cannabis as well, and replace it with a healthy body smell' ('Heroes of the Rocker Pack'). Further, he made a harsh attack on the emergent rock generation in his 'A Groovy Day' in which we learn of 'Beautiful people like Harriet Neeple who flew from a steeple and now grooves with God – an Eastern Sultana, she's found her Nirvana.'

But the most nihilistic of his songs was inspired by the failure of his Tel-El-Pal oven one evening when he was attempting, alone, to heat up a TV dinner. Little things can spark final moments and this was definitely the vanishing point:

The Notable Yacht Club of Staines

I was just about to go and warm my TV dinner,
    Mexican special, I think.
I'd been talking to a politician on the television colour set,
    But now it was on the blink.
When out of the blue popped a cable asking me, please was I able
To come and take over the reins of the notable yacht club of Staines!!!

How I Became a Rock 'n' Roll Star

And when I'm settled there in state I'll burn all their books,
Toss their cups and their caps on the embers!
I used to lay alone at night and hear those buggers getting tight!
– I hate anything that has members.
I'll make them all bright blue and panicky.
I'll issue an order for anarchy
And then I'll dismantle the club.
And we'll all go and live on the mud.
We'll thrive on good natural food
And frolic about in the nude . . .

Just then Gail (the go-go girl) came in to say that there was a
groovy party high up in the hills, near the huge letters that read
'Hollywood'. Whitcomb was easily led out and into the wide
yellow auto and soon they were cruising up twisty Beachwood
through dense oily smoke (for Los Angeles was at last really on
fire).

It was at this party that Whitcomb got his come-uppance. 'I
remember nothing about the house or its people or whether there
was a running buffet or not. But I do remember eating something,
or smoking something'. Possibly P Q W? 'Stereo speakers on all
sides pounded out a heart-beat, such a tense beat that it burst me
into atomic scraps on every pulse and I felt my brain had become
razor-thin rubber, no! nice rice paper and there's lovely rice pudding for dinner again so what is the matter with Mary Jane? Can
this be the end to be high in the hills of Hollywood with the A. A.
Milne blues again? But Alice isn't here and the explosions continue as the ceiling descends like my apartment bed and the room
turns purple and the beat seems to say, like a steam train, "back to
school, back to school, back to school" until it changes to "I wanna
die, I wanna die, I wanna die", but now, in the flickering slow-
motion of replay, a procession passes before me chanting their hits
in wavering voice: poor Stephen Foster, natty Chas. K. Harris,
swaying Jim Thornton, grave Scott Joplin clutching the score of
a ragtime opera, swaggering George M. Cohan, a thousand Alleymen, the Original Dixieland Jazz Band on a truck, Paul Whiteman
with a baton under his arm, Rudy Vallée practising tennis strokes,
Cole Porter with eyes closed in a gondola.' Slowly a voice, a
matter-of-fact one, is overlaid saying:

Our Time

OK. So groove with yesterday and the day before if that's what your thing is, get into it but don't pretend it's of any importance because it isn't except as hilarity. Why d'you relate to that dusty world so intensely? I'll tell you: because the past is no threat, you can dissect it, look at it, shuffle it about like cards, you can sit on it, trample on it, laugh at it but it's as dead as Warren G. Harding. You use the past against today but it's today that matters and tomorrow which is gonna be fantastic if we can get together as one culture making a music that bleeds and I'm tired rapping but let me say this: you can't escape us because we're gonna be all over everywhere with meaningfulness, so blah blah blah!!!

(This has been found on a tape. Whitcomb was talking to himself.)

EDITOR'S NOTE: *Steverstein trailed his subject back to Europe but when the singer reached his stone cottage on the Sussex Downs he slammed and bolted its thick oak door. Pushing a loaded shotgun through a barred window, he shouted at Steverstein: ' You can apply your stuff to America but you ain't never gonna bring it to England. I'm telling you to clear off my property sharpish or I'll blow you and your recorder clear off the White Cliffs of Dover!' A little later he fired, filling Steverstein's back-side with buckshot and blasting him in the direction of the hovercraft. From there the student set off across the sea and after that, who knows?*

Thank You

During the three years it has taken me to put this book together I have travelled widely over Britain and America looking up ragtimers, Alleymen, crooners, rockers. I have read heavily in the British Museum, London and in the Lincoln Center, New York. Many pop people have seen my figure, surrounded by file cards and felt pens, lumbering towards them. A few have hidden themselves in 'current chart business'; one or two have asked when was I going to get another hit, and was I still around. But the majority welcomed me and took time out to roam back over the history of our industry.

Chris Ellis of EMI records is one of the world's experts on popular music. From the start of my research he has always been at hand to guide and correct. He was particularly helpful on Pop's Middle Period (1920–50 approximately), taking me gently into the work of such musical comedy songwriters as Cole Porter, Rodgers and Hart, and George Gershwin. As a ragtime-rocker I'd hitherto been rather snooty about these song jewellers because I was ignorant. Now I both respect and enjoy them.

Ben Nisbet of Feldman's, Al Brackman of the Richmond Organization and Bert Jones of Francis, Day & Hunter have supplied me with rare song copies and rich stories of Alley days. Song-plugger Mickey Addy, whose experience ranges from Al Jolson to Pat Boone, wised me up to many facts. I met him in the New York HQ of *Billboard* by arrangement with Don Ovens, reviews and programming services director, who later spent hours with me describing how the charts work. Paul Ackerman, the executive director, told me about how C&W and R&B had to struggle to get respect in the forties and fifties.

295

Thank You

I got the BMI story from BMI's Russ Sanjek and the ASCAP story from ASCAP's John Craig. John Kennedy talked about his days as Tommy Steele's manager. Jack Good provided me with acres of tape on his experiences as producer of TV rock shows.

Now the artists of pop: songwriter Eubie Blake ('I'm Just Wild About Harry', 'Memories of You') demonstrated the various ragtime styles at his grand piano and described what pop life was like for a black man at the dawn of the century. Likewise Shelton Brooks ('Some of These Days', 'Darktown Strutters Ball') and the late Joe Jordan ('That Teasin' Rag', 'Lovie Joe').

Veteran Alleyman Abe Olman ('Down among the Sheltering Palms', 'Oh Johnny, Oh Johnny, Oh!') reminisced and played some of his latest rock songs. Gerald Marks ('Is It True What They Say about Dixie?', 'All of Me') provided me with many stories behind the great hit songs. Harry Warren ('Pasadena', '42nd Street', 'Shuffle Off to Buffalo', 'You're Getting to be a Habit With Me', 'Lullaby of Broadway', 'Chattanooga Choo Choo', 'You'll Never Know', etc.) described working on Hollywood musicals in the thirties and played and sang a duet with me on his 'Pasadena' hit. David Raksin ('Laura') showed me the complications of scoring film background music (he started out as arranger of *Modern Times*) and got me in to a songwriters' dinner where I heard the late Wolfe Gilbert sing 'Waiting For the Robert E. Lee', which Gilbert had written with Lewis Muir back in the ragtime era.

In London I spent days and days with Tolchard Evans ('Lady of Spain', 'Let's All Sing Like The Birdies Sing', 'There's A Lovely Lake in Loveland') whose tunes had words by my great-uncle the late Stanley Damerell. Tolchard gave me the true story of Britain's own Alley and also painted a wonderful picture in words of the late Ralph Butler ('All By Yourself in the Moonlight', 'The Sun Has Got His Hat On', 'Run Rabbit Run'), a much underrated writer.

Not counting the many rock stars I toured and chatted with during my hit days, I thank the following stars for their time spent with me: Miss Mae West, with whom I worked on an album of pop songs and who told me much about vaudeville, films and

296

stagecraft; Rudy Vallée, who let me rove through his superb museum after I had only just beaten him at tennis; Jerry Lee Lewis, who worked with me on a Jack Good special and showed me what a mesmeric performer he is. I am also most grateful to Sid Colin, now one of Britain's top comedy scriptwriters but back in the thirties a crooner/guitarist with the cream of London's hotel dance bands, for his tales.

Several writers on pop music have read my manuscript and made valuable comments: Henry Pleasants (*The Agony of Modern Music, Serious Music and All That Jazz*), Charlie Gillett (*The Sound of The City*), Rudi Blesh (*They All Played Ragtime*) and pop jazz/blues archivist and expert supreme, Brian Rust.

I also owe an enormous debt of gratitude to a number of American friends who first excited me about early American pop music – long before I started this book: 'Ragtime' Bob Darch, Max Morath, Dick Zimmerman, Earl Angevine, Robin Frost and Mr and Mrs Spencer Quinn.

You'll have noticed that the latter part of my book is garnished autobiography with many dream touches. I would like to thank the following for sticking with me through the extraordinary period of my teen-throb career: Jerry Dennon, Hal Shaper, George Sherlock, Bud Fraser, Perry Mayer, David Mallet, Mike and Carol Curb, Bob Fitzpatrick, Denny Cordell, Ray and Barbara Pohlman, Thorne Nogar, Bob Mahoney, Graham Churchill, Michael Roberts, Gil Bateman, Gloria Stavers, Steve Post.

Finally I want to thank the friends who, though mostly outside the pop business, encouraged me to keep plugging away at the wretched thing: Jeremy and Petra Lewis, Roy Moseley, Christian Roberts, Reina James, Virginia Ironside, Vicki Metherell, and Vicky Marshall.

And, of course, the family, who always assumed my project would succeed: my brother Robin, my sister Suzanne, and my mother who gave me coffee, cigars, meals, our dining room and her love in order that I might give you this book.

IAN WHITCOMB

London,
March 1972

Index of Composers, Lyricists, Writers, Songs, and Key Performers

Index

Bill Bailey, Won't You Please Come Home?, 28, 42 n.
Bimbo, Bimbo, What Ya Gonna Dooeeo?, 189
Bird in a Gilded Cage, 43, 47, 140
Blake, Eubie, 45, 296
Blue Danube Waltz, 225
Blue Moon, 136
Blue Moon of Kentucky, 229
Blue Room, 137
Blue Suede Shoes, 231
Blues in the Night, 200
Body and Soul, 168
Bolton, Guy, 133
Bond, Carrie Jacobs, 47–8, 206
Britt, Elton, 198
Broken Doll, A, 158 n.
Brooks, Shelton, 79, 296
Brother, Can You Spare a Dime?, 52, 260
Brown, Lew, 46
Brown, Nacio Herb, 120
Bryan and Piantadosi, 58
Bryan Believed in Heaven, 52
Buchanan, Jack (singer), 173, 174, 181, 186
Buck, Gene, 155 n
Bunk-A-Doodle-I-Do, 161
Burlington Bertie from Bow, 158
Burnett, Ernie, 71, 206
But in the evening no-one comes . . ., 266
Butler, Picayne (musician), 22
Butler, Ralph, 182–3, 296

California, Here I Come!, 274
Camptown Races, 12, 207
Cantor, Eddie (singer), 11, 129, 209
Carr, Michael, 182
Caryll, Ivan, 140, 159
Castle, Irene and Vernon, 34–6, 265
C'est Si Bon, 205
Chantilly Lace, 234
Charlie Brown, 234
Charmaine, 118, 127
Chattanooga Choo Choo, 200, 296
Children of the New Regime, 180 n.
Chopin, Frédéric, 51
Christy, Ed, 10, 12
Chrysanthemum, 26
Cole Smoak, 24

Cohan, George M., 14, 61, 108, 132, 133, 135, 138, 153, 206, 293
Cohn, Irving, 46
Cold Cold Heart, 215
Colin, Sid, 297
College Life, 53
Come Away with Me, Lucille . . ., 53
Come, Josephine, in My Flying Machine, 53
Comin' thru the Rye, 22
Cooking Breakfast for the One I Love, 126, 209
Coslow, Sam, 181
Coward, Noel, 119, 136, 139, 140–41, 143, 182, 241, 247
Cowards over Pearl Harbor, 198
Crazy Blues, 105
Crazy Man Crazy, 224
Crazy Words, Crazy Tune, 125
Creole Belles, 15
Crosby, Bing (singer), 89, 101, 103, 130, 149, 176, 177, 198, 201, 229, 280
Cry, 204
Cuanto le Gusta, 205
cummings, e. e., 139
Curse of an Aching Heart, The, 45

Daddy Wouldn't Buy Me a Bow Wow, 155, 158
Dallas Blues, 30
Damerell, Stanley J. (Jack Stevens), 182, 296
Dance Little Lady!, 140
Dance With Me, Henry!, 221
Dancing With Tears in my Eyes, 75
Danks, Hart, 13
Danny Boy, 166
Dapper Dan – The Sheik of Alabam, 125
Dardanella, 38, 40
Daring Young Man on the Flying Trapeze, 106
Darktown Strutters Ball, 296
Day in Venice, A, 6
Day of Jubilo, 185
Dearie, do you remember when . . . ?, 205
DeKnight, Jimmy (James Myers), 225

302

Index

305

Index

Index

Index

Index

YOU TURN ME ON

by IAN WHITCOMB.